To Flo
Happy Reading !
Elaine A. Small

Priests in the Attic

ELAINE A. SMALL

authorHOUSE®

AuthorHouse™
1663 Liberty Drive
Bloomington, IN 47403
www.authorhouse.com
Phone: 1-800-839-8640

First published by AuthorHouse 9/3/2010

ISBN: 978-1-4490-4413-8 (e)
ISBN: 978-1-4490-4411-4 (sc)
ISBN: 978-1-4490-4412-1 (hc)

Library of Congress Control Number: 2010909795

Printed in the United States of America
Bloomington, Indiana

This book is printed on acid-free paper.

ACKNOWLEDGEMENTS

Heartfelt thanks to the following professors at York University for their support in encouraging me to become a writer upon my return after a twenty year absence: Stanley Fefferman, Bruce Powe, Ian Balfour, Steve McCaffery, Marlene Kadar and Richard Teleky. I am grateful to authors Susan Swan, Sarah Sheard and Isabel Huggan who, as trusted mentors, helped to shape my journey towards the completion of this book.

Thanks go to my three children: Joanne, for her amazing recall of family matters; Craig, for his writing talent and creative suggestions regarding content; and Kevin, for his expertise in technical applications and design.

To my sister Yvonne Goostrey, thanks for her support in all of my writing endeavors and achievements, starting from my return to university and continuing to this day.

Finally, I thank my husband Richard Haeberlin for his ever-patient technical assistance, his encouragement throughout the publishing process, and his enduring confidence in my ability to write an intimate book that could be inspirational to many readers.

This book is a memoir. As such, it records the author's memories, recalled within reverie, describing emotions and impressions experienced over a lifetime. Some names have been altered and some events attributed to those named may differ from their recollections, but to such perceptions I submit that emotional truth rarely lies—and certainly not to the bearer.

This book is dedicated to my father, The Very Reverend Dr. S.W. Sawchuk—a giant of a man whose unerring influence has brought me to these pages. I love you Dad. Thank you.

And the Dead Shall Lead You Home

There were seventeen priests at my father's funeral. I know this from a blurry picture taken by my cousin from the choir loft at St. Michael's Cathedral in Winnipeg, Canada—my childhood home. I've counted the priests by squinting and tracing the silver-trimmed sleeves of their incense-bearing arms, swinging as they circle the coffin. In another picture, also lacking in detail, I see my father at rest in his open coffin. Here the outlines of his magnificent regalia, the gold-trimmed folds of his vestment and silver miter, are just visible enough to remind me of his importance and stature among those many priests who chanted the sacramental prayers for their long-time leader and friend. In the same picture, off to the right in the second row, I see myself and six of my seven siblings lined up—now a family of adult orphans. These pictures assure me that we were all there, but one, on that bitter November day some twenty-five years ago. Looking closely, I can see my pinched face turned towards the procession in what appears to be an anxious attempt to see my father's beloved face. But no, I could not see it. Access denied.

Antimin: *A cloth or stole used at every Divine Liturgy: it contains a Holy Relic of a Saint.* When a Priest dies, his face is anointed with Holy Myrrh and then his face is wrapped in his Antimin.

CONTENTS

Introduction   xiii

Part 1 — **In My Father's House**   1
1. Childhood Dreams   3
2. Crib Notes   6
3. The Chapel   13
4. The Minister's Daughter   22
5. Mama's House   34

Part 2 — **Enigmas: Pursuing the Dream**   49
6. Learning to Sing   51
7. New York: Feisty, Fabled and Fabulous   73
8. Amazing Grace   88
9. Canadian Conundrum   99
10. No Games, No Guile   125
11. Show Me the Way   140
12. Turbulent Times   155
13. Chaotic Moral Dismay   167
14. Memories, Legends and Longing   192
15. Designers of the Seventies   211
16. London Levity   226

Part 3 — **The Lost Divine**   253
17. Heartache   255
18. Love, Labor and Loss   273
19. As Time Goes By   282
20. Rock of Ages – the Blessing   290

Afterword   295

Sources   297

INTRODUCTION

Emotional Truth

By certain of its traits, childhood lasts all through life. It returns to animate broad sections of adult life…. But in waking life itself, when reverie works on our history, the childhood which is within us brings us its benefits….The imagination ceaselessly revives and illustrates the memory.
— Gaston Bachelard, "Introduction," *Poetics of Reverie*

In every life there are stories asking to be relived, yearning to be reborn in order to expose their emotional truth in the light of past circumstances. The following pages, triggered by memory, meditation and dreams, describe details of my childhood and adult life as influenced by my late father, The Very Reverend Dr. S. W. Sawchuk. My stories, written within reverie, express historical and emotional truth as seen through the subjective experience of this writer, his youngest daughter.

In documenting this memoir I have learned about the power of writing my life through the gift of *reverie*. In "Reveries Towards Childhood," *The Poetics of Reverie,* the French philosopher Gaston Bachelard describes his use of reverie to unearth emotional truth:

> *Reverie extends history precisely to the limits of the unreal. It is true in spite of all the anachronisms. It is many times true in its facts and in its values. In reverie, image values become psychological facts.*

In recalling my stories I have learned much about the essence of human love and the spiritual aspect of the human condition itself— mine and others. Personal memories, clear and retold, will never completely explain why reveries (dream-like fantasies, daydreams) which carry us back toward our childhood have such an attraction, such a soul quality. According to Bachelard, our childhood remains within us as a principle of life, in harmony with the possibilities of new beginnings. In this way, all of us possess our own emotional truth of the past and thus each of us has a unique story to tell—but who am I, that anyone should be interested in my story? Let my book tell you:

"I'm everyone who has ever taken a breath and marveled at the wonder and miracle of life. I'm everyone who has discovered their own finitude and shuddered at the concept of one day, being no more. I'm everyone who has suffered the pain of loss, the torment of regret, the desolation of loneliness, a fear of the past and a fear of the future. I'm everyone who, through an anguished cry for help, receives the possibility of a new beginning and a miracle of new life through God's immeasurable grace…. Who am I? I am one with you—and all of us have a story to tell. This is mine."

PART ONE

In My Father's House

Chapter 1

Childhood Dreams

In my Father's house are many mansions: if it were not so,
I would have told you. I go to prepare a place for you.
—King James Bible: John 14:2

The Very Reverend Dr. S. W. Sawchuk

Knowing

I still remember how good I felt, all of them looking at me and smiling … I liked it. From my high chair I could see my family sitting around the huge kitchen table, half-bathed in golden light that slanted through a window across Grandpa Dido's face, to land so warmly on my hands resting on my tray. Across, at the far end of the table, against the bright light, I could hardly make out the shadow, but I knew it was my sister Zenovia; I could tell from the shiny red

3

nails that danced in the strong sunlight beneath the shade—delicate-fingered puppets that reached out for the blue and white china teapot steaming off to her right. The eldest of seven, "Snow" always held a place of honour next to Daddy.

Still wearing my yellow sleepers after my nap, I sit quietly, staring down at the square of light that jumps around on the brown and gold linoleum each time Babka (Grandma) slides past the window to get more cookies and tea. Never stopping, she is always getting tea for those sitting around the table: Mama and Daddy, my six brothers and sisters, my Uncle Alec and my beautiful Aunt Mary, whose sparkly earrings dance as she tells stories to my darling Dido, and the student ministers who live upstairs—the priests in the attic.

My big brother Zenon is the only one missing. I'm not sure where he is, but I heard Mama telling Babka that he'd run away to join the navy and lied about his age, "and he's only seventeen, and what if something terrible happens to him?" Mama cried out; then Babka started yelling about "how bad he was to do that"—and Mama cried some more.

Everyone is talking at once, not paying any attention to me, but I don't care, because in front of me there's a big plate of cookies that I'd put tiny circles of jam on when I helped Babka bake them this morning. She'd promised me I could have first turn, so I reach over to get some, but the plate is too far from my chair. Standing up, I grab hold of Dido's shirt, but he's too busy talking to Babka, and his bristly grey head is turned away. Anyway, out I reach and down I go heading fast for the cookies staring up at me—brown faces with sticky red eyes daring me to crush them. Just then Dido grabs hold of my sleepers and in mid-air I lurch to a stop while thinking, *Oh no; I'm going to fall into the cookies and ruin them and Babka will get mad and yell at me, and everybody's going to laugh.* But Babka doesn't yell, and nobody laughs. After Dido settles me back in my chair, he pours some dark tea from his yellow mug into my favorite Brer-Rabbit cup. Wincing after my first swallow, I blurt out, "Please pass the sugar, my tea's too hot." *Now* everyone bursts out laughing. Thirteen people sat at our table laughing as Dido hugged and kissed me even though I didn't know why. What I remember most is the hugging, the kissing and the *knowing* that they liked me.

∞ ∞ ∞

My story, so far, discloses the power and ramifications of emotional truth established early on, at a critical time of childhood. In Gaston Bachelard's philosophy, childhood's truth returns in reverie: "...in waking life itself, when *reverie* works on our history, the childhood which is within us brings us its benefits."

The scene above, my childhood reverie, the *knowing* that they liked me brings with it a gift of humor, love and a joy, and, as such, provides a touchstone for the balance of my memoir. In reviewing my life and narrating my history through reverie, I have witnessed, in a personal way, Bachelard's declaration that "many a childhood feeling returns to animate broad sections of adult life." Read on....

Chapter 2

Crib Notes

I learn by going where I have to go
—Theodore Roethke, *The Waking*.

"Leaving Home," Winnipeg

The Cell

As the baby, seventh in line, I slept in a crib until I was six years old. Although my father's house, the manse of the Ukrainian Greek Orthodox Church in Winnipeg was huge, it seems that the family crib was the only place my parents could find to put me. Not only did I sleep in a crib until I was in Grade one (luckily I was short for my age), but the crib was in my mother's and father's bedroom, three feet from their bed. I remember the crib well. It was iron and heavily layered in shiny white paint (lead-laced in that day). By the time I got my turn in "the cell," the protective railing had been teethed upon by two brothers and four sisters who had merrily chewed their way down to the bare iron—a bitter taste and metallic smell permanently etched in childhood memories too pungent to forget.

Where's the Baby?

When I hear Daddy's voice so close, I open my eyes expecting him to be by my crib. But he's not.

"Where's the baby?" he says in Ukrainian, and Mama answers him in English, her voice quietly assuring him that I'm probably with Babka and Dido in their room across the hall and "please don't talk so loud, because you'll wake up everyone in the house and it's two o'clock in the morning." I can hear Mama's voice close by, but I can't see her, because it's too dark. But *where are they*, I wonder, *and why can't they see me?* It's black all around me—no light anywhere, nothing to see. Lying on my stomach, I roll over trying to sit up, but something hard hits me on top of my head and with a sharp pain back I fall....

When I wake up, it looks like morning: I can see some light under the bedroom door, but my head is hurting and it's still dark around me, and I am feeling sick and scared, and *where is everybody? Where is Daddy? Where is Mama? Where am I?* I'm afraid to move, and I don't know what to do and I soon start whimpering. That's when I see Daddy's bare feet: he's putting them into his slippers while telling Mama to wake up, telling her that I'm not in the crib, but how come he can hear me whimpering? He's still asking, "Where's the baby?"

Now I turn my head and see Mama's bare feet feeling around for her pink fuzzy slippers, while asking Daddy in Ukrainian, "What do you mean 'where's the baby'?" When I see their feet, and hear them talking, I start feeling better. It's light now, and looking straight up I see wires and wooden pieces close to my face, smelling like the pine logs Daddy brings in for the stove, and ... *ah, now I know. I'm under their bed!* The smell close to my face is the same as when I crawled under their bed searching for my yellow duck. *They probably left the bars of the crib down again. I've fallen out of my crib, rolled over and slept here all night, and they don't even know it!* Now I keep quiet, like when

7

we play hide and seek. My heart pounding, I wait to see how long it will take them to find me....

If the image revealed in the reverie above rings true, then, in Bachelard's words, it "bears witness to a soul which is discovering its world, the world where it would like to live…" In retrospect, it seems that I knew, even as a baby that I would have to work hard to get my fair share of attention in our huge bustling household. But being the youngest had its benefits.

I learned early on that, in my sisters' words, I could "get away with murder." These memories of my babyhood onwards appear to be filled with just this mode of operation. Who I was as a baby becomes the lynchpin, the cohesive element for who I would become as an adult. And, as such, these childhood images suddenly roll out of hiding to reveal snippets of emotional truth straight from the crib.

∞ ∞ ∞

In the evenings, Mum and Dad always left the bedroom door open so that they could hear me from downstairs if I fussed. As a result, I could hear everything that went on in our living room below when I was supposed to be asleep. Because the side door of the manse opened up into our private living room, used for family and personal visitors, there was always plenty of action and lots of things to be heard from my vantage point in "the cell." Mostly I could hear the radio playing the comedy of *Fibber McGee and Molly* or the serial, *The Lone Ranger*. The rest of the time a great variety of music floated through the house: soothing orchestral arrangements like Liebestraum and other symphonic classics, including Mama's favorite opera, *Carmen*, and Daddy's spiritual songs, his favorite: *Not for tomorrow and its needs, I do not pray; but keep me safe from harm, Oh Lord, just for today.* Through these various influences, music was instilled within me at an early age. Still in the crib, music became my universe of comfort and my future joy—both deeply embedded in a prolonged dream of hope and longing.

Operation Opera

On a snow-driven Saturday afternoon in January, Mama took me and my sister Daria to see the opera *Carmen* at the Winnipeg

Auditorium—a treat for my fifth birthday. There were just the three
of us, and I sensed the importance of the occasion. It was rare for
Mama to go downtown with just two of us kids, and rarer still to go
without Babka, but off we went: Mama in her black sealskin coat,
matching felt hat and galoshes, and me in my green hooded coat
and fur-lined boots with a wool scarf wrapped securely around my
face—a mask to prevent Winnipeg's notorious frost-bite.

I'd never been to the big downtown auditorium before, and upon
entering I remember staring up in awe at its high fancy ceilings and
beautiful marbled floors. Later, in grade school, I would often sing
there in the school-choir competitions at the Kiwanis Festival and
although the auditorium decreased in size as my own height and
perspective grew, I've never forgotten my gaping wonder on that first
visit. It was there, within the excitement and drama of my first opera,
Carmen, that my love of theatre was born.

I was intrigued by the sound of the orchestra, all of them making
strange noises. I told Mama that they "sounded funny," and she
explained that they were tuning-up, getting their instruments ready
and soon they would sound fine. They did. (To this day, the discordance
of instruments tuning up heralds in me a heady excitement of new
beginnings.) The dramatic overture to *Carmen* was followed by robust
clapping, which stopped and came to rest in a hushed excitement and
intrigue as the music took up the theme of the first act.

From the back row of the theatre, I watched in fascination as
the hundreds of heads in front of me, silhouetted in semidarkness,
disappeared into black with the curtain's rise. Staring in awe at the
opening scene, I watched spangled bare feet and buckled shoes emerge
into full bodies with the curtain's slow lift. But I was too short and
couldn't see well, so I whispered this to Mama and without a word
she hoisted me up on one knee, then raised it for a better view—and
what a scene! Costumes in every color filled the stage—gold sashes
flew on the male dancers as tambourines were flung high by their
lady partners, so fancy in their satin skirts of purple, orange, red and
blue. Every color in my paint box swirled by as my ears tried to take
in the jumbled voices of the soaring sopranos and pleading tenors
who sang out against the frenzied chorus as they swirled around the

market square—almost too much for my young eyes and ears to take in; and oh, the wonder of Carmen's entrance!

Shocked by her sudden appearance on stage, barefooted, in a red satin skirt and green apron topped with a shimmering white blouse, her ankles adorned with silver bracelets matched by others tinkling up and down her arm, when she opened up her voice and sang out, so beautifully, high above the chorus, I fell in love with her, the music, and singing itself.

Mama folded her coat and placed it under me, on top of her lap, for an even better view. Fascinated, staring at the stage, lost in the music and dance, I was completely unprepared for the last scene. Seeing Carmen stabbed, watching her fall with blood spurting out all over her shiny white blouse while writhing on the floor was more than I could bear. Crying out in shock, I turned to Mama with my eyes squeezed shut while I murmured into her softness about "how bad it is that the beautiful Carmen has to die."

"Don't worry," Mama whispered, hugging me close. "It's just ketchup. Carmen's not dead, but for sure her blouse is ruined...."

Later, emerging from the dark theatre, blinded by the midday sun shining sharp against the blue-white snow, I struggled back to reality. On the long streetcar ride home, neither Mama nor I spoke. Filled as I was with dreams of singing and performing, I was still in the theatre, and perhaps Mama was there too—lamenting the loss of her own singing ambition which I often heard about from Babka:

"Too many kids and no time for Mama to sing," was her guilt–laced mantra when we kids were growing up. Babka's mantra just strengthened my resolve.

At age six, still lying in that oversized crib while staring at the yellow hall-light, I loved to listen to our RCA Victor gramophone playing downstairs in the living room. The family took turns: after dinner, my older brother's jazz stuff would come on: Fats Waller, Billie Holiday, Doris Day and Buck's favorite, Peggy Lee. I still remember how I loved her calming voice. I would close my eyes and imagine myself all grown up, singing on a huge stage. I'd have silky blonde hair styled in a page-boy like the actress Veronica Lake and sparkly earrings like my beautiful Aunt Mary; I'd be wearing a shiny gold gown with silver crosses made from the fancy cloth that was stored in Daddy's office, all the way from Paris, France. Mama once showed it to me and explained,

"It's for the priests' robes, after they've finished their studies."

"And me too, when I finish school and become a famous singer?" I asked. And Mama just smiled. Six years old, I would memorize the words of Peggy Lee's low, sassy songs and soon I knew most of the other popular songs too, by heart. From that crib, I was launched into a future not fully imagined but already yearned for: I'd start somewhere big, like Toronto or New York City, where Daddy and Mama went to see The Great World Fair. When they showed me the pictures of their trip, I thought to myself, *one day I'll go there and sing* ... and one day I did.

View from the Gallery

Our big house was always full of relatives and friends, and since they congregated in our family living room, I was privy to details that were probably not meant for my young eyes or ears. Climbing over the crib bars I would sneak to the top of the stairs, and curl up small enough to position myself in the dark shadows, so that I could watch through the rails without being seen. Included in my view were physical fights between my two brothers, forbidden by Dad; secretive murmurings between my sisters and their boyfriends, definitely forbidden by Dad; excited arguments between my uncles and aunts, including my Dad; grouchy words between my grandparents, arbitrated by Dad; and endless discussions between my parents: Dad about money and Mum about the lack of it—the tone serious enough to worry a little kid imprisoned in a crib listening to Peggy Lee's succinct vocal instructions to get out, and get her some money too.

From an early age, I understood that money was important—to Mum, to Dad and later to me. Recalling the conversations heard from my crib and the scenes viewed from the top of the back stairs, I don't think I really minded my six years "doing time, in the pen." In a way, I grew up fast: I got to see, hear and learn a lot about adult life while I was still young. And there was much to learn. In the shadows of our wide walnut stairwell at the front of the house, my self-education continued. For my two older sisters and me, "the three little kids," those shadowy stairwells provided endless hours of diversion and entertainment.

Unusual by virtue of its style and size, our distinguished house, the manse, built in 1908, consisted of thirteen rooms spread over five thousand square feet of living space on four floors—all hardwood. Connecting these floors were five sets of stairs with oak banisters: two leading from the finished basement to the main floor, two from the main to the second floor where the bedrooms were located, and a final set leading up to the attic where the priests that Daddy trained lived. After school we would position ourselves in the dark landing of the front staircase and look down from our gallery into the parlor next to Daddy's office where the parishioners visited. Next to his office was the chapel—where people got married, baptized and prayed over when they were dead. I loved our chapel.

Chapter 3

The Chapel

As the hart panteth after the water brooks,
so panteth my soul after thee, Oh God.
—King James Bible: Psalms 42:1

Dad and 'the three little kids': Yvonne, myself and Daria

Going to the Chapel

Our chapel was beautiful; it had silver crosses stamped all over powdery blue wallpaper. When it was empty, it was my favorite place in the house to hide, but I also liked to be there when it was full. I liked the special family services that were held there on favored holidays like Easter and Christmas. I loved the spicy aroma of incense that curled out of Daddy's brass holder as he swung its chains toward us while chanting the blessings; I loved the tall golden candles and their honey scent that came my way as the elders passed by on their way to the altar. I loved the stained-glass windows that shone jeweled halos over the faces of the bride and groom at the Saturday morning weddings. But best of all, I loved the altar picture of Daddy.

As a little girl I knew my father was "important." After all, I would say my prayers to him every night, propped up in bed with Mama kneeling or sitting beside me holding my hand: "My Father … 'hollowed' be thy name…." But this is not about Mama, my darling Dido, or even my darling dog, Skookie, no, this is about Daddy and me, and his special picture that hangs in the chapel over the table where the silver trays and small glasses are kept for grape juice and tiny pieces of bread that Babka bakes for something called "come-you-none." I don't understand what that means but it doesn't matter 'cause we kids aren't allowed to touch or take any.

Mama says that Daddy's picture was painted by Mr. Marko, the artist who lives next door, whose crab apples we would snitch from his tree. I think he must be a good painter 'cause the beard, moustache and long dark hair look exactly right for Daddy—except for the funny looking circle of spiky leaves on his head. In the chapel, when the people pray, they say almost the same thing I do, except for the part about "our Father who art in heaven." I don't understand what they mean by that 'cause my father's right here in the house, and they know it. Still, I like it when everyone prays to him. It makes me feel proud that Daddy is so important.

∞ ∞ ∞

The chapel was usually locked, but once in a while we were allowed in for christenings, weddings and often funerals—if there were not enough people.

My favorite time in the chapel was during the weddings, which usually took place on Saturday mornings. Before the wedding, from our hideout on the front stair landing, we could see and hear everything. One time the bride's mother was crying, and, in Ukrainian, imploring her daughter adorned in a white satin gown and feathery veil "not to marry *Ainglish*, she'd be sorry." Meanwhile, not understanding the language, the groom's mother was nodding and smiling back, thinking the bride's mother was crying for joy and relief at the union—considering the bride's tangential body curve.

"A baby on its way?" my sister Yvonne had whispered, and with this remote idea we had giggled nervously and stared even harder. Now here comes Daddy, so handsome in his formal gold and silver robes, calming everyone down with his big smile while showing them to their places in the chapel and explaining that "this day they would be married in an English *and* Ukrainian wedding ceremony"— this "mixed marriages" ceremony was first introduced to the Ukrainian Orthodox Church by my father. Six months later, the same couple would be back with tearful parents and grandparents to joyfully christen their beautiful baby boy who is "so big and bouncy, so wonderful, considering he was born three months earlier than his due date!"

After the weddings, we three little kids were allowed to sweep up the confetti left around the steps and the tall imposing pillars that upheld the front verandah roof of our big house. When we were finished, Daddy would solemnly check our work and then pay us our wages—a few pennies each, just enough to buy chewy licorice babies and jelly beans, our treats for the Saturday afternoon movies at the College theatre, just three blocks away on Main Street.

Movie Mania

Around five years of age and on, while still "the baby" and a "favorite," I'd be delegated by my two older sisters to approach Dad in his office for our movie money—ten cents each. After hesitantly knocking on the etched window of the door, I'd impatiently wait to be invited in. Busy, always busy writing, typing or reading, Dad would finish his work then glance up with a worried frown that most often turned into a smile when he saw me. I reveled in Daddy's attention; his smile made me feel special. He would ask me about school; did I have any new poems to show him, and if not, what could he do for me today, pretending he didn't know. We would play our little game, and every time I emerged triumphant with three dimes squeezed in my pudgy little fist the girls would whoop and holler as if surprised by my achievement. Then off we we'd run, darting dangerously through Main Street traffic to arrive breathlessly on time for the one o'clock movie.

And oh, how I loved those Saturday afternoon movies! We'd stay in the theatre for hours, hiding under our seats between shows in order to see the same movie over and over again, "for free." In between the repeated movies, the intermission shows featured local talent on stage, some sporting their tricks with a yo-yo; and some "walking the dog," everyone's favorite, which required a steady hand. My brother Leo usually won. He was also good at paddleball, where the contestants would line up and endlessly smack a small rubber ball attached by elastic to a paddle while performing tricks that one then another would miss, until only one player would be left. I still remember Leo winning the "barrel" sweater vest patterned in wide three-inch stripes of green, black and brown; it encircled his chest for days, even weeks throughout that winter—rightfully proud of his talent, as was I!

After watching my favorite musical, the one about the Canadian Mounties with Jeanette MacDonald and Nelson Eddie, we would run home to our bedroom and eagerly mime their actions while shouting out their songs. Searching through Mama's discarded hats and our older sisters' high heels, we'd swish around in long "skirts" created from Babka's satin quilts belted tightly around our skinny waists. Happily oblivious to reality we'd act out the movie, singing and dancing in our fantasy world for hours until our two older brothers screamed out, warning us to *"can it already."* Soon after Dido would holler from two flights down to "come for dinner—*now.*" After we'd eaten, in sharp contrast to our festive before-dinner show, we'd face reality buried within the extensive cleanup required after every family meal.

Twelve or more people sitting at a table eating a meal can create quite a clutter of dirty dishes. Every evening, we each had to perform our designated tasks. Dad set up a rotational system, which was written out monthly and posted over the kitchen sink. At seven years of age, before the miracle of dishwashers and grease-cutting detergents, I'd find myself perched on a stool trying to wash our dinner dishes in thick, greasy lard-laden water, which no amount of plain soap could cure. The dish driers, even my beloved Dido, complained about my greasy dishwashing; I was embarrassed, but not enough to argue about keeping my job. After being replaced by one of my older sisters, I was then commissioned to her job of drying dishes—until I started dropping them: "But they're still too greasy, too slippery," I whined. In the end, I escaped the dishes brigade altogether. "Wait until you get bigger," Daddy said, to the relief of everyone, especially me.

After our chores, we'd rush into the living room, all scrambling for the best place to sprawl on the carpet near the family radio—anxious to hear our favorite shows: *Jack Benny, The Lone Ranger* and *Charley McCarthy*. Saturday night was an important family time and even Daddy found time to be there. I can still hear his laughter, the loudest of all, ringing out as Jack Benny's sidekick, Rochester, performed his silly pranks. But to me, the gallery seats behind the banister of the stairs overlooking the guest parlor still provided the best show of all—and it didn't cost a dime!

In the front parlor there were always meetings with visiting priests and guests, including distraught parishioners who felt free to confer with Dad at any time, day or night. Once, well towards midnight, the front bell started clanging—slowly at first, then louder, with rapid, static persistence. Of course, we three kids woke up in a flash and hustled to our places in the shadows of the stairs to watch.

As Daddy opened the front door, a grey-haired lady in a blue dressing gown and pink cat-face slippers fell into his arms, sobbing and crying out something bad about her husband. Hearing all the noise, the good minister's wife, our Mama, showed up in her best blue velour robe carrying her petite point English teapot and Babka's crisp almond cookies on a silver tray. Setting them down, she calmly invited the upset lady to have some tea, please. Seeing Mama's politeness, the nervous lady sat down and accepted the offer, chattering on in Ukrainian in-between gulps of tea and cookies—I counted four. Yes, yes, she would come back tomorrow, and no thank you, she would find her way home, "As you know, it's just around the corner and please thank the Reverend for his trouble," she stated as Mama gently guided her to the front door. Seeing the upset lady leave, I eyed the cookies and started to run down to join Mama, but my sisters stopped me, hissing that I would ruin their cover, forever. *As if Mama doesn't know we're here*, I thought; *my Mama knows a lot about a lot, but she doesn't always say so.*

As a little kid I was very responsive to my parents' moods and attitudes; this early understanding of Mama's particular wisdom was confirmed later when I entered my tumultuous teens. Apparently my acute sensitivity to general household circumstances and moods took hold early on, as attested by these next childhood reveries.

Depression Days

One beautiful Indian summer day, while walking home from school, I had an attack of the "twirlies"—a scared feeling that always creeps up on me as I head home for lunch. Seven years old, the baby of seven, I got to hear a lot of grown-up stuff I was probably not supposed to hear. There was always talk going on around me, and just the other day I'd heard Babka say "there are tough times ahead for such a big family as ours." Then she'd wondered out loud, to Mama, about "how long this depression will last." I was not sure what that meant, but whenever they talked about "depression," they looked worried, and whenever Daddy talked about the Big War going on in Europe, and how he would probably have to go there soon, Mama would look away to hide her tears. All their talk about depression scared me, and as I headed home for lunch I worried whether there would be enough food for all of us—even plain white spaghetti with bacon bits or cottage cheese would be better than nothing, I thought, as I headed to the front door.

As soon as I walked in I smelled the Varsol used for cleaning the hardwood floors and I knew that the yellow Johnson's Wax, a smell I loved, would soon follow—spread on sparingly by Mama on her hands and knees then polished by Dido with the electric polisher parked for repair beside the front door. The house was so big that they could only do one level at a time, so this work would go on for three days or more. If the polisher was not fixed in time by Saturday, Dido would relegate three of the bigger kids into helping:

"Okay kids," he'd shout, "get on your thick winter socks and come downstairs to the dining room." While waiting, he'd turn on the Saturday afternoon New York Metropolitan Opera to full volume on the radio, filling the house with soaring sopranos, tearful tenors and pleading baritones.

"Now," he'd order, "Skate! And in time with the music, please. Pretend you are skating in Central Park.... Go!" Then back and forth they would fly, laughing hysterically while jostling each other, falling down, sliding on their backsides, then, more laughing and skating until the floor was shining a bright gold. When Dido turned down the radio, Mama would know that the lower level was done—only three more to go.

Because Mama would get tired cleaning and waxing the floors, doing the laundry, ironing all the shirts and sheets and Daddy's shorts too, Babka did most of the cooking in our house—at least she was the one who cooked lunch. As I walked into the kitchen I saw my darling Dido. He was smiling and looked happy to see me, so I slid in beside him and my six brothers and sisters who were impatiently waiting for something to eat—anything.

When I was older, I learned that lunch was often late because poor Babka, in her words said, "I always had to make something out of nothing." This was usually that plain white spaghetti or "Babka's Borscht." Leftovers from the ice-box (no fridge in those days) were thrown into a huge soup pot, with a beef bone or a chicken carcass, some cut-up onions, diced potatoes, ruby-red preserved beets, tomatoes and finely shredded cabbage—cheap and handy from our own back yard. Served with this were slices of unbuttered white bread which we would roll up and dip into the borscht, fascinated by watching the purple stain inch its way across to the crust—careful not to wait too long before stuffing it down. Once I was too slow, and the soggy roll plopped into my pinafore lap, staining it purplish-red, with me wailing in embarrassment while the other kids laughed and called me "Sloppy Joe."

Aside from the usual hamburger meat and the occasional chicken, most of the food we relied on during the extended Winnipeg winters came from preserves produced from our huge vegetable garden out back, including some fruit from our neighbor's crab apple tree and our own plum tree, carefully tended by Daddy or Dido. From late August through September our kitchen hummed with canning activities as delectable odors tickled our palates.

I loved the fall days of preserving. Mama and Babka would spend the mornings sorting and chopping raw vegetables while sterilizing the Mason jars and lids. Every day after lunch, vegetables would be cooked and carefully poured into the largest jars available: golden sauerkraut, orange stewed tomatoes, purple beets, which had been peeled and shed of their grey jackets by Dido, whole garlic dills, sweet mixed pickles, string beans and finely coined carrots—my favorite. When I was young, I'd ask Mama if I could stay in the kitchen to help. I loved everything about that time, especially the different smells: sweet sauerkraut one day, savory tomatoes the next, green beans and carrots after that, and finally, the pungent garlic and vinegar scent of dill pickles—all of these invaded the basement kitchen and breathed their way upstairs where the older kids were studying, making them hungry and luring them downstairs too early to ask, "What's for dinner?"

I liked looking at and counting the colorful moist jars brimful, cooling down, waiting for Dido to tighten the lids. Most of all, I liked the way Babka and Mama worked together, their felt slippers sliding on the linoleum, gliding past and around each other, laughing and joking in Ukrainian, sometimes in German, when they didn't want me to understand—but I didn't care. I just liked all the activity and being around them. One day Daddy walked into the kitchen with two crates of store-bought peaches and green pears—on sale they were—"Not quite ripe for eating, but just right for preserving," he said. We were treated to one of our choice, which Babka said we "should place on our sunny window sills to ripen." But we ran away giggling, because we all knew they'd be gone long before we reached the third floor. We were always hungry.

During World War II, when food was rationed, we'd have to save up our allotment of food stamps all summer long to have enough sugar for preserving the fruit in the fall. The peaches and pears always came out close to their true color, but the scarlet cherries faded, their claret hue lost in the watered-down syrup. By early October, when the weeks of preserving were done, I'd sneak into the big walk-in storage cellar and marvel at the dozens of shelves loaded with an army of preserves; the tallest Mason jars filled with vegetables of high color and rank stood on the upper shelves, out of reach, while the smaller fruit jars squatted at eye level, uniformly lined up—soldiers resting in jewel colors, waiting to battle the hunger that our family fought every winter in the bitter aftermath of the Great Depression followed by World War II.

In retrospect, I guess we were poor, but as a young kid I didn't know it. We all had clean clothes to wear, albeit hand-me-downs, and although it was a struggle, three times a day there was always *something* to eat on the table. Our teeth were looked after by a dentist who attended our church. Many in our family wore prescription glasses, which could *not* be handed down, but somehow Daddy managed to regularly mend them and pay for new prescriptions when needed. Our hair was home-cut by a barber from our church and, as I recall, we did *not* go shoeless in the long Winnipeg winters or the short smoldering summers. But, because our house, the manse, was so big and impressive, people outside the church thought that we were rich.

The "White House," as it was dubbed, was more than our home, containing as it did, the rector's office, a reception parlor, a busy chapel and three additional floors including the attic, where the priests lived. Built at the turn of the century before 1908, the wonderful dwelling at #7 St. John's Avenue in Winnipeg is now gone—torn down by a zealous builder who felt he could improve on what was an established landmark during our residency there fifty years ago. The front of the grand manse boasted four white Grecian pillars extending to the roof line and these are what made the house so impressive and architecturally interesting. Byzantine in flavor, situated on a shady green acre surrounded by an eight-foot honeysuckle hedge, our house was the most distinctive of the six homes on our cul-de-sac facing St. John's Park—in those days a safe haven, where, as a young girl, my play hours were spent with my darling grandpa, Dido, the only one in the family who had time to watch over me. And so the years passed.

Immersed in the fantasies of childhood, teen trials, and soon enough the ambitions of adulthood, the time came for this minister's daughter to leave her father's house. In doing so, I may have left Dad's immediate presence, but, as I soon found out, never his imposing influence.

Chapter 4

The Minister's Daughter

One needs, and sometimes it is very good, to live with the child which he
has been. From such living he achieves a consciousness of roots, and the
entire tree of his being takes comfort from it.
—Gaston Bachelard, "Introduction," *Poetics of Reverie*

Dad and Mum: 7 St. John's Ave, 1942

An Imposing Influence

What's in a title?—that which conveys meaning. In a desire to
write about my muddled life, in searching back through a multitude
of careers, marriages and children, I have finally found the connective
thread that ties this bundle of events together. The connection can be
found within the phrase "the minister's daughter." This title comes

to me as I rifle through a box of pictures retrieved from my father's house after he died in October, 1983. On top of the pile is a picture of Dad and me taken when he was already sick with lung-cancer. He'd been formally diagnosed at the Winnipeg Clinic in early June and had been sent home, in essence, "to get his house in order."

The day after he was formally diagnosed, a Saturday in early June, 1983, Dad did not get dressed. He spent the whole day in his dressing gown talking on the phone in Ukrainian and English, calling his friends and colleagues across Canada giving them the dire news. From childhood on, I had never seen my father not get dressed for a full day. Although I could not understand every word he said on the phone, I knew that he had accepted his inevitable fate and was now getting his church house in order. I also noticed that, almost overnight, he appeared fragile and small ... no longer the giant of my childhood whose imposing influence shadowed my every move. I was worried. But early the next morning, Dad was up and dressed in his Sunday best. Walking tall and looking handsome in his black clerical suit and formal gold cross, he asked if I would like to accompany him to church. "Oh yes," I replied enthusiastically, so happy to see him looking fine again.

Nearing the entrance to Holy Trinity Cathedral, Dad gallantly offered me his arm. As we walked into church I felt wrapped in a closeness of love that was intimate, holy—joy mingled with sadness at the thought that this may be the last time I would accompany my father into the church of my childhood. It was.

∞ ∞ ∞

Reaching again into the jumbled box of black and white photos I come across a picture taken forty years earlier. Mum is standing with Dad in his army uniform outside our big manse across from St. John's Park. She is standing close to Dad, smiling demurely and looking pretty, but still, it is Dad's stalwart military stance that overtakes the landscape. Backed by the tall white Grecian pillars of our century manse, my father's imposing presence overshadows all.

Another picture shows me at three years of age. With suitcase in hand, the minister's daughter is apparently leaving home. Surprisingly, I remember this occasion and, as the black-and-white photos jump back in time, my once-blurred childhood comes into focus. Going through the pictures, I can see, feel and smell the past in a child's world that was ever still—the endless hours spent in St. John's Park across the street, the green grass sweet and damp with morning dew as I lay back contemplating the swift-moving clouds—now locked in time. Breaking through my reverie, I would hear my father's commanding voice cutting across the park, shouting from our front door: "Lunch is ready, now!" Resentful of his intrusion, I would nevertheless leap up and run towards our house, jolted into a demanding reality where I was once again the obedient minister's daughter.

Looking back, I see that the title "the minister's daughter" framed my life and held it in a firm identity in photos and concrete feelings tied to my father, his house and his church. I can see the aggregate evidence of a lifetime informed by the phrase itself. When, as a young adult I left home, this identity paled to make room for diverse careers and ambitions, but now, in later years, it has reappeared as the driving force behind my current search for spiritual understanding—first planted as a baby, its roots carefully nurtured by the influence of my father's deep faith. In spreading out my life, reviewing its process and reaching into my psyche through meditation and dreams, this insightful phrase, "the minister's daughter," illumines then defines a shadowed self lying in wait ... and everywhere I look I see my father's face.

Daddy's Face

I have three distinct memories of my father's face. In the first one he is sitting in his blue armchair in the living room, his face deep in his newspaper. As a young girl, around four, I walk quietly into the room to see him. He probably hears me come in, but he doesn't look up, so I sit down on the footstool under the window and wait. From where I am sitting, I see the late afternoon sun slant golden across the upper part of Daddy's forehead, circling his head in an aura of light that for a moment looks like a crown—and to me he appears as a king. As he turns in his chair, the fading sun shadows his face, and though he looks tired, his eyes light up as he holds out his arms for my hug. Sitting on his knee, I stare into his face, touching the deep laugh lines between his full mouth and long uneven nose; here

I stop to trace my thumb along its side, gently tracking the sharp bump before searching my own face for the match. Then I run my fingers along the thin moustache that curves down to join his silky dark beard, my favorite part of his face. As I do this I look into his eyes. They have changed color: at first they were greenish-grey with points of light that danced when they saw me but now they are dark, far away, in some other place. As Daddy's eyes turn into shiny mirrors I watch myself vanish from view.

I remember Mama telling all seven of us that morning, "Don't bother Daddy today. He's far too busy, so much on his mind with the war and all." With this thought in mind, I slip out of Daddy's arms. Pausing as I reach the door, I wait, but he does not look up. I quietly walk away.

∞ ∞ ∞

Three decades later was the next time I looked closely into my father's face. Dad was visiting me in Toronto after a church trip to Ukraine. He was searching for a canonical Ukrainian bishop who would be willing to take on the much needed position in Canada of leading the Ukrainian Orthodox Church into the future. Although past eighty years of age, Dad was still keeping very busy, "…to keep from missing Mama so much," he said, his eyes turning misty. Without warning, Mom had passed away in her sleep in Winnipeg, two years earlier, June 26, 1976. We were all so shocked by the suddenness of her death. Because I was living in Toronto at the time, I wasn't close at hand when she died. Here is my sister Yvonne's account:

> I was awakened by a telephone call at 6 AM on June 26, 1976. It was my sister Snow, calling to tell me that Mum had died at around 1 AM that morning. I was immobilized by the shocking news and could barely assimilate the instructions that I should get ready immediately, because her friend Ross was on his way to pick me up to drive us to Dad's house near the university. The shock was so profound that while trying to get dressed, I could not extend my arms to put on a blouse and skirt and was still struggling when they arrived.

25

I could hardly believe that, only hours earlier, at 10 PM that previous night I had phoned my mother. We chatted together for about ten minutes, laughing and joking as well as exchanging the latest family news. Four hours later, when Dad went up to the bedroom after watching television and listening to the late night news, he found her dead from a heart attack. She had been reading and appeared only to be asleep, her hands still holding the book now resting on her body. Dad tried, but was unable to revive her. Rather than call for an ambulance at that hour, he sat and visited with her throughout the night before he called Snow. The rest you know ... Yvonne trailed off.

∞ ∞ ∞

The last time I looked into my father's face was in the early spring of 1983. We were having late afternoon tea in a restaurant at the top of the Park Plaza Hotel in Toronto. Dad was telling me about his affiliation with St. Andrew's College and his continuing interests, which included ongoing ecclesiastical duties and an active role in the formation of a national coordinating body, the Ukrainian Canadian Committee. *So, Dad's as busy as ever,* I thought. *Nothing has changed except that now we are both a lot older.*

Dad's face looked wan and spent. Dark shadows sharpened his deep laugh lines and exaggerated the fine lines around his eyes. His once-light skin now appeared sallow and his full dark hair, once salted with grey, was now completely white. Set against his high cheek bones and patrician nose, his features had reassembled to give him the look of an aristocrat—or an elder statesman, perhaps. But it was Dad's solemn grey eyes, framed by his dark eyebrows in a concentrated frown that told me something was wrong.

"Dad, you look so tired. Are you sure you're alright?" I asked. But he just took my hand and smiled. We finished our tea in relaxed silence. *Finally,* I thought, *he has some time for me*—how little I could hardly guess. Three months later, in June of 1983, I got the call. Dad was really sick—a smoker for many years, although he had already quit, there was now a malignant tumor on his left lung. Here it was emphasized that I SHOULD TRY TO COME HOME TO WINNIPEG AT ONCE.

∞ ∞ ∞

The final time I studied my father's face was just before his funeral on November 3ʳᵈ, 1983. When I got close enough to see him in the casket, I saw the features of a stranger. Gone were the deep lines around his once laughing mouth, gone the fine lines around his intuitive eyes, gone, the open greeting and ready grin, all lost in the geography of time. In their place was a marble mask, smooth and impervious, unlined—finally worry-free.

Sitting stone silent next to my brothers and sisters throughout that solemn funeral (all of us present except my sister Lessia, far away in Australia) I was deeply immersed in thoughts of family life in our father's unconventional house. In retrospect I realized that the effects of our high energy manse had shaped my future in ways I was unaware of at the time and had barely thought of since, but with Dad's passing, seeing all of the priests at the funeral—some the same students he had trained in our manse, now seasoned priests in their own right—a door burst open to release forgotten fragments of my past. Harbored for decades, remote scenes and unrelated moments of childhood in my father's house surfaced and took on new meaning

Priests in the Attic

While still young, maybe seven, I remember sitting at Babka's knee while she sewed clothes for everyone in the family, including my hand-me-down dolls. There were fancy banquet gowns for Mama, silky going-out dresses for my beautiful Aunt Mary, pinafores for us three little kids, skirts and blouses for my big sisters, and vestments for the priests in the attic. At that time I didn't understand much about why student priests, two or three at a time, were living in the attic on the upper floor. This fourth floor of the manse contained two large bedrooms, both finished with fine hardwood floors, separated by a hallway and a shared bathroom. I was told by Babka that the students were there because Daddy was teaching them all about the Holy Bible and how to be good priests.

"This house is, after all, a seminary," she sternly reminded me.

In retrospect, I now see that for me, the priests were a reflection of my father, who he was and what he believed in, as in the Easter film he showed us when I was barely three years old—the one with the bearded man dragging a cross. The mysterious feeling I got then is the best way I can describe the "otherness" of my father's world. That feeling was deepened when, as a little girl, I would sneak into our empty chapel; as young as I was, I remember being overtaken by a special feeling of comfort and belonging upon entering that secluded room. Today, I can describe the power the chapel had over me, but as a little kid it was all about feelings.

The chapel was startling in its beauty on a sunny day. From the rainbow colors of the stained glass window spilling onto the gold polished floor, and the sky-blue walls winged with silver crosses, to the elaborate icons on the altar—sculpted candelabra supporting huge gold candles next to a gleaming silver chalice—all held me transfixed. Enveloped by the pungent scent of incense, my eyes would be drawn to the onyx-framed picture of Christ hanging behind the pulpit—the one that looked like, in fact, in my young mind, *was* my father. I would nearly swoon from the effect of that beautiful room coupled with the excitement of being there all alone in the middle of the day. We kids were not allowed inside the chapel on our own, and the few times I was caught, my brothers were bemused:

"We found the baby in the chapel again," they would snitch at the dinner table, adding, "What does she do in there, anyway?"

Dad would say nothing, but I would see him glance at Mama with a half-smile. Today I know that in some deep way he was pleased by my interest in the chapel at such an early age.

Within this memory, I see that it was our small chapel, shrouded as it was in mystery that first aroused my feelings to do with prayer and spiritual matters. Back then I didn't understand any of this and no one explained it, but for me, the priests in the attic seemed to be part of the same mystery—something big. I was curious, "Too curious for my own good," my first grade teacher had noted. Since none of my other friends had "strangers" living in their house, and certainly no priests, I wondered why. I used to hide in the shadows of the stairs and watch them heading up to the attic, whispering to each other in Ukrainian, sometimes nodding my way.

Today, I view our manse, the chapel and the priests in the attic as symbols of my father's unshakeable belief that he was doing God's work and therefore, family sacrifices must be made. It was our unconventional household, coupled with Dad's sizable influence on me during those formative years which instilled within me the precious seed of faith that lead to my early spiritual awakening and errant, yet determined, quest for conviction in all matters of faith and discernment—still active today.

My dear Mom, Dad's constant helpmate, was always by his side, sustaining him through arduous decades as a resourceful leader who helped create a national identity through the early growth of the first Ukrainian Greek Orthodox Church in Canada. But Dad's house was different to Mama's house. Mama's house was all about us kids and Daddy's house was all about church and business.

Daddy's House

My father's house was called the Consistory: "a governing body of a local congregation in certain reformed churches." As the first administrator of the Ukrainian Orthodox Church in Canada, Dad was always meeting with priests and colleagues in his office situated on the main floor of our home, next to the chapel—both unusual situations for that day. In due time, as I grew older, I became familiar with his office and its contents. Beside the large, cluttered oak desk, stood eight wooden glass-fronted bookshelves crammed with volumes in both Ukrainian and English. My older sister Snow tells me that there were many classics scattered throughout Dad's collection of books—in fact, she remembers reading half of Tolstoy's *Anna Karenina* at the age of thirteen! We all read like mad in our house.

My sister Yvonne was the most avid reader of the bunch. The oldest of the three little kids, she was never without a book; all she wanted to do was hide in her room and read—before school, after school and at night under the bedcovers with a flashlight. We could hardly get her down to dinner. That's why Yvonne was so skinny. We all called her Mahatma Gandhi. When "Mahatma" grew up, she became a respected English teacher in Winnipeg, preaching her love of Shakespeare to high school students for thirty years before retiring to her hidden passion—the performing arts. As a senior, my sister started dancing her way into a healthy future, learning to tap dance and clog. As well, she spent much time studying foreign languages—learning to read and write German and Ancient Greek. These interests developed early in a household open to learning and knowledge, compatible with Dad's edict that in Canada, an advanced education opened the door to a successful future.

Whenever I visited Dad's office, always knocking first, I felt that I was in a special place—a sanctum from the rest of the house. Maybe that's why he spent so much time there. Privacy was at a premium in our rambunctious rectory: everyone was always looking for a place to hide, to be alone. Because I was so little, the first thing I would see whenever I entered the office was the floor. The threadbare Persian carpet was hardly visible, covered as it was with books and papers piled everywhere, spilling over and under the enormous oak desk where Dad himself sat tall and stern, preoccupied, always reading, writing or picking away at his typewriter. For me, barely eye-level, the desk appeared huge, overwhelming and loaded with square wire baskets full of letters and copies of the paper Dad edited, *The Ukrainian Voice,* the newspaper of the Orthodox church. On the floor beside Dad's swivel chair, on which I loved to twirl, was a large wire waste basket where, waveringly balanced, sat back copies of *The Winnipeg Free Press.* Here the editorials were circled in thick red or black ink, depending on Dad's agreement or disagreement— the colors indicating condemnations or compliments. Many times Dad would type late into the night, a steady two-fingered tap that lulled me to sleep, his office being below the bedroom where he and Mama slept, with me in the crib nearby. I rarely heard Dad come up to bed, but I knew when he didn't. In the morning I would see his side of the bed still smooth while Mama's side was crumpled. By that I would know that he had worked in his office all night, and now Mama was downstairs in the kitchen cooking him an early breakfast.

In addition to his office and the chapel, next in the line of importance in Daddy's house was the front parlor, which could be entered from the front entrance door. The reception parlor, for parishioners, dignitaries and visiting priests, included a turn-of-the-century wicker sofa with a wicker tea table to match and two chairs in green velour. Against one wall stood a dark walnut china cabinet, unusual for its day with glass on three sides, which housed Mama's best china—Limoges from France—an anniversary gift from the church. That china cabinet was involved in a terrible accident involving my sister Daria, the details of which are as vivid today as over sixty years ago. What was I thinking? Nothing, I guess, in the way of all five-year-olds who are where they are not supposed to be: in the reception room of the manse playing crazy parlor games.

The Conga Caper

In pursuit of originality in games for the three little kids, I'd already exhausted their interest in the conga dance, which consisted of me leading them around the parlor dancing while chanting a conga rhythm, with a heavy accent on the fourth beat where each leg must be kicked out vigorously, first to the right then to the left. "Too easy," they soon wailed in unison, so I upped the ante. Now they had to follow me *onto* the furniture: around we'd dance, onto the sofa, down to the floor, over the chair, then down the kitchen stairs past Dido, who would barely look up from his newspaper as we each tapped his outstretched legs in turn, not missing a single conga beat on the way. Laconically he would tell us to "Please stop the noise; Mama's resting with one of her headaches." After a few circuits, the girls announced that this game was also too boring.

"Think up something better," they demanded.

"Okay, okay, I've got it," I said, desperate to retain my ringleader status.

"Now we've got to do the whole thing over again; but this time—backwards," I haltingly announced in my best bossy voice, hoping they wouldn't see the stupidity of the plan. They didn't, and off we went: me pushing them backwards, reminding them to kick out strongly on the fourth beat. Apparently this is what they did, because that's when I heard the crash—flat out, on the fourth beat. The noise of breaking glass and a piercing scream followed by a heavy thud sounded a frenzied alarm throughout the house that brought everyone running with Mama in the lead.

Oh yes, here's trouble: broken glass from Mama's beloved china cabinet all over the floor and my sister Daria writhing on her stomach, blood spurting out of her side where a jagged piece of glass at least three inches long protruded from her back. And the scene! Yvonne screaming and frightened (being the oldest, she was meant to take care of us), and I, so scared, crying in surprised shock.

Mama, white-faced, clutching a cold washcloth to her head, saw the mess on my sister's back and was about to pull out the glass when a resounding "No!" was shouted out by Dido with such fervor that her hand stopped in mid-air. Turning too quickly and losing her balance, she started to fall onto Daria's outstretched body—the shard locked in place where rivulets of blood came trickling out—a ready weapon rising towards another victim. Luckily, Dido caught Mama going down; slumped in his arms, her face a pasty white, he carefully placed her on the floor.

"I'm afraid she's fainted," Dido said, as Daddy, having been notified by one of the priests, came running in from the Cathedral two blocks away. Close behind we could hear the ambulance from the Sick Kid's Hospital, its siren screaming its approach and its brakes squealing its arrival. Here, two white-coated men came running in and upon seeing Daria lying on the floor on her stomach they authoritatively announced,

"You were right not to move her, or touch the glass." Lifting her carefully, still on her stomach, they placed her onto the stretcher.

"And what about her?" they asked, nodding towards Mama—her eyes closed, stretched out on Daddy's lap as he sat on the floor stroking her forehead.

"Do we take her too?" Daddy shook his head indicating no. "We'll soon follow."

Lifting the stretcher to leave, they asked who was coming with them, and Dido offered.

"But what really happened, and where are the girls?" Daddy asked Dido as he was putting on his coat. Grandpa mumbled that he didn't exactly know and left with the attendants.

During the commotion we'd snuck up to the gallery, and, trembling in the shadows, watched the tableau below. Seeing all the trouble we'd caused, we were scared, really scared.

Today, my sister Daria still bears the physical scar of that accident. Writing this memory in its metamorphosis from jolly to sad, I find that I too carry a scar, newly discovered. As the emotional truth of this reverie is revealed to me, I am informed in an objective way of the "me" of my childhood. Was this minister's daughter sometimes bossy, often headlong and even imprudent at times? Yes—it seems all of the above.

I can't recall the punishment, nor can Yvonne. Personally, I well remember feeling guilty about all the damage caused in the parlor. In the end, it was Mama's concern for Daria's injury that took precedence over all—and rightly so, for this was Mama's way.

Chapter 5

Mama's House

Time held me green and dying, though I sang in my chains like the sea.
—Epitaph: Westminster Abbey, Dylan Thomas, *Fern Hill*

Mama: Olga Sawchuk, circa 1942

Domesticity

It was Mama's job to keep our huge church house and her seven children, soon to be eight, tidy and presentable to visitors every day of the week, including Sunday. In other words, she was chained to the house; with the responsibility of all of those rooms to clean and all of us kids to look after, it's no wonder Mama got tired. For a while Dad was able to afford an outside cleaner, but in the early forties, during the war years, money was short and that's when Babka and Dido came to live full-time with us to help out. Everyone had to pitch in doing dishes, dusting, vacuuming and shoveling the snow on the long sidewalk to the front door. Knee-high by November, the snow bank would freeze over. It grew with daily snowfalls, reaching waist-high by February. In early April, the spring thaw would slowly melt the packed snow creating a miniature lake in place of a sidewalk. If it turned cold again, the icy walk became a skating rink—a hazardous challenge to all in their efforts to reach the front door. That precarious walkway told us little kids plenty about our family's behavior. We always knew if our older brothers were fighting by their intrusions on the crusty banks lining the walk; we also knew how icy it was when one of our older sisters would limp in, irritated, after trying to navigate in high-heeled fashionable galoshes "that skating rink out there". By the end of April, when all of the snow had melted, the serious spring spruce-up would begin.

Every day, throughout every season, and all year round, cleaning and maintaining our huge house was a full-time job. By now, our house was over-crowded with Babka, Dido, Aunt Mary, all of us kids and the priests in the attic. "Too much housework and, no time for singing," Babka would say again, and I would cringe. I decided early on that Mama's busy life so full of housework was *not* going to be my life. Oh no; I'd find another way, in another world, far away from endless domestic chores.

Mama's Space

The central point of Mama's activity was the kitchen—for her, the most important room in the house. Although I loved watching Mama and Babka as they prepared copious amounts of porridge for breakfast in between chopping vegetables for the huge pot of borscht already simmering for lunch, I knew in my heart of hearts I would never want their life.

Babka always told us that Mama loved music and would have become a singer were it not for having all of us kids. This always made me feel guilty—for being born seventh in line, and for having been born a girl.

"It was time for a boy!" I'd heard Babka say when I was still a baby. And it's true, I should have been a boy; at age nine I *yearned* to be a boy. Then I would grow up to be a busy man like Daddy—

always on the go, talking with people, helping them get started in their new world, doing important work, instead of being tied to the house, in Babka's words, "…with a bunch of kids and endless tasks." Mama fell in love with Daddy, married him at seventeen when he was twenty-five and then had me, the seventh baby, when she was just thirty. Babka's mantra: "Too many babies, too much work, and no time for singing," was true. But perhaps this is putting Mama's life too simply.

Today, in retrospect, I see my mother as a hero. I remember how hard she worked. Not only in the house with us kids, doing the shopping, preparing the meals, cleaning endlessly, but outside of the house too: the church duties, heading up the Women's Club, setting up teas and accompanying Daddy to business meetings and banquets. When I was little, after the dinner dishes were washed and put away and the other kids were all studying or listening to Lux Theatre on the radio, Mama would go up to her bedroom, where I had slept in the crib almost six years, and let me visit with her while she got all dressed up to go out with Daddy.

First she would put on her pink corset, "to hold her stomach in after seven babies," she explained. Then she pulled on her silk stockings and her slippery pink satin slip before choosing one of the going-out dresses that Grandma Babka had sewn up for her. I best remember her royal blue silky dress, the one with long tight sleeves and the skirt cut on the bias, draped to one side where Babka had sewn a sparkly rhinestone broach. When Mama wore that dress, I knew she was going to a special party with Daddy—a "real banquet," she called it.

Mama's eyes would always shine when she was dressing up to go out "fancy." I would perch myself on her bed and watch as she spread Pond's cold cream all over her face then wiped it off to puff on rosy powder, her eyes shut tight. When she finally opened her eyes, she would delicately dab light grey shadow on her lids to match her hair which was already grey at thirty—"…from too much worry", Babka said. Then Mama would dab on light pink lipstick using a Kleenex to blot the shine. When I asked her why she did that, explaining that Aunt Mary and my sister Snow always wore lots of red shiny lipstick, she stated, "It doesn't suit the minister's wife to wear too much strong color." She never wore makeup during the day. When Mama finally put on her pearl and silver earrings, I thought she looked beautiful, like the Queen of England, and I told her so. By then she was smiling at me, and I knew it was a good time to ask for a visit with my doll.

Being the seventh in line, everything in my life was a hand-me-down. The blue and red checked pinafores with their matching white blouses that were sewn by Babka for my older sisters were washed and starched before being passed down to me. "None the worse for wear," Mama said. The pearl-grey wool dress with red trim and matching buttons sewn especially for my sister Yvonne, Babka's favorite grandchild, was also lovingly passed down after being dry-cleaned at home in a big keg of cleaning-fluid—varsol, I think. At that point, nearly everything I owned was a hand-me-down—except for my doll.

The Doll's House

To start with, I did not have free access to my doll. Oh no, my very own "Eaton's Beauty" doll was so precious that she was kept out of sight and out of reach, high up in a closet in Mama's bedroom. There she was stored and kept safe, propped up on the closet shelf staring out at me in a cut-off stocking—in Mama's words, "protected from other children who might try to tear out her beautiful blue eyes and silky lashes, or even ruin her shiny blonde ringlets by washing her hair in real water."

"Or dirty her pretty pink party dress with sticky fingers while trying to pull off her lace panties," I added. I once saw my brother do that with my sister's doll, but I didn't tell Mama.

My doll was very special. She was new, she was not a 'hand-me-down,' she was mine, truly mine, and when I was allowed to play with her, I left this world.... Off I would drift, dreaming about my doll's glamorous future: she would grow up to be beautiful, with a special voice for singing sad songs about love and everyone would adore her and want to be with her. One day she would meet a handsome man with a beautiful deep voice whose eyes would shine like diamonds every time he saw her. Oh yes, my doll's life as a performer would be perfect ... but would mine?

I have always known my musical limits, but not readily accepted them. This goes back to grade two and my first stint with the performance arts. Apparently I was short for my age and I was made aware of this by reason of the stool the stagehands brought out for me to stand on when I was conducting the percussion band at the Kiwanis Music Festival in the Winnipeg Auditorium. Replete in my official school uniform: navy tunic, white cotton blouse, black crinkled stockings on pin-thin legs, my hair in tightly plaited pigtails with shiny red bows, I would climb smartly up onto the box, raise my hands with authority and signal for the ready. Crisp on the downbeat, we'd launch off into a rollicking version of Bring the Good Old Bugle Boys, rendered with gay abandon, in a 4/4 rhythm. This was usually followed by the genteel melody, Down Yonder Green Valley, a slow legato in a 3/4 rhythm. I never had any trouble differentiating time values and since it was only a percussion band I figured I was tenured for life—well, through grade school, at least. Not so. When I was unexpectedly asked to share the podium with Alan Dectar my nemesis for standing first in class, I was first mortified, then chagrined. Declining, I grandly stated: "No thank you, Miss Lush, I prefer to step down. I will take up the triangle instead."

As reverie works on my history, it allows me to see early signs of independence, resolve and yes, a little arrogance—a formidable mix in a seven-year old. Here, my curiosity is aroused. In making choices, facing losses, and in determination and resolve in reaching goals—what, and who, have been my influences? In writing my childhood memories, they always seem to fall within the landscape of my father, who was often away, rather than my dear mother—the true constant in my life.

Dad's Continuing Influence

My father always figured strongly in my life. I inherited his nose, which as a teenager I hated. There were tortured hours spent in front of the mirror examining my nose in profile, trying to flatten the bump with my thumb. My obsession continued into my early teens when, as an over-wrought teenager, disaster struck again—this time in the form of extreme myopia. Within six months I couldn't see the black board, the passing traffic or my friends across the street. Of course I wouldn't wear my glasses! We developed signal signs: two arms raised high meant that I would meet them at Kelekis' Fish and Chips on Main Street, and one arm meant I'd see them at the playground after school, at St. John's Tech. Meanwhile, my already blurred teenage identity became even more tortured as I blamed my father for inheriting his long nose, short-sighted vision and extreme skinniness, all of which I was cursed with. I wanted to look like my best friend, Joanie Bergman, who was of Icelandic descent, from Gimli, Manitoba. I envied her. Her short pert nose, naturally curly hair, cute figure along with a perky personality, garnered chronic praise from my mother, all of which, in an obvious reversal of intention added to my woes. Luckily, my gangly figure and sharply proportioned face eventually softened, as did my teen-age angst and resentment towards Dad. By the time I grew out of my teens, I grew out of my "phase." I had more important things to worry about, such as what to do with the rest of my life ... but my basic insecurity about my looks and my unorthodox background never faded.

Brought up in a fancy house which we didn't own, I was born into a myth—a confused identity and a social veneer I little understood in my youth. Today, triggered by photos, songs and meditations, many of those early feelings are being revealed to me. As a consequence, I have found that writing about my life provides a means of ferreting out and understanding my emotional truth as a child, young adult, a middle-aged woman grappling with self-expectations and guilt and finally, as a senior, happily living out my life on the growing edge—still in wonder, still learning, still asking questions and still looking back to learn from the past.

For example, I now know from letters going back decades between Mum and Dad, passed on to me by my older sister, that my parents struggled financially from the time they were married in 1920 right through to the 1970s—fifty years. The first baby, my oldest sister Zenovia (Snow), arrived a year after they were married, followed by six others in rapid succession: Zenon (Buck), Lessia (Laddie), Leo, Yvonne, Daria, and me trailed years later by my brother Simeon (Joe). Born curious, the youngest of seven for eleven years, I was acutely aware of everything around me, including the emotional dynamics in our household. Everyone's feelings—Dad, Mum's, my brothers and sisters—all of their moods affected me, as these next Easter reflections reveal.

Easter Morning

I remember how cold, miserable and hungry I would be after fasting from early evening on through the night before church service, Easter morning. I remember that time, just past three years old, Mama nudging me in the crib to awaken me. Getting dressed very early while still dark outside, the boys would fight about their lost socks, the girls would fight for their turn in the bathroom and Babka would complain about "those noisy kids." Mama braided our hair and tried to shush everybody quiet, so as not to upset Daddy, who has been working on his sermon all night. Finally dressed, we would all trundle off to church, walking fast through the slushy April snow in order to stand (no church pews then) over two hours listening to the choir and the priests chant a service in Ukrainian that I could barely understand. After the lengthy service inside, we would congregate outside huddling in Winnipeg's cold, damp, April air. Clutching our baskets full of Easter fare, soon to be our festive breakfast, we would form a procession behind the chanting priests who led a walk around the church three times in honor of the Holy trinity—an abiding precept of the Ukrainian Greek Orthodox faith. In pre-dawn light we would uncover our baskets and raise them toward the priests to be blessed. Singing soulful hymns while circling the church, we would patiently wait for the sun to rise, its warm rays heralding the official dawn of Easter. Everyone seemed happy when it was finally time to go home. I'm not sure that any of the other kids, especially my brothers, liked Easter very much. I suppose they remember all the arguments and bad tempers those mornings when we were awakened at four AM and told by Mama to "Hurry up, we'll be late for church, and you know Daddy will get mad." What I remember best is that I loved Easter and Daddy rarely got mad at me. I guess that's because I was the baby.

Easter Breakfast

Easter morning after church, we take our usual place at the table. We giggle and talk while waiting for others, including the priests in the attic, to come in; but when Daddy enters, we all hush up. We are dressed in our Sunday best: my sisters in their blue-checked pinafores with crisp white blouses and shiny red ribbons around their pig tails that I watched Mama braid this morning, when it was still dark outside. Every time they move their heads, the ribbons sparkle against the light of the silver candles that are flickering shadows on the dining room wall. I tell my darling Dido to look, and he says they are dancing and waving Happy Easter to me. I like that. I look around the table and see that everyone has calmed down. Mama looks happy and so does Daddy—so I am happy too.

At Easter breakfast, Mama cracks open the boiled eggs with her sharp knife then cuts them in half and passes them around the table—me first, because I always sit next to her in the big dining room. Next, she passes around two big plates, one with sweet ham and pineapple rings and the other with garlic *kolbassa* sausage, sliced thin and carefully placed in a circle around the *paska* bread which I watched Babka bake last night.

First she tosses and pounds the thick white dough until it's long and flat; then she shapes it into three long ropes that she braids and cuts into loaves, brushing them with melted butter for "...the shine," she explains, before popping them into the oven. As she lifts the steaming loaves onto the table to cool, I can hear the other kids flying down the front and back stairs, three steps at a time from the third floor where the delicious aroma of baking bread has already reached. They arrive breathless, in Dido's words, "...hungry as wolves, but sounding more like a herd of elephants." When Babka takes the loaves out of the oven my brothers beg for a taste, but she tells them, "No, you have to wait for Easter breakfast after church tomorrow." Now they swing me between them, laughing as we all try to squeeze through the dining room doors at once, racing each other back upstairs to be the first to reach the living room in order to grab the best spot near the radio for our favorite Saturday evening programs.

∞ ∞ ∞

After our Easter breakfast is eaten and the many dishes had been cleared away and washed, we are ushered back into the big dining room, which is so large it was once used for my sister Lessia's formal graduation party. Now we all sit in chairs that have been lined up in rows, like at the movies, staring at a white sheet that Daddy has draped over the tall bookshelf at the far end of the dining room.

Propped up on Mama's lap I can see the whole family: Daddy, my six brothers and sisters, my darling Dido, Babka, the student priests from the attic and my Aunt Mary, who always smells nice and wears lots of shiny bracelets that jingle when she tickles my stomach. I am finally warm after shivering for such a long time inside and outside of Daddy's church earlier this morning.

"April, and still ice on the bony trees," Grandma had complained as we filed through lumpy ice-slush on our way home from church at 6 AM. I still remember clinging tightly to Grandpa's arm for support and safety as I gazed up at the "bone trees"—black and scary against the yellow dawn light, I was afraid their skinny branches would reach out and grab me. But now I'm happy to be at home in our warm dining room snuggled close on Mama's lap.

Even though the lights in the dining room were off and the blinds closed, I could still see what was going on around me because of a pale light coming from the back. When I heard a whirring noise behind, I leaned around to see Daddy fiddling with two wheels and a black box with a light flickering in it. I was going to ask Mama what he was doing, but she was paying attention to my big brothers who had started fighting and fidgeting. The priests were whispering to them, "Keep it down, please." My two brothers stopped for a minute but soon they started poking at each other again, getting noisier and rougher until the priests finally spoke up and told them, "Keep quiet, or else…" I knew the boys didn't like the priests. They called them the conscience-cops. I wondered what that meant but I was afraid to ask because I didn't want them to think "the baby" was dumb. I was hoping they would listen to the cops, but they just kept talking louder. I was expecting trouble, and it soon came when Daddy's voice hissed a loud "Shhh" from behind. Scared by this, I turned around to look; I could tell he was mad. The light from the box was shining up onto to his face in a way that made his nose, dark beard and mustache look pointy and scary—like the masks my brothers wore on Halloween. And when the light in the black box started jumping around I couldn't stop looking because Daddy's face looked even scarier. When I started to whimper, Mama turned me around and told me to look at the picture on the white sheet. I did, but that was scary too.

What I saw was a man dressed in a long white robe like Daddy wears when he stands in front of everybody at church and prays. But Daddy's robe is clean and it has a beautiful gold tie-belt and gold braid around the neck and sleeves. I've watched my Babka make his robes, and because she's so good at it—she sews our pinafores, Mama's dresses and even Daddy's jackets—she was chosen to make up the official robes, she called vestments, for all of the priests in the Orthodox Church across Canada. She uses a special cloth that comes from France: shiny and beautiful, with gold and silver crosses. It is kept hidden away safe in Daddy's office, where once I was allowed to see it and touch it. I loved the shine and the feel of that cloth and I told Mama that one day I'd have a fancy dress made out of it to sing in. Daddy just patted my head but Mama smiled. She knew I meant it.

The man moving on the white sheet, which Mama calls a screen, has the same dark beard and hair like Daddy's, but his robe is dirty with dark stains on it. He is stooped down, dragging something that looks like a tree trunk with a piece of wood nailed across it. Lots of people are standing around staring at the poor man, who has trouble walking and keeps falling down. Thick chains circle his ankles and when his robe falls away I can see lots of dark stripes that look like blood on his back. All of the people watching him are moaning and crying, so I start crying too. Mama holds me closer and tells me that it's okay for me to cry because it's such a sad thing that is happening to this man, whose name is Jesus. I don't understand, but because the man looks so much like my Daddy, I am afraid that this bad thing could happen to him too. So I squeeze my eyes shut to make it all stop. When I finally open them, the lights are on and everybody is leaving except Daddy, who now looks nice again. He is standing in front of me, smiling and reaching out long arms, ready to catch me. I jump into them, and hugging him tightly I stare into his eyes so close—feeling happy and safe again, wrapped in Daddy's arms.

Themes Transcending Time

Here, writing one of my earliest memories, putting my feelings into words through reverie, I now comprehend the importance of my early Christian experience—the indelible image of Christ's tortuous walk to Golgotha. I see it as the key experience in the birth of my quest for spiritual knowledge—a profound image indelibly printed onto a child's psyche becoming an integral part of a faith journey. I pause in wonder. How is it, that certain childhood memories can be visibly restored, fully wrapped in the same feelings and emotions which were present at their inception? How and why does our memory select particular childhood events to be resurrected six decades later? Can these memories be cited and held ransom towards an understanding that the "who" we were as children will help formulate *who* we will become as adults? In *Reveries toward Childhood*, Gaston Bachelard explains:

"In reverie, image values become psychological facts…. All of our childhood dreams have to be taken up again so that they will take on their full poetic flight." In other words, Bachelard believes we must take on our childhood dreams and ambitions in order to accomplish the full potential of our future.

Reverie's Child

At the time Daddy went overseas during the Second World War, I was in grade one at Machray school. My teacher had told my parents that I was a good student, but I asked too many questions. It's true. I decided early on that the only way to learn things was by asking questions. Every day, at school and at home, my head buzzed with new information. My curiosity knew no bounds.

Flattened against the darkened corner at the top of the kitchen stairs, I could see and hear everything Mama and Babka were saying even though they often whispered. This one time they were talking about a baby that was coming, and later, when I asked *who* the baby was coming *to*, and where was it was coming *from*, Mama just smiled. She knew I'd been listening, so she changed the subject and started talking about Daddy, who was back in England after a short visit home in January of 1942. Mama explained that as a chaplain in the regular army, ranked as a captain, he was in the middle of the war zone and in danger from the German bombs like any other soldier. I tried to imagine Daddy all dressed up in his uniform and cap, waving his bat-stick around, shouting and telling everybody what to do, but Mama told me it wasn't like that. He was there helping out the nurses, doctors, ambulance drivers and soldiers as a spiritual leader. She said, "They need someone to pray for the sick, the dying, and the soldiers in danger." Since Daddy was praying for everyone else, I decided to pray for him—that he would come home safe and in time for that new baby that I'd heard was coming to our house. He did, and the new baby turned out to be my younger brother, who permanently over threw my status as "the baby." Over half of my life had been spent in a worn-out crib that would be dragged out again for the eighth baby named Simeon by Mum and Dad. Disliking the name, on his first day of school, my little brother was re-named Joe (by Joe). Meanwhile, having lost my baby status, I was growing into a high-strung teenybopper replete with all the interests and crazy fads of the day.

Immigrant Experience

As a young girl, our stately manse affected every facet of my life—at times a rainbow arcing over my childhood with energy and light, at other times infusing my dreams with darkness and dashed hope. In retrospection, as old feelings are revived, I feel again that early contradiction between the outer self of my cultural circumstances and the inner self of my desires and dreams. It was a dichotomy created by the conditions of my birth as a Canadian-born daughter of a Ukrainian immigrant living within a diverse, divided neighborhood.

Brought up in an all-Jewish community in the north end of Winnipeg during WW II, my sense of self was confused and disjointed from early school years on. This confusion was exacerbated in our small adjoining Ukrainian community by my Dad's position as a high profile priest. As a leader of the Ukrainian Greek Orthodox Church in Canada, my father expected me and my six brothers and sisters to behave with decorum at all times, outside and inside the house.

Outside, geographically embedded within a Jewish community, we were expected to be high achievers in school, stay out of trouble and "be happy" while immersed in a social and cultural community into which we were not allowed to fully integrate. At home, in the manse, we were expected to follow the old-world language, faith and customs of Ukraine and always be well-behaved and respectful to the myriad of callers who came to see Dad in his office beside the chapel. These were two separate worlds with opposing languages, faiths and cultural customs. As early as grade school, I sensed the dichotomy between my inner life at home and my outer life of circumstance, i.e., life inside my father's house, heavily invested in the practice of an Ukrainian Orthodox faith, and life outside, in a primarily Jewish community that did not openly oppose our culture but returned the same covert feelings of separateness practiced by our equally distanced Ukrainian group.

As a budding teenager, I found it difficult to meet my father's expectations. Unable to synthesize my home life with the real world outside, I never discussed my Ukrainian activities outside the home, in fact, I hid them, for fear I would be seen as "less Canadian" by my Jewish friends, who were, themselves, immersed in an opposing immigrant experience and practice. For this reason, I spent most of my teenage years in a state of disconnectedness, a confusing reality that eventually caused me to turn inward for solace and outward in search of a new identity. Although not mistreated by Ukrainians or Jews, I felt displaced within both communities—a double immigrant in my own homeland.

Like many Eastern European immigrants to Canada, my father valued education as a way of gaining acceptance in the Anglo-Saxon protestant world. For him, an advanced education allowed certain recognition by Canadian hybrid society as a whole. And so, while growing up Ukrainian in the north end of Winnipeg, Canada, I made plans: After graduation I would leave Winnipeg and find my own place beside bona fide Canadians—who must be out there somewhere. After all, being born in Canada, was I not a Canadian first, before anything else? While waiting to take my leave, I maintained a loving relationship with my parents who, I've been often told by my six older siblings, spoiled me rotten because I was the baby.

As will be seen, my story is not one of atrocities or deprivation. Rather it is a confessional story centered on my search in childhood for a feeling of self-worth, first filtered through my earthly father, then onto my heavenly Father in the hope of gaining a generous acceptance of myself and others. Unlike Saint Augustine, I do not consider myself a great sinner, but, like him, I do search for *divine guidance* in writing this memoir: "With your eyes upon me, my God, my memory can safely recall those days."

PART TWO

Enigmas: Pursuing the Dream

Chapter 6

Learning to Sing

Out beyond ideas of wrongdoing and rightdoing,
there is a field. I'll meet you there.

—Jalal ud Din Rumi

Singing with the Jimmy King Trio in Winnipeg,
with Lenny Breau on guitar and Dave Shaw on bass.

My Singing Blues

While working at my first job as an x-ray technician in Edmonton, Alberta, I initiated a childhood dream. The city was hot—too darn hot. There was little air-conditioning in those days and my nurse's uniform soon clung like an airtight nylon sheath; freshly washed and ready-to-wear each morning, it stopped breathing by noon and by night it had to be peeled off like a wet condom. I was twenty-one years old, homesick and bored. I liked my job well enough, but

I didn't like my current boyfriend much. Most of my friends were getting married. In the late fifties, twenty-one was the expected age for girls to settle down—but not me. I wasn't ready. I still had things to do. Emotionally and financially free, the time felt right; I was finally in a position to get serious about my long-held fantasy.

All my life, I've loved to sing. "Your daughter has a lovely voice," the music teacher told my parents upon my completion of grade six. "You should consider sending her for singing lessons." My parents "considered," but it seems my teeth came out ahead in more ways than one.

"There is something new on the market that could straighten out your daughter's buck teeth quickly, and in a natural way" the orthodontist explained. In my father's regal ministerial manner and as the responsible dad of seven, he quickly bit into that promise and signed up for what he thought would be a quick cure for my toothy grin. But in between the chronic discomfort of bleeding gums from the elastic-bearing hooks and other mishaps, including loss of product, Dad ended up with four years of monthly payments he could ill-afford to the dentist. Gallant to the end, he would cover his financial stress by joking, "After all, only the best is good enough," and Mum, the obliging minister's wife, would laugh in between tears of love for Dad and her chronic concern over our family's relentless money worries.

Years later, as a young woman with an expensive smile and a love for the stage, it was finally time to pursue my singing dream: But how? Where? I was determined to find a way.

I decided to start with a change of scenery. I quit my boyfriend, my job and the hot city and headed for the hills: the Rocky Mountains and The Banff School of Fine Arts. This decision was based on information from my first singing teacher, Madame Carmichael—a jolly robust woman of Italian descent with a penchant for purple: monochromic layers that included the wallpaper, the sofa and a series of floral dresses in various shades of purple ranging from violet to puce. Her carefully coiffed hair-do was dyed a mauve-beige, replete with a purple bow to match her beloved miniature poodle, Mimi—who chronically occupied Madame's ample lap and all of her attention, leaving little time for me and my first fragile attempts at singing.

"Ah, but I cannot hear you, my darling," she would say, "You must sing out; you must open the throat; you must push out the lungs; you must take the deep breath—but first, you must find the note!"

"Okay, okay, I know I can do this, but can we practice it in B flat above middle C? It's the only note I'm sure to find today. Here we go: *mah ... moh ... mooh ... mayh ... meeh.* There; is that better? Did I get it? Maybe now I can sing a song right through?"

"No, no, my darling, you cannot," Madame said, distracted as usual, and shifting her monocle to her other mauve-shaded eyelid while searching for Mimi, who was now parked near the front door, panting to get out. "We know there are many more notes in the scale; we must find them. Now, take the deep breath," she commanded and the piano would loudly sound the chord.

But after searching for three weeks and "finding" only three notes, I knew I had to leave. *I don't have time for this,* I thought. *Twenty-one is probably too late anyway, but I must keep trying or my dream will die in the agony of one tremulous note.* And so, with time and Mimi yipping at my heels, I found enough courage to march out of Madame Carmichael's door into a musical future fraught with anticipation, high ambitions and deep resolve. With a positive mantra pounding in my ears (in B flat), a bullish determination was born. *Now is the time,* I thought. *My singing dream must be fully pursued or fully dropped.*

Somewhere Different

Imposing mountains leaning against a crystal blue sky not only enhanced the power of the orchestral music played on my first day at The Banff School of Fine Arts but also, for me, brought on a new bravado. Light-headed from the thin mountain air coupled with the excitement of being in such a prestigious environment, I was giddy enough to dare to perform in the open concert proposed by the alumni teachers that night. What or how I sang eludes me now, but what I do remember is an unfamiliar feeling of happiness accompanied by an unfamiliar serenity. I loved breathing the pure mountain air. Just being in that pristine environment, surrounded by friendly musicians, away from the city's clamor, I was able to concentrate on developing my voice. Yes, I finally "found" the notes—all eight of them!

Early that week, I was lucky enough to encounter a special singing teacher, a respected maestro, Dr. Ernesto Vinci, the visiting voice coach from Toronto's Royal Conservatory of Music. I later found out that Dr.Vinci was the teacher of Robert Goulet, a handsome young baritone who, after attending opera school at the Toronto conservatory, soon found great fame and fortune in the movies— the first one, *Camelot,* with Elizabeth Taylor and Richard Burton. *Hmm,* I thought, *this Dr.Vinci must be good; Toronto, eh? Yes, somewhere different, a bigger dot on the map of musical opportunity.*

The next day, when asked to sing for the maestro, excited and nervous as I was, I had my wits about me to ask the accompanist to play "Un Bel Die," from Puccini's *Madame Butterfly,* "In the *medium* key, please," I stated, "not in *high,* as written." I knew that being an inexperienced soloist with only one flawless note of merit, B flat above middle C, my knees could well turn to water. They did. But my one note prevailed, and, with the help of its foundlings I sang out with new-found conviction and bravado. Halfway through, Dr.Vinci commented to his accompanist, "Hidden somewhere deep within this smiling young woman, there is a voice that can be developed, and I'm the one to do it!" That's all I needed to hear. At the end of the course I returned to Edmonton and started packing.

Toronto the Good

Spoken in typical Western aversion to the East, Dad warns me in Ukrainian "When you get to Toronto, hold your nose high." I think he meant to say hold your *head* high. Possessing a smaller version of his hawk nose, I smiled at the reference and understood that it was his way of protecting me by citing expected prejudices against me and my European background in the big city. But I was unconcerned. I'd been around: from Winnipeg to Edmonton, Calgary and then Banff. My co-workers and friends were of various backgrounds, mostly Anglo-Saxon, and thinking of myself sophisticated in the ways of big cities, I had no anxieties. In the late fifties and sixties, Toronto was still "Toronto the Good."

In my first years in Toronto, I lived at the Fudger House Club, an all-girls' residence on Sherbourne Street, a short walk and streetcar run to Yonge Street, the General Hospital and the Toronto conservatory—the triangular space of my x-ray work, musical training and social life for the next three years. It was early spring when I first arrived in Toronto, and as April stretched into May it brought along a torrid heat wave that invaded the city and burned relentlessly through spring and summer into late fall.

There was little air conditioning at the hospital or at home, but as the city rallied so did we. In the first months of unrelenting heat, with the temperature running high, our patience ran low, but we soon found ways to manage. In between work and music, we crowded the beaches, malls and movies in search of cool relief. As such, a spirit of friendliness, support and general good fun pervaded our lives at the General Hospital and the Conservatory that first dogged-out Toronto summer until a personal tragedy struck. Simply put, I'd fallen in love, for the first time. He was studying at the conservatory; a dark handsome Italian baritone with a beautiful romantic voice. This was not kid stuff—not for me, anyway. We were absorbed with our music first and each other second, in that order. In the late fifties, in Toronto, there were still many social boundaries of propriety and conventions to be observed, but not for us. We were, after all, "artists." Love led to lust, and that, added to the hot temperatures in the city, kept us in a state of prevailing heat, inside and outside, for months.

And the newness of it all! Such a state of yearning, longing, jealousy and ambition, all powered by the gods of music. Their ability to raise the spirits of love that infused the very air we breathed came out in an ecstasy of song; *Te voglio bene assai*, "I love you very much," he sang in a tearful lyric baritone, as much to himself as to me. Desire, driven by a zealous combination of carnality and music continued to fill our hours in a torpid dream-state until, wearied and exhausted, summer finally waned—as did our love. The leaves began to blow and precipitated by the bleakness of autumn's languor, our love notes fell flat. Unable to combine with our vanities and separate ambitions, they took on a sharpness of pain that soon turned into a piercing falsetto.

He left for another.

While the fates of love took their slow, distressful leave, Music, my loyal mistress, stood patiently outside the gate, waiting … singing low. Finally, when the sting of desire had subsided, Music sang, *Dio, comme ti amo,* "God how much I love you," intoned in a lovely soprano voice that renewed my ambition and my strength. I was restored. Although my summer love had departed, Music, my true soul-mate remained. Healing through song, re-opening my numbed soul, she turned that distressful winter into a spring of hope and soon another love appeared, one who would inhabit my future but not my dreams—they were too crowded. Clamoring for attention, they would hold me in sway for years.

Auditioning for Life

After that summer of feckless love and the soulful winter that followed, I met another baritone who also studied at the Toronto conservatory. He was tall and handsome, in the way of the popular actor Robert Mitchum, with steely blue eyes and lids in repose— shades half drawn, allowing some light in but always keeping cool. We met in Buffalo on a steamy June day, both at auditions for the prestigious outdoor summer musicals performed at the *Theater under the Stars.*

After a rigorous day of auditioning hundreds of would-be singers and dancers, the directors were finally down to twelve women hopefuls and as many men. Early on, after the initial weeding-out process had been completed, we'd been advised that only eight out of each group would be selected. At this point, Michael Steele and I were still part of the pared-down groups, nine in each. By now, my nerves were frazzled and my dance steps frayed. Not having studied formal dance since my short-lived foray into tap-dancing when I was five years old (the group classes cost twenty-five cents a session!), I figured I'd probably trip up. I did.

"Thank you for trying out," the director said, smiling politely. Disappointed and dismayed I could see Michael off to the side looking at me. I watched him as he sauntered over:

"Hey, kid, what's the story?" he asked.

Trying to be pleasant I jauntily replied, "The story is, I've been dumped, and you?" After a slight pause, he started laughing too.

"Ditto—but that's show-biz, huh? Anyway, that's the bad news. The good news is you've got a lift back to Toronto—what do you say?"

"Why not"? I answered, smiling nonchalantly at this tall attractive man. *Maybe a failed audition is a blessing in disguise,* I thought, as we walked towards the car.

After that inauspicious meeting, we started dating and a year and half later we got married in a small but elegant Anglican church in Michael's hometown, Montreal. I wore my sister Lessia's made-to-order ecru satin gown, which looked beautiful on her, but for me was too short. Not to worry. I delved deep into a bin in Eaton's basement, dug out some white satin ballet-type shoes, and by using my Babka's trick colored them ecru by dipping them in strong tea and danced off to the church—a little late, as usual. I don't remember much about the ceremony, but I've recently found a picture of us exiting the church, smiling under a cloud of confetti, so it must have gone well. What I *do* remember with clarity, is standing over a hot stove an hour before the wedding, stirring a huge pot of chicken-a-la-king for the reception, which was attended by fifty guests. While everyone else was at the hairdressers' this bride, with monetary vigilance, was cooking.

And so our marital saga began. Embedded in lack from the start, it ended seven years later, book-ended in the same emotional and financial state in which it started. In between our poverty, arguments, genuine care and grief, I nurtured my dream of a singing career. Oh yes, the yearning was still there and, as the words of Peggy Lee's latest hit, "Is That All There Is?" pounded through my inconstant soul, I pondered my next move.

Back to Reality

Soon after the wedding, poor and jobless, we decided to leave Toronto and seek our musical fortunes back home in the smaller show biz pond of Winnipeg. By now I was aware that my late-trained soprano voice had limitations—it would never be good enough for the competitive world of opera, but I wasn't ready to give up; I still dreamed of performing.

We arrived in Winnipeg in the dead of winter and stayed in Mum's basement while looking for musically related jobs. In between sporadic leads with no results I had time to think back. I remembered Peggy Lee pouring out her songs on the record player to my brother Buck while I was still in my crib. Loving the music and rhythm, in childlike wisdom I memorized the words, as though one day I myself would sing them on stage. In light of that reverie, I decided that my natural interest in popular music would be a sound route to success.

Looking to contemporary artists like Judy Garland, Doris Day and the newly discovered Barbara Streisand, I bought their records and listened intently to the melodies and words while trying to mimic their styles. With no piano access, my circular pitch-pipe of conservatory days was a must-have item in my purse at all times. Searching the keynote, I would quietly hum or sing along, depending on where I was. But it was tough and tougher still when, after a month, my dear mother, in Ukrainian, gently queried, "Perhaps your husband should consider getting a job, *any* job, to carry you both through until the big day of success arrives?"

I was mortified, as well I should be. In the late fifties, by the age of twenty-one, usually one was done with school and *everyone* worked—especially a married man! Always independent, I was a worker from my early teens on—my first job was at Eaton's cosmetics counter when I was barely sixteen—my "problem-solver" personality emerged with a vengeance.

"That's it!" I announced to Mike at breakfast the next morning. "Get dressed. We're going back to my old "Alma Mater," Eaton's, to get jobs."

And we did: Mike in the furniture department and me in the sewing machine department. Within a week we were able to move out of Mum's basement to the French-speaking district of St. Boniface across the frozen Red River where the rents were cheaper. And throughout Winnipeg's famous March ice storms, enduring the tedious streetcar rides to work and back to our meager apartment, I memorized and practiced the current hit songs in my head, preparing ... for what? One song in particular haunted me: "The Party's Over," the Judy Holliday song from the Broadway hit, *The Bells are Ringing;*

it repeated itself as a mantra in my head until I started taking the words to heart. *Was* my party over?

Standing in high heels all day long, selling sewing machines at Eaton's department store, heading home in snow storms and lugging groceries up two flights of stairs, cooking dinner on a two-burner stove, completing all the domestic chores that married women of my era were singly burdened with, I'd finally collapse into bed and dream *the dream*—the one I'd been having throughout my adult life. The feelings are always the same—only the people and places change.

The Dream

And the nightmare is simple ... in this ambiguous space,
the mind has lost its geometrical homeland and the spirit is drifting.
—Gaston Bachelard, "The 'Cogito' of the Dreamer,"
Poetics of Reverie

I'm usually in an airport or a train station waiting for someone. I see them coming; I look down briefly to pick up my suitcase, and when I look up again, they're gone. I search the crowd. *Where are they?* In my dream, the "twirlies" start and my stomach curls itself into a crunch. I look down again and see that my small bag with all of my money is gone. *What's happening? Where are they? Where's the hotel? What should I do? Walk around or wait right here?* I need to do something, but I can't move. My legs are either cut off or made of lead. I search the crowd again: faceless shadows all walking away. I feel helpless, lost and alone... no way out. The terror wakes me up.

∞ ∞ ∞

According to Bachelard, "often it is in the *heart* of the being that being is in errancy." In other words the terror in a dream does not come from the outside nor is it composed of old memories. It has no past, no physiology ... here, fear is being itself. As in the excerpt above, "the mind has lost its geographical homeland, and as such the spirit is drifting.... Within the nocturnal dream the "I" dissolves and is lost."

As will be seen, this wilderness of loss and concurrent fear is chronicled throughout this memoir from my early adult years onwards. My "spirit is drifting" and apparently it will continue to do so within

59

my quest, as through *reverie* (daydream), not *rêve* (nocturnal dream), I hunt for the emotional truth of my past, in order to reconcile it with my present.

A Winnipeg Wasteland

The stylish lightweight winter coat I bought from Wilson Brothers while modeling in Toronto to help pay for my music lessons proved worthless. In the midst of a bitter Winnipeg winter, looking good doesn't count for a thing. No one is ever going to notice your silly three-inch calfskin boots, a frivolous buy while still in love, or the expensive matching carryall now toting a brown-bag lunch with extra tea bags (Eaton's doesn't charge for a cup of hot water). My weighty handbag contained a bulky makeup kit and a pocket songbook, both essentials for this ambitious singer trying to look her best while standing around Eaton's selling sewing machines, always smiling, but inwardly frustrated—bored beyond endurance. *This is torture,* I thought. *What am I doing here? I'm wasting my life. I have to get out!* Thoroughly discouraged, I could feel angry tears welling up, ready to spill. Grabbing my handbag, I head across the floor to the ladies' washroom. Hiding in a booth, increasingly upset and exasperated with my life, I prayed. *Just give me a sign,* I asked, *anything to give me some new direction and hope.* I waited…. Within seconds, calmness came.

As the tears subsided, and while rummaging through my purse for my makeup kit, I saw my round silver pitch pipe smiling up at me with its toothy grin from the cavern of my cluttered bag. Just seeing its happy face helped me relax. *Yes,* I thought, *this is what I need to do. Singing always makes me feel better.* So I pulled out my pocket songbook and began to hum Doris Day's current hit song, "Just in Time." The lyrics described her being lost, with nowhere to go. *Hmm,* I thought, *sounds just like my current ongoing dream.*

Carried away, singing out in an energetic voice, I was suddenly interrupted by a loud flushing sound in the cubicle next to me. Looking down, I saw a familiar pair of shoes, Tender Tootsies, the sensible shoes of my floor supervisor, a great gal, who loudly stated: "Whoever you are, you should be singing professionally."

Shocked and amazed by this ready answer to prayer, I started crying all over again, this time laughing in between. After my supervisor left, I waited a few minutes then hurried back to the sales floor, gave her a big hug, handed in my notice and quit on the spot—I guess she never knew why, but *I* knew.... *Angels are everywhere.*

Performance Promises

That summer, after successfully auditioning and performing professionally for two months in Winnipeg's outdoor theatre, Rainbow Stage, I managed to get some club dates and radio work on CBC. While there, I met up with some local musicians including Jimmy King, a talented and amiable pianist working part-time at Eaton's selling pianos.

Through the years Jimmy became a very successful and popular full-time musician, one who played the xylophone and keyboard with equal dexterity. Making up Jimmy's trio was Del Wagner, a fine drummer whose work was complimented by a young creative guitarist, Lenny Breau—who, at age twenty, was already recognized by his peers as a musical genius. Lenny was a Canadian prodigy, who left his mark on generations of musicians to come. In 1979, Chet Atkins, an American guitarist and record producer, pronounced Lenny "the greatest guitar player in the world today." To this day, thirty years later, his innovative work is still respected and admired by guitarists nationwide. Sadly, in 1984, at age forty-three, Lenny Breau was found murdered at the bottom of an LA swimming pool. Today, his case remains unsolved.

In retrospect, I see that my professional singing career started and was honed with those fine musicians in Winnipeg—a winter wasteland to some, but at that time home to many fine artists who not only survived but flourished. Winnipeg's verdant artistic centre included the Royal Winnipeg Ballet, founded in 1939—an early home to Veronica Tennent of ballet fame. There was The Manitoba Theater Center, whose individual artists went on to world-wide fame and fortune, including the late John Hirsch, a talented director at The Stratford Festival of Canada and Gorden Pinsent, originally from Newfoundland, a fine film actor who wrote and starred in the well received movie, *Rowdyman,* later appeared in *Shipping News* and more recently in *Away from You* to name only a few.

In the early fall of 1960, after my first stint as a professional singer in Winnipeg and a full-hearted attempt at weathering those dreadful winters, upon Michael's urging, we decided to move back to Montreal to find "real work," settle down and raise a family. Mike left first, on a balmy day in mid-September, but I had to stay behind for some minor surgery on my foot which I had injured while dancing in the last musical of the summer, "Damn Yankees." Unfortunately the surgery was botched and required three more visits to the Winnipeg General Hospital. I had to stay behind with Mum for a few weeks that turned into five months when the site of the surgery got infected and wouldn't heal. September turned into November, and I soon found out that trying to maneuver crutches through slippery ice, streetcars and buses, in a Winnipeg winter was impossible, so I took a small apartment downtown near the hospital. For the next three months I managed financially by playing club dates with the Jimmy King trio. At first, I could barely hobble out to sing, but once I was settled on a high stool, the performance style of that day, I managed quite nicely. I worked with Lenny Breau and Jimmy's eminent trio at various venues around town, including the best hotels—the Marlborough and Royal Alex supper clubs—private parties and weddings, as well as live appearances on a musical variety show produced by the early television station in Winnipeg, CJAY and I will never forget performing at the Flin Flon Festival way up in northern Manitoba in early June. As I remember, there was a golf tournament that teed off at midnight—it was that light outside!

Those were great days; I loved the music world and performing in general. As my performance skills improved so did my small-town success, but soon my ambitions outgrew my ventures. I felt ready to plunge into a larger performance pool. But after two hospitalizations and three skin grafts, and finally able to walk without crutches, I also knew it was time to face reality—join Michael in Montreal in an effort to retrofit the pieces of our wobbly marriage. My guilty self, beleaguered by the status quo of the early sixties, convinced me that this was *the right thing to do,* and so another race to the future was on. But what was I running toward? And what of my heart's desire?

Cloudy Dreams

Our life together, in Montreal, started out badly. My marriage was falling apart; pieces of me as a professional singer, potential mother and faithful wife had gone adrift after Michael left Winnipeg, the previous fall. Being alone, I'd had too much time to think … and all I thought about was music. A hit song popular in the sixties, Carly Simon's "You're So Vain," pounded on my radio by day and insistently behind my dreams at night. The lyrics, about dreams, clouds and coffee reverberated through my psyche endlessly. Why?

Yes, as the song suggests, I had some dreams. At this point they were free-floating and if I didn't net them soon they'd sink forever. The truth is my dreams were not about Michael or our marriage; they were about music. In Winnipeg, I'd had a taste of being a professional singer, and I loved it. In my time there, without Michael, music was my rock of reality; I grabbed it and held on, afraid of losing my grip and drifting off into obscurity. No, I wouldn't let that happen. I would perfect what talent I had. I'd find a coach, one who would understand my natural voice and work with me to create a professional club act that would include the show tunes and ballads of the day. I decided that this was the only way to get what I wanted—a full-time singing career.

∞ ∞ ∞

His name was Johnny Gallant; he was not only a terrific pianist and accompanist, he was also interested in coaching me and preparing a viable supper-club act. In between working on our act, I did showroom modeling in the garment district of Montreal in order to contribute towards our sparse basement apartment and household needs. At this point Michael was working with CJOH-TV as a floor director, a job that would eventually lead to an excellent long-time career as a TV producer of such well-known shows as *Stars on Ice* and the immensely popular *Ian and Sylvia Show*. While Mike built his career, Johnny and I worked together building mine.

After a year, when I was, in Johnny's words, "…ready," he arranged an audition for me with the Paul Notar Trio, for whom he was the pianist, at the fancy Ritz Carlton Cafe on Sherbrooke Street—at the time the most expensive supper club in Montreal. On the day of the audition, in late July, 1961, I woke up feeling queasy. I put it down to the humid heat that hung over my every move. Before my shower and even after, I was still perspiring heavily and by the time I left the apartment I was to the point of nausea—first at the idea of *not* getting something that I'd worked over a year for and also the fear of embarrassing Johnny after all his help and faith in me. Obviously it was a severe case of audition nerves. Knowing my propensity for perspiring under pressure, in an effort to protect the hot-pink sundress I'd borrowed from my last modeling job, I placed thin wedges of Kleenex under each armpit to prevent staining. Mindful of the expensive dress which had to be returned, I chose not to sit down or raise my arms during the hot, tedious bus-ride downtown. But nervousness prevailed. I was running late, and by the time I reached the hotel, I was damp and dizzy with fear.

Johnny was anxiously waiting for me, and after a smile and perfunctory hug, he introduced me to the club owners. He then turned to the piano and launched into to my opening song, the one we'd resolutely rehearsed through that long winter of work. Unprepared for this immediate call, but upon hearing my familiar introduction played, I lunged forward and, in something akin to a spasm started belting out my opening number from the Broadway show, *Wildcat*, titled "Hey Look Me Over." In full voice, I sang out that well-known popular song and once started, I forgot everything else. I performed the way we'd rehearsed it so many times, carrying my enthusiasm right through to the end. Finishing the last rousing line, I ended by throwing my arms high and wide in an audience embrace just the way we'd choreographed it. Happy with my performance and the fact that it was over, I joined Johnny, who laughingly hugged me and stated with controlled humor, that even though I was "snowing Kleenex" the whole time, the job was mine: I would be singing at the Ritz Carlton Café in early April the following spring. Embarrassed, though happily relieved and thrilled with the news of what could be my big break, I sat down and laughed. Later that week, after visiting the doctor for my ongoing nausea, I sat down and cried—joy combined with panic. After five years of marriage I was pregnant. The baby was due in early March, 1962, less than four weeks before I was to make my grand Montreal debut at the Ritz Carlton Café in early April.

Montreal Flashback

Thirty-eight years later, looking through my huge "Do Not Open: Memory Box" during a Toronto move, I came across a photo album from those early days in Montreal when I trundled around on buses and streetcars in a very pregnant state waiting for my first-born son to make his appearance. He was late! Counting off the days on the calendar had stopped by March 2nd the baby's due date. He was already overdue by twelve days, which meant that I was less than three weeks away from my opening night at the Ritz Carlton Cafe! I panicked.

Entering Johnny Gallant's apartment, hair askew, dripping wet from a March ice storm, I burst into tears. "Johnny, what *are* we going to do? Why are we rehearsing? I can't possibly be ready! How pregnant *do* I look? Do you know that a guy on the streetcar actually offered me his seat! I was so amazed, that I refused his offer. You know I've only gained eighteen pounds—the doctor said that was as much as I was allowed. Anyway, where *is* this baby? Why doesn't he come out?"

Johnny was not his usual calm self, because he was, after all, responsible for the music *and* the show, and so he had his own problems to deal with.

"Don't panic," he murmured, as much to himself as to me. "Your voice sounds good, and because you're basically thin, I'm sure that everything will fall back into place quickly—pardon the pun. By the way, how are the gowns coming along?"

"I've already missed two final fittings! Oh, Johnny, what are we going to do? My nerves are shot." Then the idea came: "I've got it! We're going to call the doctor and tell him that we have got to have this baby right away; right now! Okay? Where's the phone?"

That same day, the good doctor sent me off to the drugstore to buy the oldest remedy in the world. "A healthy dollop of castor oil should do it," were his words. On March 14th, 1962, after twenty-eight hours of labor, my reluctant baby, Craig Anthony Torrington Steele, beautiful and healthy, was born. This left me less than three weeks to get my costumes and act ready for my big debut at the Ritz Carlton Café in Montreal. Could I do it?

∞ ∞ ∞

Looking further into the photo album from my Montreal days, I come across a full-length picture, the one that was used for the Ritz Carlton ads. I'm in a tight-fitting slinky gown, flashy in cobalt blue and matching earrings with an early sixties' hair-do teased high, singing in front of a standing microphone, arms out-stretched, mouth open—a candid shot. *Wow,* I thought, *this looks like I'm singing my heart out, probably my final number,* "I Wish You Love." Remembering the song, I start humming to myself: "Goodbye ...", and with the familiar words nostalgic feelings return. In retrospect, did I know that this was a portent of things to come? That this was where my marriage would end?

Turning the photo over, I search for the date: April, 1962. *Oh my God, it's so long ago; and what a nerve I had, trying to have it all: a successful marriage, a baby and a singing career too ... maybe in this millennium, but not way back then.* Ready to terminate my indulgent reverie, a large glossy photo falls out of the tattered album and arcs to the floor, landing face up. Smiling up benignly, it holds me firmly in the past. I look closely:

"Kevin," I call out to my youngest son who is visiting me in Toronto for the weekend. "Come and see your Mom 'putting on the Ritz.' It's that picture I was looking for. Do you remember me telling you about 7 St John's Avenue, in Winnipeg, how, when I was a little girl, I fell in love with the cloth of gold from Paris, France, that Babka used to sew the vestments for the priests in the attic? It was patterned in pale silver crosses, and it was so expensive that it was kept under lock and key in Daddy's office. I told Mama that one day I would have a gown made out of it, and I would wear it to sing in all of the big cities. Remember?"

"Well, sort of, but why?"

"Cause, here's the gown. Take a look. Isn't that something? I'm singing at the fancy, dancy Ritz Carlton Café in Montreal at five-hundred-and fifty-dollars a week—a huge amount of money in those days; I never made that much singing before or since, even at the

Royal York Hotel in Toronto. Anyway, here I am, wearing a gown made out of vestment material rifled from your Grandpa's office. Mum snitched it for me—crazy, huh?"

"It *does* sound crazy—a gown with crosses all over it ... in a night club?"

"Supper club," I correct him. "But look at the picture again: the cloth is in a brocade design. You can't *really* tell that those are crosses, can you?"

"Why did you do it?" Kevin asks, ignoring my question regarding the obvious crosses.

"I had no choice; I couldn't afford a store-bought gown, what with your older brother Craig just weeks old. There were the hospital bills to pay and all the other stuff that a baby needs. Anyway, I phoned my mother in a panic. I would never ask her outright for money, but if I explained the problem she would always offer good advice or a little financial help."

Mama, Help!

Mom was so great when I called her: I told her how out of shape I was after the baby and how there were only two weeks left to put together a new wardrobe for the Ritz Carlton Café. I further explained that while searching for a gown at around hundred dollars, all I could afford, I found that everything looked terrible on my distorted shape.

"After all, Mom, the baby's only two weeks old" I wailed. What do they expect?"

"Okay, okay, calm down," Mom chided me. "Now, tell me, who's *they?*"

I explained that once I realized I had to have a dress made for me, I found a Montreal dressmaker, but I couldn't find the right material. It was all so hard and I was so scared about the show at the Ritz, and after all, when I auditioned last summer for the show this spring I didn't know that I was already pregnant, did I? I mean, I just thought that I was nauseous with nerves—

"Okay, calm down," Mom interrupted, this time in her "we'll solve this," unruffled voice. "Now, tell me more about the 'they.'" So I started describing the couture dressmaker's reaction when she was first taking my measurements: "Mon dieu," Madam Dressmaker had murmured, "zer is no derriere. Zee bebe, ee take it away. We must fix zis—now," she announced, before whispering some instructions in French to her assistant.

I further explained to Mom that I understood French well enough to get the idea, and while I was mulling over how I was going to pull my protruding stomach in while curving my concave backside out, in ran the assistant waving a slab of foam rubber. Setting it down, she carefully cut it into two matching round pieces, sizing and shaping them to fit my flat derriere, all the while talking to the dressmaker about how fancy the Ritz Carlton Hotel was and how they will have to do everything to make me look *très jolie.*

"After all," she said, in broken English, "their reputation as haute couture designers was 'at the stake'." Just telling my mother the story got me laughing and then she started laughing too. Finally, both of us, in peals of laughter, Mom asked,

"So, tell me, Olanna, what else is false?"

"Everything, from top to bottom: the false hairpiece, the false rubber eyelashes, the false beauty-spot placed in the way of Liz Taylor's—you know I met her on the elevator once in Toronto, when I was singing at the King Edward Hotel—the contact lenses, the boobs, and now the famous derriere." More laughter....

∞ ∞ ∞

"Anyway, Kev, it was my Mom's idea to send out the gold-cross cloth from Winnipeg, 'for your fancy haute couture dress and *new* derriere'," she'd emphasized. Here, just telling *how* my Mom said it, Kev and I both burst out laughing.

"So," I said, turning to Kev, "that's my story about the gold and silver-cross dress. What do you think?"

"I think this picture doesn't look like you, and *now* I know why," he said, still laughing.

"Wait a minute, that was forty years ago," I remind him in protest.

"Yikes, Mom, I guess it wasn't you, even then. Besides, I thought this picture was taken in New York."

"It was, but that's another story—so what?"

"So that's why you look so good, that's what. Those showbiz guys in New York can make anyone look good. You and your stories," he said, laughing and shaking his head in his good-natured way as he left the room. "You know you're too much, but I still love you," he shouted over his shoulder, still chuckling.

"I know," I hollered after him; "but just remember, 'the apple doesn't fall far from the tree!'" Smiling when I heard his guffaw from the other room, I closed the album and put my reverie away.

∞ ∞ ∞

Thinking back to the struggle of it all, I wonder what kept my dream alive. After my first son Craig's birth, I should have been ready to pack it all in, but I wasn't. The two-week stint at the Ritz Carlton had brought favorable reviews in the dailies and *Variety* magazine, and after that taste of success, I was more determined than ever to go on. There were more offers in Montreal, but with my limited French (I memorized the songs) I soon knew there would not be enough work to build a real career. So I struggled on, frustrated, trying to enhance our bleak basement apartment and enjoy my motherhood the way societal standards of the day suggested. But I was missing the work.

Be Happy!

Now, digging deeper into my memory box, I come across more pictures of me in Montreal, in those hectic days in the early sixties, just after I'd fulfilled my engagement at the Ritz. In the first picture, I'm in our sparse apartment, looking through our narrow basement window at Craig's baby carriage, placed just outside, within reach. I was following the doctor's orders: "Lots of fresh air. At four months old, that's all this colicky baby needs." The same picture shows me in a black, low cut dress, replete with high teased hair and drop rhinestone earrings; *but where in the world would I be going, in such an outfit in the middle of the day,* I wonder. Thinking back, I remember: I was headed for a modeling job, some runway work at one of the hotels. The designer had said: "Show up early, looking glamorous, so you can work the room serving drinks before the show," and that's what I did.

I remember being stared at in the blazing summer sun while waiting for the bus, and again at the streetcar stop (by now I was in Montreal rush-hour), not for my looks but for my bold outfit at that time of day. Later, after the job, I'd had misgivings about spending money for the cab-ride back home but it was so late and I was so tired. *Don't always be so hard on yourself,* my self-critic chided, but I still felt guilty. Arriving home well after dark, confronted with the babysitter's exorbitant fee, almost three dollars, I wondered if the modeling work-in was worth the meager pay-out. Our one-bedroom basement apartment cost ninety dollars, exactly one week of Michael's monthly pay check at the television station Twenty-five percent went towards rent—those were the rules of survival in 1962. Between the thriftiness of Babka's Borscht and my innovative ways with pasta and rice, we managed to survive, but I couldn't get past my singing dream. *"Grow up!"* my rational self said. *"This is it—all there is. This is your life, and it's what it's supposed to be. Accept it."*

"Wait a minute, not so fast," my heart's yearning countered. *"What about my dream, my truth?"*

"Society says you have to forget them. Be a good wife, a good mother— and be happy!"

"I can't give up my dream—I won't," I stated out loud.

And so the inner conflict continued, full tilt, veering back and forth for months until finally sinking under my weighty indecision, I gave in to depression's gloom. I started moving through my days in numbness, unable to appreciate life's smallest joys.

"Don't worry," my pediatrician said. "It's very normal for a new mother to feel depressed. It will soon pass." But it didn't. I stumbled along for months wrapped in a grey cloak of sadness, my heart mourning its lost dream. Feeling my energy deteriorate and my youth passing me by, I reached out for comfort in prayer. And, as had happened before, my dilemma's prayer was answered in its own unique way. The decision was made for me. Craig's dad, Michael, who'd been working at the entry level in Montreal television, was hired by CFTO in Toronto as a cameraman. This would prove to be a major step in his successful climb towards excellence in television production. At the time I was too close to my own frustrated ambitions to fully appreciate this aspect of his life.

Aah, here's prayer's answer, I thought. Why, it should have been obvious all along. When things aren't working out your way, just wait ... *God's time isn't your time*. But now, apparently, it was. We were finally getting out of the basement apartment *and* Montreal. *A good move on both accounts*, I thought as my mood lifted.

With renewed vigor, we packed up and in just two days left Montreal for "Toronto the Good" with baby, music and my Dad's favorite prayer-song in hand: "And, keep me safe from harm, oh Lord, just for today." Amen.

∞ ∞ ∞

Upon our arrival back in Toronto, I found that nothing much had changed. Things did *not* get better, in fact, in some ways they got worse. Now, on top of my career frustrations, I was very lonely. We had no friends or family in Toronto, and we could not afford to live downtown, not only because of the inflated rent prices, but, more importantly, because the doctor had advised us that the air was too polluted for Craig's ongoing allergies. So we ended up in the suburbs, east of the city's downtown core, away from the CBC and all the music action.

It was tedious travelling to auditions and modeling jobs downtown without a car, but I persisted—on buses and subways, again over-dressed—and for a while things seemed to be okay. But once we were settled, I could sense another spiral of depression hovering near my frustration, getting ready to pounce in and pummel my singing dream again. This time I knew I had to fight back, so I re-entered that safe familiar place, my music—first for the love of it, and then for some success: I would find a vocal coach in Toronto to perfect my technique and heighten my confidence so that every audition would count as a job. I'd spend less time modeling for a pittance and invest what little money I had in new arrangements in order to enhance my act, which at that point needed to be refreshed.

Working with a Toronto accompanist and paying for new music sheets that involved big band arrangements, still popular in the sixties, took up a lot of time and money. By now I had a new agent/manager who maneuvered me into CBC and the better supper clubs in Toronto, but it was still a struggle. Without a car and travelling downtown by bus, I juggled my energies between full-time motherhood, wifehood and a career—not being able to give up one or the other. This worked for a while, but soon enough it proved to be too much.

Depressed by the poverty of guidance and lack of mentoring in becoming a star in Canada, I was getting ready to pack the whole thing in—when I got *the sign*: blasting out on the radio was Barbra Streisand's hit song, "Don't Rain on my Parade," from the new Broadway show, *Funny Girl*. Upon hearing that compelling tune, with my heart beating in time with the music, I jumped up and joined in its rhythm—singing out the words in full tilt with a voice that sure sounded like Broadway to me. The title song said it all; no one was going to ruin my parade or my career, until I was good and ready.

This was the sign I'd been looking for. I wasn't giving up and I wasn't getting out. I was heading to New York to savor a bite of success in the only place where musical fame *really* counts—the "Big Apple."

Chapter 7

New York: Feisty, Fabled and Fabulous

I will extol You, O Lord, for You have lifted me up,
And have not let my foes rejoice over me.
O Lord my God, I cried out to you, And You healed me.
—Bible; New King James Version: Psalm 30:1-2

Elaine Steele: Chanteuse

New York, spring: 1964

I was scared, really scared—but ready, prepared, I thought. *After all, the baby will be fine with Grandma Steele. Michael's mother is coming from Montreal tomorrow, the house in Scarborough that Mike has rented has a nice big back yard; they'll probably get a dog, and soon Craig will be in pre-kindergarten. Grandma Steele always takes good care of him; she's*

*a great cook, she loves him dearly, and Craig absolutely adores her. There
... now, get on with your packing.*

And, I kept talking to myself. "Don't think, just keep moving;
soon you'll get your chance. Lady Liberty awaits you, her torch held
high, offering success to you and your dreams. In New York, music
is everywhere—arms open, cajoling, luring you in. Soon you will be
dancing on Broadway's golden streets, leaping through high hoops
of hope towards a contract that will finally fulfill your dreams." *Let
it be so.* Of course, everyone thought I was crazy.

When my Toronto manager, Paul Simmons, heard my plan, he
bellowed, "What's the matter with you? I can get you lots of work....
I have contracts waiting for you right here on my desk. Just sign! And
you'll be off to South America in the next two weeks. And there's
that job in Cleveland, Ohio—you know, "Night in Budapest," with
Mitzi Gaynor and other big stars and oh, Joe Pasternak, Hollywood's
top movie producer will be there; it's just a matter of time, trust me."
Sure, Paul. And then, later that week, there was my concerned Mom
on the phone, calling from Winnipeg, talking excitedly in Ukrainian,
"New York? Why? Is everything alright? Are you okay? Are things
bad at home again? Who's with the baby? What are you going to do
in New York? More practicing, studying? Where will you stay? Do
you need money? Tell me..."

"Cause New York's where it's at, Mom. Yes, yes and yes, to the
first three questions. The baby's with his Grandma Steele; don't
worry, she's crazy about him, and he about her. Everything's alright,
I'm leaving tomorrow. I'll be staying with my friend Eleanor—no,
not our cousin Eleanore—a girl I met at the conservatory years ago.
No, Mom, I don't need money, not now, anyway. I've got to go. You
know I love you, and please don't worry. Okay?" Now calm, Mom
speaks English.

"Okay, but I'll be praying for your safety; it *is* New York you
know."

"I know. Give Dad my love. He's at a meeting? Okay. I'll call
soon. Love you too, 'bye."

Streetscapes

New York looks and sounds just as I've seen it and heard it in my dreams: a frenetic circus of dissonant noise emitting from narrow streetscapes; yellow cabs honking their way into the heart of the city; pale sunlight shadowed out by huge horizontal buildings and tall vertical heights; glass and steel gleaming over the ant colonies of people below. In awe, I crane my neck, and for the first few days, sleep is out of the question. There's too much to see, too much to do and too much reality to avoid.

"But what *are* you planning to do?" my friend Eleanor finally asks after a few days in her apartment.

"Everything," I reply out loud.... *Everything that's important to me,* I murmur to myself. No, I didn't visit the Empire State Building, the United Nations or the Statue of Liberty. I stayed in my own area, 150 West 58th Street, within walking distance of Broadway, Carnegie Hall, Radio City Music Hall, Fifth Avenue and Macy's.

I'd started my New York sojourn in the fancy St. Moritz Hotel across from Central Park, upon the invitation of a rich Texan fan and his wife, but, after two days of high living as their guest, I moved down the accommodations ladder to my friend Eleanor's place. Those first days with her were time enough to find my way around my part of New York: prowling the theatre district, searching out a trustworthy agent, inquiring about an "interested" coach and finding the best cafeterias at the lowest price. Within a week, sensing Eleanor's impatience, I agreeably moved a few doors down the street to a typical Manhattan brownstone with the compulsory New York doorman standing in the doorway, typical of the sixties, who was surprisingly friendly when I approached him.

Looking alright from the outside, inside the building bore witness to the hopeful hunters of show-biz fame and fortune who had frequented the premises and left, probably no less scarred than the peeling paint and stained wallpaper facing me now. *Nope, I'm not going to be one of them,* I thought, as I turned the worn brass key and stepped inside the room. Switching on the main light, I thankfully saw there was a window, which now cast a two-foot square of light on the bed. *This will do,* I thought, *at least I'll know day from night, and*

I can shut New York out or let her in, any time, depending on my mood. And so my love/hate affair with New York began.

"Missy, it's after midnight," the doorman would caution, "where are you going?"

"To the Deli, I'm starving."

"Again?" he marvels. "Okay, but go to the corner one where I can see you. I'll watch."

"Thanks—you're wonderful," I said, really meaning it.

"Everything is so exciting, so 'New Yorkish,'" I told my mother, speaking into the grimy telephone now scrubbed clean with an old toothbrush. She understood, having been there, she reminded me, back in 1939, for the New York World's Fair with Daddy.

"Too much," I exclaimed. "I remember you telling me about it when I was little, still in the crib. Imagine Daddy taking you, the minister's wife, all the way from Winnipeg, Canada, to New York City, way back in *those* days; He was really something then, wasn't he?

"Your Dad is still something, in *these* days. Now he's off to Europe to seek out a new Bishop, and then after that, on to Australia, to visit your dear sister, Larissa."

Larissa's Theme

Larissa (Lessia or Laddie, in English) was my second oldest sister. After she got married in Canada, in 1957, her *Anglaish* (born in England) husband whisked her off to Australia. She lived there for the rest of her life with too few visits home, the plane fare being prohibitive in those days. Mom never really forgave Lessia's husband for taking her darling daughter so far away.

For a while Lessia (or "Luscious," as I called her) and I were roommates at the rectory, on #7 St. John's Avenue. I was nine and she was eighteen. A smart student, already studying Home Economics at the University of Manitoba, she was pretty and very popular. I loved watching her dress for her dates. All the fussing that went on! For one date, that was apparently serious, Laddie decided she absolutely *needed* a pale pink angora sweater with short sleeves, all the rage in those days, to wear on her date with Conrad the next night. Of course, "store-bought" was too expensive, so Babka and

Mama decided they would knit one. On the very same day as her announcement, after a long streetcar ride to Eaton's to buy the fancy angora wool on sale, they began knitting. All that evening and half the night they knitted; one worked on the front of the sweater and the other on the back. The next morning they took off time to cook a huge pot of borscht and a side of boiled potatoes, both left to simmer all day so that we could help ourselves.

By late afternoon on d-day (date day), the sweater was still not finished. Panic set in:

"Why can't she wear something else?" my brothers, irritated by now, wailed. But we, the three little kids (girls) knew better. We would see it through.

Back and forth we ran, sliding across the polished hardwood floor between the front and back stairs, watching for signs of Conrad, before reporting back to the knitters. Peering down from the back gallery, staring at their needles flying furiously as each one worked on a sleeve, we placed bets:

"Bet they don't finish," Daria said negatively.

"Bet they don't finish, and she'll have to wear the same as last time," Yvonne added—by this time, bored.

"Bet they *do* finish" I pipe up. "And "Luscious" will look gorgeous and Conrad will fall in love and they'll get married and stay together forever and ever," I shout behind me, already running to sneak a peek at the front door as the bell jangles ominously.

"He's here," I hiss hoarsely to the gallery.

"He's early!" whispers Laddie, overhearing me on her way to the bathroom with more makeup and hairspray in hand "and, I'm nowhere near ready" she adds, barely controlling her panic.

"So what should we do?" I uneasily ask my roommate, my pal, my big sister.

"Just ask the knitters to knit faster, and ask Yvonne to go out front and visit with Conrad.

"Okay knitters, keep knitting," I call down to the silver streaks of flying needles.

"Everything's fine up here," I add deceitfully, not wanting to add to the knitters' visible stress.

Clearly Yvonne and Conrad found plenty to talk about, because it was an hour before she returned to the gallery, just in time to see Conrad gazing fondly at Laddie, a sparkle in his eyes when she sauntered in—dark hair shining, looking so pretty and cuddly in her pink fuzzy sweater. We all breathed in and released a unified sigh of relief, including the knitters. *Such a to-do over a sweater,* I thought. But wait, there was that "look" in his eyes—what I call the "diamond look." *Okay, it was all worth it.*

Apparently that "look" was well worth the *to-do* for Mama and Babka, now digging into large bowls of purple borscht laced with buttery boiled potatoes and huge dollops of sour cream. Looking tired after six hours of knitting, I could see that they were happy with themselves and their accomplishment, especially since Lessia looked so pretty. I was happy too. "Luscious" was special. We kids always thought Mom loved her the most, after she got rheumatic fever and nearly died but we didn't mind; we felt she deserved to be the favorite for having been so sick.

New York Angst

Recalling the telephone conversations with my mother expressing my hopefulness to her when I first lived alone in New York brings back dark moments that led me to some hard truths about the world I was engaged in—show business in another country, so far away from home. Slowly, insidiously, the heady excitement of being in New York that first summer wore off to be replaced by loneliness and high-wired nervousness that stretched into nightmares echoing self-doubt over my musical career, my motherhood and soon a fear of life itself. Every morning, despite New York's chronic heat wave, I'd wake up shivering, staring at the nicotine-stained ceiling, unable to move while waiting for the first wave of anxiety to finish its slide across my belly. Not ready to face the day upright, I'd roll over, sink to my knees alongside the bed and start praying—head down, hands crumpled under my chin as when I was a little girl with Mama teaching me the prayer words in Ukrainian—those same words coming back to me in between sobs. Finally, gaining temporary courage, I'd start getting ready.

First, I would run the tap to help shoo the silver bristletails down the drain before stepping into the stained tub, its shower spraying tepid water, rusty then clear, in the way of all Manhattan pipes not retrofitted with copper. After a cold uncomfortable shower, I'd wait for the small tea kettle to boil while holding bread over the other burner with a fork—the way Dido taught me years ago before we owned a toaster. All I ever ate for breakfast was tea and toast, and this morning, as a treat, I used up the last of my strawberry jam, hoping for a little sugar lift. By now I was quite thin, skimping on lunches to save money for that rainy day hiding around every corner—*hopefully not today*, I thought

Finally ready, in my lightest summer suit, I'd step out into the blazing midday heat and a deluge of standard New York sounds and smells: horns blowing, dogs barking, kids screaming, while ethnic restaurants with open doors released pungent odors of lunchtime offerings to jar the senses and start the juices flowing. While I was striving to cross the busy street, wind currents would propel cigarette wrappers against my legs and trifle ominously with my new hairdo, teased high in the beehive style of the day, as soot-laden drafts smudged my careful makeup.

It's all too much, I thought. *I can't stand this constant wind ... it's the tall buildings that do it. They create wind tunnels and all the sooty street stuff blows around. Now, here I am, half a morning getting dressed, my face already smeared, my hair looking messy and still so far from that manager's office. Never mind ... get a cab, you'll be late!*

"Taxi" I shouted, optimistically holding my music high while anxiously checking my hair and make-up in a store window's reflection. Squinting through contacts lenses now burning with soot, I wonder why I should find all of this so hard. I try to relax in the cab, but I find I'm unable to shut out the clicking sound of the meter that resolutely carries on even at a dead stop while snarled in noon-day traffic. Finally arriving at the manager's building, after paying the cabbie what was probably a fair price but felt exorbitant to me, I struggle against the lunchtime crowd while searching for the elevator. By now, exhausted from nerves and frustration, I'm ready to turn back.

Something's wrong, I think. *I'm scared, nervous and annoyed—but why ... at whom?* Ready to answer as usual, my critical voice, *Sinc*, jumps in. I'd finally named my inner critic/censor "Sinc" in keeping with his synchronicity *and* propensity for being painfully honest and succinct whenever he shows up—like now.

Smarten up, lady; this is your dream, remember? Representation by a manager in New York—someone who likes you, respects you, does not hit on you and gets you some great singing dates. This is what you want—go!

∞ ∞ ∞

"No, my dear," coos the manager. "You don't have to sing for me. I've received your pictures from Maurice Seymour here in New York, and they're great. It doesn't really matter about the voice; I've seen your write-ups in the Canadian *Variety*, and I'm sure we'll be able to work together. I have a club in mind, not far from here, and if you agree, I'll take you there to check it out—see how you like it. What about tomorrow night. Are you free?"

All of this took place with me facing him seated at a huge leather-inlaid desk. Wearing a grey silk shirt and dark glasses, pitched high on his balding hairline, the manager smiled to himself, while sifting through my pictures and write-ups—each fluttering down to join the mess of files and photos strewn across his cluttered desk. Meanwhile, the phone kept ringing, punctuated by short buzzes from the hassled middle-aged receptionist I met on the way in. Each time, he'd pick up the phone, bark "Later, Jean," and promptly bang down. *He's either very rude, or I'm very important*, I thought. *Maybe he really does see something in me.*

Manhattan Malarkey

The next night, all dressed up, I was chatting with my friendly doorman, Lou, about my "date," when a shiny black coupe pulled up curbside. I couldn't see in, but assuming it was the manager, I started for the car, turning to wave at Lou just in time to hear his warning grunt to "Be careful." I nodded and smiled back. *Just like my father*, I thought—*a worrier.*

The evening started out pleasantly enough. I was excited. Maybe, just maybe, this would be it. Finally, after all my hard work, a real shot at the big time. All of a sudden, New York appeared to me as it did when I first arrived six months ago. The late August heat had cooled down to a balmy evening, and I was dressed just right: my pale green pongee silk suit flattered my hazel eyes and was understated enough for a chic supper club in downtown Manhattan. I felt that I looked reserved yet attractive enough to merit attention and approval from the club owner.

After a lengthy ride in the showy black coupe, we finally arrived at what I guessed was the club. *Okay, don't panic*, I cautioned myself; these clubs downtown all look alike, but they can be quite lovely inside with high ceilings, velvet drapes and small intimate tables flickering amber candles, their light so flattering to mature women over forty—the chic clientele of supper clubs so prevalent in New York during the sixties.

Upon entering the dark interior, my fears dwindled. The club was fine inside, just as I had imagined it. The musicians, a trio, were seated at the far right in the shadows, headless beneath the low smoke-fogged ceiling. When my eyes grew accustomed to the dark I was surprised and pleased to see that the keyboard player was a woman. From the name on the display card near the piano it appeared that this was *her* trio, and this also surprised me because I'd never worked with a female lead before. She gave the nod to the percussionist and the bass player, and when the tempo revved up I could tell by their jazz riffs that they were good—really good. They were playing one of my favorite tunes, Cole Porter's "You Do Something to Me," and since this was already in my repertoire, I relaxed, hope rising that this gig might just work out to be right for me. Concentrating on the band, I didn't notice the shadowy figure that slid silently into the chair beside me. My attention was on the trio and it wasn't until the song was finished, that I realized the manager, sitting opposite me, had just introduced the club owner, apparently named "Joe."

"She looks okay to me," muttered Joe, leaning in as his chair scraped closer—*too close*, I thought while viewing his face just inches away, impassive and pasty in the flickering candlelight.

"Okay, here's the thing," my potential manager said. "Joe has another club a little further north, in the Bronx. He'd like to work out a deal for appearances in both clubs. I can't go with you I've got another appointment, so I've asked Joe to drive you out to see his other club. You take a look, and if you're alright with it, then we'll work out a contract. Okay?"

It wasn't exactly "okay" with me, but I murmured a response, while trying to figure out what to do next. The whole thing sounded weird, certainly not the way my Toronto agent, Paul Simmons, operated; but then again, this is New York, and I wanted the job badly. Anyway, it was too late to say, or do, anything. Rising abruptly, Joe shook the manager's hand then reached over and took hold of my arm, half-pulling me up to indicate that we were leaving. Clutching me firmly by my elbow, he hustled me past the dimly lit tables, their occupants chortling over drinks, to a door leading into a small alleyway where a red convertible was waiting with its motor running.

At first, on the way up to the Bronx, this Joe guy seemed alright. Starting out we'd chatted about New York show business and other mundane stuff, but I could soon tell that he didn't have a clue about Canada, never mind Toronto, so halfway up I stopped talking and let him take the lead. Of course, the first thing he asked was if I was married. By now, used to this question, I answered him in the offhand manner I had adopted for these occasions:

"Yes, but in the biblical sense only," I said, thinking this would shut him up or at least give him pause for thought. Usually, if a guy has any sensibility or humor at all, he moves on to another subject, but not this one. He just clamped down—not a word. I took this as a warning that he was angry, and by the time we got to the Bronx my alert button had shifted to orange.

The club turned out to be a roadhouse with an office and nightclub at the front attached to a sprawling motor-inn behind. Seeing the neon lights in front stating Day Rates in bright yellow, my alert button revved up to red, raising my apprehension to all-out anxiety. Getting out of the car, Joe waved at the burly doorman and shouted at him to park in the usual spot, then, the motor still running, he circled around the front and unfastened my door.

"Let's go," he ordered, ushering, no, shoving me through the main door into a small lobby that led through another door into the adjoining night club. Assailed by raucous laughter and a wall of dense smoke that briefly sent my contacts burning, my eyes quickly adjusted to make out a small band, the cymbals reflecting light as the drummer picked up one stick and gave a perfunctory nod our way. Stopping briefly, Joe waved back, and hurriedly pushed me towards the bar. *Whoa,* I thought, *this doesn't feel good; if he offers you a drink, say no.*

There was nowhere to sit at the bar. Most of the stools were occupied by jazzy looking women on the dark side of forty with heavy makeup and jangling earrings, all who smiled at Joe in a knowing way. Waving back, he didn't stop but just kept urging me forward. Now his arm was around my waist, the familiarity signaling an impropriety that sent my anxiety level to flashing red in a full-blown panic.

"Well, what do you think of the club?" Joe asked, not looking to me for an answer, rather searching out the bartender, who, while pouring tap beer, looked up questioningly. Releasing my waist, Joe pointed to a half-mickey of bourbon behind the bar, and after taking an eye measure of its contents, the bartender handed over the bottle without a word. Quickly pocketing the booze, Joe shoved me towards a dark glass door at the end of the bar and pushed me through. Blinking at the sudden bright lights, expecting to be in his office, I could see that we were, in fact, in a narrow corridor leading through to the motel rooms. Panicked, I stopped.

"Okay, what's going on?" I asked. Without answering, Joe grabbed my arm and started steering, no, pushing me down the narrow hallway. By now I knew I was heading for real trouble. Trying to stop, I braked and reached out to the stucco wall with my right hand while trying to wrench my other arm free, but he just tightened his clasp and pulled me along even faster. Afraid of falling, I stumbled behind, dragging my right hand along the wall's rough surface, looking for something to grab onto. The harder Joe pulled, the more I held back—stumbling, falling, getting up again—all the while pleading for him to *Stop! Please!* Finally, in a combination of anger and fear, I yelled out, tentatively at first then louder, as loud as my soprano–trained voice could scream. Tightening his grip on my arm, Joe stopped at a door with a tarnished number three, tried the knob, angrily muttered something about that damn key, then wheeled around, his other hand raised high:

"Stop screaming," he hollered, "or else!" I stopped.

"What the hell's the matter with you?" he snarled, his face close, breathing stale whiskey. "I thought you were a professional. Do you want the job or not? And what's the matter with your hand? It's bleeding all over the wall." At that point, I'd slumped to the floor, sobbing.

"No, I don't want the job—not like this. Right now, I just want to go home."

"Okay, lady, that's exactly where you're going," he muttered, as he hauled me up.

Driving home in the convertible, this time with the top up, Joe never said a word. At a stop sign near my building he turned and looked at me for a long time—I was slumped against the passenger door, nursing my hand in a serviette blotched with blood—then, shaking his head negatively, disapprovingly, he drove past my entrance on West 58th and, without a full stop reached over, opened my door and shoved me out. Luckily, my doorman, Lou, saw the red convertible pass by. Sprawled on the pavement, I could see him running towards me....

∞ ∞ ∞

Two days later, on a fine Saturday afternoon in September, I found myself drifting aimlessly along Fifth Avenue, nursing my hand and my wounded pride, both still hurting from the flagrant behavior of the club owner on that unhappy night in the Bronx. Unable to shake off Joe's nastiness, I was in a grey zone stuck between anger and disappointment—anger at the agent for putting me in a compromising position with an abusive club manager, and disappointed with myself for being so naively tricked into what was obviously an "either-or" plan.

Being who I am, a minister's daughter with a certain inbred morality, I realized that I must make a choice. For a long time, I'd been driven by my heart's desire—a music-love dream that stayed alive through childhood fantasies, adult ambition and, in New York, determined pursuit. In the past, I'd been able to dodge the unsavory part of show business with a decent voice, a modicum of charm and a dollop of humor; but now things had gone too far. Exactly how far down would I let my performance addiction drag me?

My dream of singing in Manhattan was close, within my grasp, but the price was too high. Still angry at my stupidity in letting things go as far as they did, I realized, more importantly, that my burning ambition was out of control. It had put me in real danger—both physically and morally. *The stakes have gone up*, I thought. *I have to fold, but where to go? What to do?* "Show me the way," I whispered.

St. Patrick's Cathedral

Peace I leave with you; my peace I give you. I do not give to you as the world gives.
Do not let your hearts be troubled and do not be afraid.
—NIV: John 14: 27

Stumbling along Fifth Avenue, eyes blurred by stinging tears, I push my way through hordes of Saturday afternoon shoppers to find myself in front of St. Patrick's Cathedral. Distraught, looking for answers, I fumble my way up the broad steps to the huge oak door, fully expecting it to be closed. As I clutch at the worn brass handle, the formidable door swings open, and I step inside. Immediately the scent of offertory prayer candles near the entrance bring back comforting memories of the chapel in my father's house and I am transported to Winnipeg, Canada—a safe place, my home. Nostalgically, I am propelled toward the lofty stained-glass windows, their rainbow colors shining onto the altar, lighting up the silver cross leading my way. Exhausted by the emotions of the week coupled with tears of confusion and increasing self-doubt, I collapse in a front pew. Time passes....

Finally my frustrated tears subside; I feel peaceful, safe in a place of stillness and serenity—another sphere. Transfixed, I want to stay within this realm forever. Falling into a prayer-like meditation, I silently ask for some direction, *any* direction away from the loneliness and guilt I am mired in. Silence....

Then a draft ... ever so slight, followed by the merest whisper: "Elaine"—I hear my name uttered softly in my ear, a light touch on my shoulder. "I will never leave you, nor forsake you. You'll never be alone again."

Opening my eyes, I looked around. I'd just heard the kindest words I'll ever know, but from where, from whom? Although the candle-lit cathedral was still fairly dark, I could see that it was as empty as it had been when I first walked in. Immobilized, I contemplated the experience of the voice, the touch, and the promise. How long I sat, I do not remember.

Emerging into the late-day sun, I was shocked to see how the vista had changed. Fifth Avenue shoppers were still milling about, but now they appeared less tense, relaxed, unveiled of their aggressive behavior. They smiled. I smiled back.

The autumn leaves presented startling colors as soft breezes danced them about. And, how did the sky take on such crystal blueness in the few hours I was in church? All appeared as new: a blaze of color infused with love and hope, promise and peace. As I strolled back to my apartment, my thoughts were finely focused; I knew with certainty what I had to do.

Two days later I was on a Greyhound bus northbound to Canada, heading home to Toronto, my son Craig and whatever else the future might hold. The transition from loneliness, confusion and desperation, to peace and an understanding of what I must do, had been swift. All dreams die upon awakening, as did mine, in its own sacred light, that Saturday afternoon in St. Patrick's Cathedral. In less time than an eyelid's blink, my dream volume was switched down from a demanding shriek to a low palatable hum. Although I'd heard no clear warnings, there were, in retrospect, incidents and signs that prophetically led to that moment when my life story changed.

As I stared out of the bus window, marveling at the kaleidoscope of autumn colors streaking by, I started thinking about what had happened that night in the Bronx. The chronic anxiety that had been dogging me for months was brought to a head. First through anger, and then through confusion and pain, I was led to St. Patrick's Cathedral to cry out for help. Through an amazing touch of undeserved grace, I came to realize that if getting ahead in New York's show business meant giving in to compromising demands, than that city was not for me. Looking at the brilliant colors of my new world, feeling clean, reborn and at peace, I smiled and picked up my pen to write:

Heading Home
Past the holly hedge – around the corner,
Crimson pink against a pale gold sky;
a rose ... new-born
beauty
glistening with fresh rain,
Isolated: facing
a northern latitude
within
meridians
of
longitude,
rising
towards
the
Holy
—

towards
Home.

Chapter 8

Amazing Grace

I have swept away your offences like a cloud,
your sins, like the morning mist.
Return to me, for I have redeemed you.
—NIV Bible: Isaiah 44:22

A tear in every stitch

A Difficult Gig

Back in Toronto, after explaining some of my reasons for leaving New York, my agent Paul Simmons made no judgments, just shook his head in disgust upon hearing my diluted report of the club owner Joe's unsavory behavior. He then arranged some singing engagements to help me out in my present position of having no apartment, no job and no money. Thinking about what happened in New York could still stir up my anger and while Joe's behavior in the Bronx was awful, in many ways it epitomized the way women were regarded in show business everywhere in the mid-sixties— not just New York. For example, not long after I got home, in December of 1964, Paul booked me an out-of-town engagement in Ohio, USA. Needing the money, I accepted the job gratefully. Akron would turn out to be a difficult gig. I would be away from the family throughout Christmas and New Year's, and even before I left, I was already missing Craig. The name of the club eludes me now, but the phenomenon that took place there during the last weeks of December, 1964, does not.

On a bitterly cold, snow-driven day, one week before Christmas, I left Toronto and headed for the airport, leaving Craig in the care of his beloved Nanny Steele; I was worried about his asthma, his coughing spells and sleepless nights, but I had to leave. This was, after all, my job—the only one I had. Singing and performing in better supper clubs, two twenty-minute solo appearances each night, was how I had supported myself during the last year of my marriage to Michael, Craig's dad. It had been rough going in New York and now it was the same in Toronto, albeit safer. When I moved out of our meager Scarborough apartment to downtown Toronto, I took nothing but a small round kitchen table, two matching chairs and a small Danish living room armchair. Pride and a desire for independence prevented me from asking for anything else, although I'd worked most of our seven-year marriage and was certainly entitled to more. I soon found out that the law provided little sympathy and almost no financial help for separated mothers who had left the family home. Six dollars a month, the government's newly created baby bonus, is the only financial support I walked away with.

The four meager pieces of furniture just fit into my cousin Eleanore's petite Nash Metropolitan. The rest of the limited space was taken up with boxes of music and my wardrobe, mostly gowns and shoes and wigs of various styles—so popular in the sixties. When I moved into the first apartment on Jarvis Street, I did not have a bed, dresser or night table. Although I'd sung in better dinner clubs, including The Royal York Hotel in Toronto, I found, that in spite of my successful engagement at the Ritz Carlton Cafe in Montreal, I could not manage on less than eight club engagements a year in addition to appearances on CBC radio, television and performing in the occasional commercial. I realized I would have to make some serious changes in order to establish a home for Craig and myself. I wanted him with me—this desire is what gave impetus to my sudden exodus from New York. The club owner Joe's disgusting behavior was the trigger that propelled me into St. Patrick's Cathedral where Divine intervention miraculously released me from my performance obsession. Maybe I should thank "jaundiced Joe" for my miracle! No. As previously stated God works in weird and wonderful ways. Since my miraculous visitation in St. Patrick's, I'd been on a mission and characteristically, I had mapped out a plan. I knew what I needed in order to gain full custody of Craig: a home, a car and a "real" job—in that order. I had my apartment and now I was heading out of town to work for the car. Two out of three is an acceptable start.

Singing over Christmas and New Year's in Akron, Ohio, was tough. I was lonely and riddled with guilt at leaving Craig again. The separation hearing and legal agreement had created ill feelings between Michael and me; mutual accusations had flown high, scattering seeds of renewed anger within Michael and fresh remorse and guilt within me.

'What kind of mother are you? Sinc, my ever vigilant self-critic, asked. *Why can't you be like everyone else? What are you looking for?*

I don't know, I'd respond, deep in thought. *I'm not ready to quit. I love the singing, but I hate the life. I have to leave town in order to work and so I have to leave Craig. But if I leave him for too long I'll lose him; I can't bear the idea of that. But what should I do? Where should I go? Back to x-ray; back to Michael?* No answer.

It didn't help that the club manager in Akron, Ohio, made a pass at me the minute I arrived—disheveled, struggling with my music case, luggage and wig-box in hand. He repeated the move many times thereafter. Every night, in a tightly fitted sequined gown, I had to safely maneuver past his office, and, in four-inch satin heels gingerly step through the kitchen with its greasy tiles to finally appear on stage unspotted and ready to perform. After carrying out two shows every night, the last one finishing well after midnight, it usually took me two to three hours to relax enough to get to sleep. As I was covered for only one meal in my contract with the hotel, I saved that for after the last show, just before the kitchen closed; I was always hungry. If I was lucky, one of the fellows in the trio (it was always piano, bass and drums in the smaller clubs) would join me, trying to jolly me up. It helped for a while, but when I got back to the room, thoughts of home and Craig would bring on tears. I was always alone; when I finally got to sleep and woke up, the day was half gone as were the fast-food breakfasts. Waking up in the middle of the day, all I wanted was breakfast; I was not about to spend my hard-won earnings on food, when my mission was to save every penny for a car. So I bought a big box of cornflakes, sugar and milk, which I stored by the icy window, and ate breakfast without having to leave the hotel on a midday search for food—it was, after all, Ohio, in the dead of winter.

Since I didn't know anyone except the musicians, who were all local and had their own families and interests, I put in my afternoons knitting a sweater for Craig. It was a lovely grey-green, the color of his eyes and as I stared at the wool while knitting, a tear in every stitch, I'd think about him—*how I missed him, and why was I not at home with him? And what in the world was I doing here freezing in a hotel room, alone at Christmas, in Akron, Ohio?*

Soon I stopped going out of the hotel altogether. Within days a curtain of depression descended and clinging tenaciously, it blinded my eyes to past joys, current resolve and future plans. Moving slowly, I struggled through the oppression of my days—a somnambulist under water reaching out for help against a seawall of guilt. Immobilized by sadness, I silently prayed, unwilling to speak the words out loud for fear they'd vanish before received. And in between the knitting, the singing and the praying, I waited ... waited for the miracle to come.

Faith, Miracles and a Change of Heart

Listen ... hear it; a harmonic wave, fragile as an egret's plume, infusing consciousness, infiltrating my grey world with hope while engaging my mind with a song from the past—a hymn heard years ago in a Southern Baptist church, a hymn confronting guilt:

> *There is a fountain full of blood, Drawn from Emmanuel's Wings.*
> *And sinners plunged beneath that blood lose all their guilty stains....*
> —William Cowper, c.1771

As the music progressed, the words spilled out and under their power I could feel myself relaxing. Closing my eyes, I repeated my mantra prayer, "show me the way," over and over and soon the guilty thoughts were vanquished—pushed aside by a tunnel of white light speeding towards me beneath an iridescent horizon of blue. Answers came in riddles, coupled with promises whispered within silent prayers:

Show me the way, I implored, *that's all I ask.*

"I already have."

Oh? When?

"Yesterday, today and tomorrow; you've been listening but you haven't heard."

Today, I have.

"Good, now listen again, and hear. There's a new song coming and a new dance too. Go with it. I'll guide you through, one step at a time. Soon you'll be singing out your life to *my* music, in *my* time; I promise."

Within these words, I felt the energy of change, a reversal of attitude. Even as they were spiritually uttered, I could sense a change of heart, a freeing of my old self away from me. I was opened to a fresh overflowing of love for Craig and a belief that I would truly be led into a new life—where or how, I had no idea. I had to sing and walk in faith, one song and one step at a time. For the first time in my life, my spirit was opened to the true meaning of Christmas. Yes, a Savior, *my* Savior was born! I sang freely and joyfully for the next eight days, including a boisterous celebration on New Year's Eve. Nothing could upset me. I felt saved from myself—from my burning ambition and my insatiable drive to be a professional singer no matter the cost.

After a raucous New Year's celebration with the musicians and their wives, I crawled into bed by dawn's light, pleased with myself at a job well done. Later that day, thoroughly exhausted, I happily headed home clutching a hard-earned pay check. Anxious to see Craig, I was counting on my "new" used yellow Toyota, held under a small deposit, to drive me to Scarborough the next day. Arriving in Toronto, I called my friends:

"What's up?" they asked. "You sound better."

"I *am* better, and guess what ... I'm quitting."

"No way...!"

"You'll see."

Succinct Synchronicity

Three decades later, rummaging through our basement looking for stuff for the church sale, I discover the large cardboard box—the one I've been lugging around through countless moves for countless years. It is huge, around three feet high and two across. Pushed back into a deep corner, it's been resting there since our move to Tara Hall, our B&B in Wellington, Ontario—eons ago in emotional time but fifteen years in real time. With great effort I shimmy the box a few feet towards me, into a slot of window light, to check its contents. First, I see a blanket of feathery grey dust over the sealed top. Looking closer, I see a few spiders buried underneath. *Hmm,* I think, *they're dead or sleeping—either way, they're warm under their dusty coat.* Unlike some people, I like spiders. They have ambition, they work hard, and they build gossamer ladders to high places. On the other hand they're easy to destroy. One swipe at their cobwebs and they plunge to their destiny. Yep, this last part reminds me of when I lived in New York.

Okay, enough; remember, you're on a new mission, my censor's voice pipes up—rising high from that low place he lives. *Forget your past disappointments,* Sinc chides. *Just because you're writing about New York doesn't mean you have to relive it. You're supposed to find usable stuff for the church sale and you have to get on with your writing—all morning, you promised yourself, remember?*

"Okay, okay, I remember," I mutter out loud. *Damn, I wonder where my censor Sinc, has been hiding these last happy years. I thought he'd retired.*

"But what if there's something important in the box," I whine out loud. "You know some memory that will trigger my next pages?"

I don't think so, Sinc replies impatiently. *You know darn well what's in the box. Look at the label. See what you wrote those years ago when you were so agitated and distraught? Walk away from this box. There's nothing in there for you; trust me.*

Looking around to the other side of the box, I see, boldly printed with a thick red pen, in my own hand: "Lives Past: Do Not Open on Penalty of Death." *Oh sure, dramatic as usual,* I think, as I pull the box closer. Grabbing a cloth, I swipe at the spiders' final resting place to get inside. Aggressively ripping off the cover, I peer inside to see a pile of picture albums, some old, others older.

Lying near the top, in a large plastic envelope, there's a full-colored newspaper photo of me on the cover of *Canadian Weekly* published by *Toronto Star,* for their magazine insert dated May 8-14, 1965. The caption reads "Singer Elaine Steele Reveals 'Why I Quit the Merry-Go-Round.'"

Oh no, I thought, *I haven't seen this article in thirty years. I can hardly remember it. I'm curious to read it, but it's going to be hard. Too many dreams lost, and tears found, in that lifetime. And there's the picture of me knitting Craig's sweater in the hotel room. Did I ever finish it?*

You're right, don't read it, whispers Sinc. *Just think about "the cat." You know, you've always been too curious, always asking too many questions; like they told you back in grade school: "Curiosity killed the"*—but I blocked off my censor's voice before he could finish the time-worn adage.

"Actually Sinc, *I'm* the one who killed 'the cat,'" I respond out loud with annoyance, "years ago, with *my* curiosity, when I was still in the crib. From that time on, everything I was interested in took on a 'need to know' basis." *There,* I thought; *that should do it. My curiosity goes further back than his censorship. Sinc won't like that.* I waited ... silence. Good, now I can finish going through this box.

Reveling in Reverie

Reaching into the box, I could feel some fabric; one side satin-smooth while the other felt metallic and rough. As I pulled out the cloth, I recognized my tear-away singing skirt—pink and silver brocade on the outside, hot pink satin inside. *Wow,* I thought. *So this is where it's been hiding all of these years.* This is the gown that my dear choreographer, Roger Palmer, designed and sewed for me when I was invited back to sing at the beautiful Hotel Duverney in Quebec, nearly forty years ago. I well remember that after we signed the contract, Roger turned to me and announced, "Well, of course, my dear, a return engagement requires you to have at least one new gown. It won't do for you to look outdated, you know."

"But Roger, you know we can't afford to buy another gown."

"Not to worry; I'll design and sew it myself. We'll take the sewing machine with us. By the way, where is that darling little portable you brought with you when you ran away from Eaton's sewing machine department in Winnipeg?"

"I didn't exactly run, you know; it was more like crawling, what with my foot surgery and all. The machine's in the bedroom, but Craig's asleep right now. Really Roger, it's too much to expect you to—" Interrupting my protest, Roger stood up tall in a first position ballet pose, took a deep breath with arms fully extended, did a quick toe twirl and with an extravagant flourish leaned forward into a deep bow at my slippered feet.

"Always at your service, my dear," he smiled up at me. Laughing with pleasure, I hugged him. He was my absolute best friend: generous to a fault, always funny—and safely gay.

∞ ∞ ∞

Having enjoyed my reverie, I return to the present and reach deeper into my memory box, searching for Roger's PR pamphlet. Poking around, I find it near the photo album from my singing days in Toronto. Holding it up to the light, I see that it still looks good after all of these years in the basement. I've always loved Roger's distinctive pamphlet: it boldly consists of nothing but a set of gorgeous legs in high satin pumps and mesh hose—sexy, but classy. These legs are supposed to belong to GwenVerdon—the lead dancer in the movie "Damn Yankees," a big star off Broadway and in Hollywood. At one time Roger danced with her and later worked with her when he was a choreographer at the CBC in Toronto. I was very lucky that he was willing to choreograph my act, as my friend and without charge. Seeing his pamphlet took me back to the great times we had together on the road, forty years ago....

Roses and Roast

It was the early sixties. Michael, Craig and I were still together in a low-cost apartment in Scarborough, a Toronto suburb. Roger and I were getting ready for the Hotel Duverney gig. Craig, not quite two years old, was sleeping and his dad, Mike, was at work at CFTO television, off highway 401, in East Toronto. Roger and I would be driving to Hull, Quebec, later that same evening with music, gowns and sewing machine in hand, so we had to work quickly and quietly to get the choreography ready for my new song.

Grabbing two side panels of hot-pink chiffon from my half-sewn gown, Roger put on the record, "Canto Karabali," my new song for the show—a haunting melody with a jungle beat that builds up to an exciting crescendo then fades back in the final bars. Swaying slowly with the music, hips, then arms and feet, Roger closes his eyes and, in a dancer's warm-up, moves lithely around the small room measuring out the compact space of the stage that I would be working on.

"Okay," he says, "hum it quietly, and watch me—this is what you're going to do. Raise your arms high and hold the pink chiffon panels up, hands together, like this, in a tented veil that covers your face. Stand very still and wait. The club lights are off, and you're a silhouette, dark and mysterious, just like the music that has started in a low jungle beat. After a couple of bars the piano brings in the melody. Bathed in a baby pink spotlight, you start singing in Spanish—low, mysteriously, "Karabali...." As the music builds, so do the lights. Singing more intensely, you release the veil and the panels flutter down beautifully, dramatically. See how they reach the floor on each side, still attached to the back bodice of your gown? With your arms free you take the microphone with your left hand while reaching out with the other toward the patrons who, entranced, have stopped eating and drinking to watch you as you sing passionately, longingly, for your lost love. Swaying leisurely with the music, you slowly start this dance step I've just created; it's perfect for the 2/4 rhythm. Now here's the tricky part. You must first move one hip up and out and then the other the same, sensually, in time with the music, while standing spot still in front of the microphone, *comme ça*. You've been singing in a subdued sultry way but now your voice builds up in intensity as the drums beat out their crescendo, then, as the lights dim, you turn slowly to the right with that same hip movement ... don't rush.

Now facing the band, you replace the mike, and on cue, with a dramatic drum roll, you reach to your left waist and rip off your skirt (see, it's attached by Velcro). It flies, abandoned, to the floor. Now, in your pink-and-silver sequined leotard à la the Hollywood dancer Cyd Charisse, you slowly raise the chiffon panels while circling around to face the audience again. Fully veiled, back in your original pose, legs slightly astride, head thrown back and arms up in full surrender to your lover, the audience and the music, the house lights dim to black, and away you slip ... leaving the darkened stage to the sound of applause. Okay, what do you think?" Roger asks.

I am mesmerized. I don't hear the door open, I don't hear the baby crying, and I don't notice Mike standing in the door way:

"Looks great, sounds great," Mike answers, while taking three long strides across the small living room toward the baby's cry.

"Oh, here," he says, tossing me a brown bundle tied with butcher's string on his way through. "I bought you something to celebrate your new show, a nice standing rib roast. You can cook it for Sunday dinner tonight, before you leave."

Roger, seeing me with my mouth agape, looks at Mike and snickers: "She wants roses, he brings her a roast." Aah, dear Roger—so wise and wonderful; I wonder where he is now.

∞ ∞ ∞

Thinking back to those crazy hard times when Michael and I were still together and Craig was a baby, I must admit, Roger was right. I *did* want roses, not a roast. I wanted the singing career, the excitement, the action, and all of the celebrity that goes with it. But I wanted Craig too. The marriage was floundering—lurching between two opposing forces: my singing dream and Michael's flourishing career in television production. Stymied, unable to face giving up Craig *or* the career, I kept trying to have it all. And I was tired. Tired of juggling my time, energy and money; tired of fighting off the recurring sexual proposals by managers; tired of the increasing loneliness in the marriage; and tired of the guilt I felt every time I left Craig. Thinking back, I guess I was just plain tired of trying to balance the desire for the music career and the longing to be with Craig. But then, that's exactly what kept me going.

Apparently, those many years ago, in Toronto, I still wasn't ready to give up my singing dream. I was close but I was not quite there.

Keep Digging

Still in the basement, digging deeper into my memory box, I come across a huge stack of orchestrated music. *Whoa, look at this.* I'd forgotten about those great arrangements done for the cross-Canada CBC radio show. Aah, but I remember that time very well. I was happy with my career. Finally, I was singing with a full orchestra and an excellent musical director.

While sifting through the music I come across a song I've always loved but haven't heard in many years. It was new in the sixties, and everyone was singing it. Quietly humming to myself, deep in memory, I recall how that song came to be one of my favorite numbers. I sang it at *The Night in Budapest* show at the Sheraton Hotel in Cleveland, Ohio, when I opened for Mitzi Gaynor—a popular singer, dancer and actress in Hollywood. As I hum, the musical memory takes me back to one day in late December, 1964, when I was headed downtown for a rehearsal at CBC, on Jarvis Street, in Toronto:

"Do you think this one will work?" I ask Lucio Agostini, the well-known and respected musical director at CBC. He reaches for the sheet music and starts to hum the popular title tune, "The Sweetest Sounds," from the Broadway musical *No Strings*, lyrics and music by Richard Rogers.

I love the words," I murmur; "they're written for me, you know." He smiles benevolently and slides over on the piano bench indicating for me to sit down.

"Let's hear it—start easy…. Okay, sounds good," says the Maestro Agostini. Let's do it. I'll have it written up in fourteen parts. Lots of schmaltzy violins … should be great."

And it was great—the experience of singing with a full orchestra on CBC radio across Canada. I felt I'd finally arrived—but *where?*

Chapter 9

Canadian Conundrum

Sell your cleverness and buy bewilderment.
—Jalal ud-Din Rumi: Sufi Mystic Poet.

APPEARING NIGHTLY
in the
OAK ROOM
Monday thru Friday 9:45 p.m.
and Midnite
Saturday 10:15 in the
VICTORIA ROOM
•
THE GLAMOROUS
ELAINE STEELE
SULTRY AND EXCITING
NEW SUPPER CLUB STAR
•
FEBRUARY 3 TO FEBRUARY 15
•
NO COVER CHARGE
Monday Thru Thursday
Friday and Saturday
$1.00 Per Person

Singing at the King Edward Hotel, Toronto, Canada, 1965

Tell It Like It Is

Around the time of the CBC radio show with Lucio Agostini, I was also singing at the Oak Room, in the King Edward Sheraton Hotel in Toronto. While there, I was interviewed by their publicity department. The transcript is dated January 21, 1965. Reading over the interview by Robert R. Rowe, I am amazed at the frankness with which I answered his questions. Today, doing research for this book, unedited, word for word excerpts from that interview help me understand exactly where I was at that point in my life and career.

Interview:

Rowe: You have entertained both in Canada and the United States, Miss Steele. How do Canadian audiences compare with American ones?

Steele: Not too well, I'm afraid. After many years in show business here, I find a clearly marked apathy on the part of the Canadian public towards our entertainers. If you were born in New York, Boston, Miami or Los Angeles you'd have a far better chance of getting audiences and coverage in Toronto than if you were born in, say, Regina, or in Winnipeg, as I was.

Rowe: What do you think is the cause of this apathy?

Steele: Canada has no star-makers. No one cares enough about all of the wonderful talent to be found in Canada to take an interest in us and help bring us to the attention of the public. Then, too, word-of- mouth is a very over-rated method of communication; we really need more attention from the reviewers.

Rowe: What do you find to be the greatest problem for female entertainers in a show-business life?

Steele: That's an easy one. Trying to retain some sense of balance; trying not to be a phony. This is a shallow sort of business— it's not easy to keep a check-rein on oneself, to decide which path to take. Then, too, if a girl isn't inclined to "co-operate," things become even more difficult.

Rowe: Is it necessary for a girl to "cooperate" in order to get ahead as you imply?

Steele: Not always of course, but it's a great deal more prevalent than anyone could possibly imagine. One well-known producer I met in New York, sitting in an elegant office with his feet up on his desk, drawled to me:

"My dear, all the talent and all the good looks in the world are no good to you unless you cooperate. There are thousands and thousands of good-looking, talented girls already in New York.... You will have to *co-operate.*"

Well, this sounded so much like a movie script that I inadvertently started laughing. Nonplussed, the producer promptly invited me out for the evening. I've heard stories like this often enough to realize that this is a very serious problem in the life of any female entertainer trying to make the grade.

Rowe: What do you think can be done to get more recognition here and to help our own Canadian entertainers?

Steele: First, I believe we badly need those star-makers I mentioned. Someone who is willing to find out all about a performer – to teach her to avoid any pitfalls such as playing in the wrong type of atmosphere for her act, or, through ignorance, blundering into performing at the wrong places and so damaging her reputation. Take Robert Goulet – I remember the days when he wandered around the Toronto Conservatory in leather jacket and jeans – he finally gave up in disgust and headed for New York; then, came Camelot! The States did for him what Canada should have done.

Rowe: But you still seem to like being an entertainer, Miss Steele, in spite of your disappointment in it. Why, then, do you stay in this business?

Steele: Because I *am* a performer, Mr. Rowe. It's a field I've wanted to be in all of my life. I started out as an x-ray technician, but when you're as outgoing as I am, that isn't enough. That's why I trained at the Banff School of Fine Arts, and then went on to the Toronto Conservatory of Music. I can't seem to get enough of the show-business life.

Rowe: Don't you find it a lonely life for a girl?

Steele: Sometimes, yes. Sometimes I could go mad from loneliness. For example, I had an engagement which meant I had to be away from home last Christmas. And on Christmas day I found that I couldn't get any food in the hotel, so I spent the day in my room eating cornflakes and watching the only TV set the hotel could scrounge up for me. Then I made the fatal error of telephoning home—it took just a few words with my 2-1/2 year old son to reduce me to tears! But there are so many compensations.

Rowe: For instance?

Steele: Hearing a man like Harry Belafonte speak as he did on the very serious Negro issue which has been plaguing the United States. Mr. Belafonte is an honest, sincere person, and it was a great honour for me to meet him and appear with him and other stars on the same stage at Massey Hall. I've met so many fascinating people in my travels that it would take me hours to even begin listing them all! It's a hard thing to be a mother, and still have this urge to get out, go places and do things. I can cope in only one way. I try to make the best of what I have–to enjoy both my home world and my work. I'm convinced it can be done, without neglecting either.

Rowe: What are your plans for the future, Miss Steele? What do you feel you can gain in this business?

Steele: I don't expect a lot, knowing how things are in Canada right now. But I do hope with all my heart that things will change here for our people – that they will get the recognition so many of them really deserve. We must get the help we need before we lose any more of our number to other countries with more foresight!

∞ ∞ ∞

Re-reading the Rowe interview, I quickly recognize that my "light" tone was an attempt to trivialize my degrading experiences in New York. In retrospect, I see that I exemplified the shame and guilt prevalent in the sixties in most accounts of abuse or rape—highlighting the narrow attitude toward these matters well over forty years ago. Most encounters were not discussed, and if they were, the victim was simply not believed. Obviously I wasn't ready to give the unsavory details of my New York experience to my Toronto manager or anyone else. Today, in retrospect I see that my reluctance to give an account stemmed from a sense of shame, but why? In those days I was considered "different"—a maverick, independent in thought and action—someone who resisted the dictates of standard society, and show-biz society too. Although "compromising myself" was never an option, I distinctly remember my inner conflict:

"What's wrong with you?" I'd ask myself. "Why are you so 'different'?" Why can't you be like everyone else?" *Why, indeed*, echoed Sinc.

Reality's Roar

The initial excitement of being back in Toronto after New York was short-lived. Picking up the yellow Toyota after successfully wrangling with the bank for a car loan—a daring challenge for a single mother in the sixties—I drove out to Scarborough to visit my darling Craig. As I expected, there were tears all around when I came in, tears when I left and more tears while driving home after dark—heading for my empty apartment on Jarvis Street in mid-town Toronto. Craig, now going on three, was living with his Grandmother and father, instead of me. Since we still had joint custody, I was determined to get Craig back with me as soon as possible.

Driving down the Don Valley Parkway in a late March snowstorm I could feel myself getting progressively upset and nervous—upset about leaving Craig behind again and nervous about driving my "new" car on the icy highway. These thoughts were distracting enough, but added to them, my critical self, Sinc, now shrouded in the guise of reality, reared his head in syncopation, readily coming up from that shallow place where he resides:

Okay, you have an apartment empty of furniture to pay for; you own only one third of a car, the bank owns the rest; you have no money, you have no job; you have no family in Toronto to help you; and now Michael is preparing to sue for custody. What are you going to do?"

"I have no idea," I muttered.... Do you?"

"Accidentally" Saved

Drawing on the comforting words spoken to me in St. Patrick's Cathedral and the epiphany in my hotel room in Akron, Ohio, I knew I had to walk in faith. I had come this far and now I would again have to depend on God's help, in whatever form it would take, to lead me through my desert. Remembering how, after my visitation in St. Patrick's, certain bible verses jumped off the page as though written for me personally, later tonight, at home, I would seek such guidance through my bible—but "later" came too soon.

I was looking down, trying to adjust the windshield wipers, not too sure how to work them, when my car was *walloped* from behind, hard, so that my head jerked back and then forward to crash face first onto the steering wheel. Inexperienced as a driver, I braked too hard—and black ice did the rest. Out of control, my yellow Toyota careened sideways over two lanes, did a full spin and came to rest with its rear on the shoulder, its nose *facing* traffic in a nasty sleet-driven storm. When I looked up, all I could see and hear were headlights heading towards me, brakes screeching, cars lurching then veering by—probably as shocked as I was, by my inappropriate presence.

I realized I had to get out of the way, and fast. Confused, feeling something salty trickling into my mouth, I groped for my Kleenex box on the passenger's side. While reaching over I could see another set of headlights, large, bug-eyed, heading directly toward me with no sign of turning off. I could do nothing but brace for the impact: the sand truck, travelling slowly, finally veered, swiping my bumper and headlight before coming to a screeching, full stop. After being hit twice in as many minutes, I knew I had to do something. Forcing the mangled door open, I lurched out. Still stunned, I watched as a police car skidded round the same curve then slithered to a stop—like me, now facing ongoing traffic.

Propped up against my crushed fender and clutching a wad of Kleenex to my bleeding nose, I watched the scene before me galvanize into slow motion. Through a surreal focus, I saw two officers as they struggled across the littered highway, the March wind pushing them off-balance. By now, the driver that had hit me from behind and the truck driver who had hit me head-on had walked over. Huddled together for warmth, we silently watched the two policemen heading towards us. Tottering in my high-heeled fashion boots with my knees rattling in a combination of cold and shock I had trouble keeping my balance. Throughout all, the blizzard was yowling so hard that I could hardly hear the officers ask for my insurance. I knew that the Toyota was near the end of a ten-day temporary policy and this pulled up a new anxiety as to whether or not my car was even covered. But the officers had other concerns regarding the cars.

"They'll have to stay put until the morning," they explained, gesturing at our cars. They further explained that there had been over two hundred accidents that night, and they were sorry to inform us that they could only drive us to the nearest streetcar line. "After that you'll have to find your own way home, or to a hospital," one announced. In a daze, we piled into the cruiser car, and after dumping us off at the nearest King streetcar stop, the officer left us on our own.

Confused, my head pounding, I headed north on the subway and east on a streetcar to Jarvis, where I disembarked onto a dark, deserted street. It was now past midnight. Still in shock, and worried about my car, my only financial asset, and my face, which I hoped was still a performing asset, I nervously skirted the icy sidewalks in wobbly boots, grabbing onto wrought-iron railings along the way—a skater without skates. In this way, I inched my way up Jarvis Street to the Wellesley Hospital. But I was still in trouble. Once there, seeing its infamous steep driveway covered in ice, I had no choice but to slide down on my backside—a sledder without a sled speeding towards the front glass doors. Just in time, the emergency doors opened wide for a patient exiting, who gallantly stepped aside for my unruly entrance.

After an hour's wait, I was told that indeed my nose was broken, "...but there's nothing we can do for you. Go home, take two Aspirins and call your doctor in the morning," was the intern's sage advice. By now fully fatigued, I had to creep home grabbing at iron railings all the way to stop from falling flat onto my broken nose while half-crawling along the icy sidewalk in my red ski pants—now torn from my dramatic entrance through the front doors of the hospital.

In sheer relief at finally arriving home, still wearing my soaked ski jacket, frayed ski pants and salt-stained boots, I collapsed into my only chair—the uncomfortable Scandinavian one from our apartment in Scarborough. Too tired to move, I glanced around the room: first at the roll-away bed that Roger had dug up for me—from where, I was afraid to ask; then at the faux bed-side table created from the beer-box left over from the house-warming my cousin Eleanore had organized. Constructed of wood, it made a fine night table when covered with the peach cloth my mother had sent from Winnipeg. Completing the décor was my two-dollar lamp from Goodwill, now casting a warm glow on the bare hardwood floor. After I removed my pesky fashion boots, I staggered over to the bed and collapsed.

The next morning when I stared at my face in the bathroom mirror and viewed the damage under the harsh fluorescent lighting, I was shocked. Here was a fighter's face: nose widely expanded tinged with dried blood, and eyes bruised red through purple ringed with shades of yellow. The first thing I thought was how lucky I was not to be performing at the time. *It's not important what I look like*, I thought—*today, tomorrow or next week*. In a way I was grateful for my unusual calmness. I took it as a sign that my stressful indecision was coming to an end.

Around that time, **The Toronto Star** had featured a full-page cover picture of me and a three-page spread titled "**Why I Quit the Merry-Go-Round**." This article and the accident would be the stopgap I needed to truly accept my arduous decision to quit singing.

The gestation period of my idea to quit, first born in St. Patrick's Cathedral after my incident with the New York showbiz czars, had progressed through my spiritual awakening in Akron, Ohio, to culminate with my last engagement in the Oak Room at the Sheraton Hotel in Toronto. In retrospect, the accident and the near loss of my car should have been a devastating blow. I remember that I *did* feel desolate over the car, but I had, after all, escaped serious physical injury twice, in as many minutes. Although confused and exhausted following the mishap, I did *not* feel alone. True to the promise whispered in St Patrick's Cathedral, *someone* was with me, at that time and in the days that followed. Yes, my accident was a terrifying test of faith, but I passed.

Something's Coming

When my Toronto agent, Paul Simmons, saw the bold picture and cover story of me in the *Toronto Canadian Weekly* magazine he called up in surprise: "What's up, kiddo? You're quitting without telling me?"

"I guess so ... I'm not sure. That business in New York was disheartening—you don't know the half of it. But you know me well enough to know I'm just not playing that game. What is it you call me in secret? Something like, 'The Ice Queen,' or is it 'The Perplexing Princess?'"

"Whatever," said Paul half-chuckling. "Okay, so what are you planning to do now?"

"I don't know. I want to get Craig back, but I can't do that if I'm not working."

"Listen, come in tomorrow and we'll talk. Maybe I can come up with something. Okay?"

"Okay, Paul, but don't fall down when you see me. I've been in a car accident—actually two—and I look ridiculous," I said humorlessly.

"That's okay, Elaine, you'll never look bad to me. See you tomorrow" and he rang off.

By the time I arrived at Paul's office the following day, I was looking and feeling a lot better. The Avenue Road specialist that I'd been lucky enough to get an immediate appointment with assured me that with a little "home-work" I'd be fine.

"Here, take this adjustable gizmo home with you," he said, handing me a chrome nose cast. "Now, when you're sitting around watching television or resting, hold this cast firmly around your nose. It will bring down the swelling and help to re-shape the soft tissue. If there's any bone damage, say a chip or something, we'll find it in a couple of months. And don't worry about the raccoon eyes; they'll be gone by next week. By the way, aren't you that singer that was featured on the cover of *The Canadian Weekly* a week ago? The article said something about 'Quitting the Merry-go-Round?'"

"Yes and no," I answered truthfully. "So much has happened since that article, I hardly recognize that person as me."

"Oh, don't worry, you'll be fine ... but the article said that you're quitting show business. So then, what are you up to now?" Dr. Inquiry asked.

"Well, actually, I'm on my way to see my agent, Paul Simmons. He's just up the street on Davenport Road. He's asked me to work with him in his office, a glorified secretary, I guess, although I don't even type. He's really a very nice guy and a good agent too ... not like that gang of wolves in New York," I muttered.

"Hmm, must be quite a comedown for you. Is the money any good?" Dr. Nosey inquired.

"Well, not really: about one-fifth of what I was making in the singing business, around forty dollars a week—just enough to cover the rent and some groceries. But, you know something? In some ways I'm happier than I've been in years. You see I'm a believer, and I just know that something's coming, something good ... just around the corner."

"Well, okay; let me know if there's any trouble, a blockage or something," purred Dr. Concern.

Feeling good, I left the doctor's office humming the opening song, "Something's Coming," from the Broadway hit, *West Side Story*. Once inside the empty elevator, I opened up and sang the promising words out loud, and for the first time in a long time I felt great!

The next day, when I walked into my manager's office the phone was ringing. "It's for you," Paul said, looking up with a questioning smile at the gizmo I was holding over my nose.

"Thanks, I'll take it in my *office*," I said smoothly, knowing he would smile at the reference, considering my "office" occupied one corner of the reception desk—public and accessible to all.

"Hello, yes, yes, it's me. Who am I speaking to ... who? Oh, Mr. Graham, from the T. Eaton Company. We had an interview a year ago, when I was looking for work? Oh yes, of course I remember," I fibbed. "You'd like to see me ... for what? Not selling sewing machines," I joked, hoping for a chuckle. Happily, it was there.

"You'd like to talk to me, this Thursday? Sure, why not. Lunch sounds great."

Paul was looking at me quizzically from his desk across the entrance hall. I'd just started working for him and already I was getting personal calls—not good.

"It's nothing, Paul," I explained. "Remember last year, when I was living in Scarborough, and so lonely and depressed? Well, I decided I should get out of show business and find a real job, so I hiked myself downtown to Simpson's at Queen and Yonge and marched up to *The Room's* head buyer whose name happened to be Miss Steele, the same as mine. Naively, I thought that this would give me an amusing 'in' with her, but as powerful and busy as she is, there's no time for humor. All I got was a polite explanation that they were not looking for anyone at this time, '...but why not try across the street?' Increasingly depressed, I dragged myself over to Eaton's. The initial interview took place in the personnel department. Filling out the customary forms, I remember thinking: *So this is how my dream ends? Back at Eaton's selling sewing machines?* Just as I got up to leave, an attractive 'suit,' a Mr. Graham, walked over, introduced himself, and invited me into his office. Apparently he was the regional manager of the Ladies Better Fashions, and, after a short interview, he asked if I would be interested in working for him. Forcing a smile, I explained that at this point I wasn't sure that I was finished with my singing career; then, not to waste the trip, I filled out a cursory application form, thanked him and left. And that's the last I heard from Eaton's until today. Now, guess what? That was Mr. Graham on the phone. It turns out that he'd seen my cover picture in *the Star*, read the article, remembered me from the interview a year ago and decided to call—weird huh?"

"Sure is," Paul agreed. While in Paul's office explaining everything, I resolved that Mr. Graham's phone call, coming out of the blue because of a magazine article, was a *sign* that should be given some attention. Maybe it will be as the song from *West Side Story*, "Something's Coming" suggests—maybe, just maybe, it will be something great! Let it be so.

"Well," said Paul, as I was leaving his office at the end the day. "I hope the Eaton's interview goes well for you. You know, my dear, I wish only the best for you."

I had never given Paul the full details of my New York misadventure, but I'm sure he got the picture on his own. I'd always found him to be a gentleman and a friend and I was assured that he meant what he said. It was a comforting end to an exciting day.

When I got back to my apartment, I found a lengthy letter from Mom. Apparently she'd seen my picture on the *Canadian Weekly* staring out at her from the news box in front of Eaton's in Winnipeg. At first she didn't recognize me, but, as she tells it, the telephone in my hand was the dead giveaway—not the low-cut dress. (At home, I was *always* on the phone.) After reading her letter, I decided I'd call her the next day after my lunch with Mr. Graham. I was anxious to tell her about the interview with Eaton's—my Alma Mater, Winnipeg's "Institute of Higher Selling"—and of course I would tell her about Craig and how he would soon be with me.

∞ ∞ ∞

The interview was great, the job sounded great, Mr. Graham was great and I was feeling great.

"Hi Mom, it's me," I announced. Why she should know who "me" is, when she has four other daughters who all sound the same, shows my vanity and my mother's exquisite understanding of her five daughters' individuality.

"*Olanna!*" Mom says my name in Ukrainian, then, "How are you doing?" in English. "Great. I got your letter yesterday. So what did you *really* think about the article?"

"I think you are the only entertainer I know who gets a cover story when she's quitting!"

"I know; weird, huh? Well, at least something good has come of it. Do you remember last year, when I was so depressed? Craig was around a year and a half, and I felt that I had to get a 'real job,' one with stability, to get out on my own. Things weren't great at home and you said, 'Why not go back to Eaton's?' and I just scoffed. Well, guess what, I got desperate and took your advice, but nothing came of it. After that, I decided to go to New York—but that's another story."

"Now," I continued, "this same guy, Mr. Graham has offered me a job as assistant to the buyer, a Doreen Maxwell, who's been with the store for eons. Actually, in your words, she's 'engaged' to Eaton's; she's wearing a 'twenty-five years of service' diamond ring on her finger. She's the head buyer for Better Dresses, which includes wedding gowns, for all of Ontario so there are quite a few stores involved. Seems she's a little difficult to work with, and after trying out a few in-store employees, Mr. Graham has turned to hiring from outside. *Voilà—c'est moi!*"

"Wait a minute," Mom interrupted. "Don't you need a degree in merchandising or something like that? I mean, what kind of experience does this job require?"

"Well, I told Mr. Graham that I knew all about fabrics from my grandma who designed and sewed vestments for Daddy and the priests in the attic. I explained that Babka sewed all the clothes for herself, Mom and us kids, especially for all five of us girls. And then I told him that I've been designing and sewing my own clothes since I was a kid. Remember that white pique cap-sleeved blouse I made, with the hand-painted colored buttons that I ran all over town looking for?—I think I was eleven at the time. I also told Mr. Graham that I had designed and sewed my gowns for my early singing dates. Do you remember that black silk chiffon dress embroidered with birds of paradise that I designed and sewed at St. John's Avenue in Winnipeg when I was already pregnant with Craig? I wanted to keep singing and I didn't want to show my condition, so I designed an overskirt with a waistband of Velcro that could be released as my waistline increased. I was almost five months pregnant when I sang at the Royal Alexandra, your fancy CPR hotel in Winnipeg—in fact you and Dad came to see me there."

"Okay, I understand," Mom said, now laughing. "In other words, you bamboozled your way into the job. So, when do you start? What's the pay and, what about your clothes? Even you can't get away wearing a fancy sequined gown and four-inch heels to work at Eaton's."

"I've thought about all that. I start a week Monday. As far as the pay goes, you'll love this: After I got the feeling that Mr. Graham was definitely hiring me, I was going to mention Craig, but I changed my mind. You may not know this, Mom, but now, in the sixties, when we think we're so modern in the corporate world and big business, no one wants to hear about your kids. Even though many women, the 'libbers,' are fighting for some kind of equality, still it's really tough out there. A woman with ambition is supposed to quietly juggle it all—husband, job, housework and family and never even talk about it. Although I'm not exactly a libber, I've learned to fight the system in my own way. When Mr. Graham told me that this semi-executive position, which Eaton's would train me for, was paying seventy-five dollars a week to start, I simply said, 'that won't do.' Honestly, those were my exact words. Well, I was lucky, I admit; at first he looked at me in surprise, then with a little smile asked me how much I was looking for. I told him I required eighty-five dollars a week, because that's my monthly rent, and everyone knows the rule about allotting twenty-five percent of your monthly income towards rent. Still smiling, he said that he would have to get personnel's approval, but when I was leaving he shook my hand and said 'welcome to Eaton's.' That's when I knew I was in! Anyway, now I'll have some money for a good lawyer to help me get Craig back. So, Mom, what do you think?"

"I think you sound better, happier. I'm sending you ten dollars for a pair of comfortable shoes for your new job. Get good ones, all leather, on sale of course, and don't spend the money on music or makeup like you did the last time!" With that, we said our goodbyes.

After that lengthy conversation, I decided to re-read the *Canadian Weekly* interview that was quietly changing my life. Mom's right: *I always do things backwards*, I thought, as I opened the article to the last page. There, the final lines read:

Q: "Do you have any regrets?"
Elaine: "No, none whatsoever."
Q: "Would you do it all over again?"
Elaine: "Yes, I certainly would."

Doing What Comes Naturally

I remember everything about my first week at Eaton's as a demi-executive in the fashion world. It's not something I could easily forget. When Mr. Graham first interviewed me, he told me that I would find the fashion world very exciting. I didn't believe him.

I remember my response, "But not as exciting as show business, I'm sure; if 'all the world's a stage,' what could be more exciting than being stage centre in *that* world, the world of *make-believe*?" Here, I paused for his comment—none, so I went on: "Being in a related business, like fashion, would be like working in the shadows, in the wings of a big stage production—doing all the doggie work but never getting to chew on the bone." No comment. *Okay*, I thought, *let it go. Either he doesn't get the show-biz lingo or he doesn't think I'm funny.* (Although I thought I saw his eyes twinkle.) *Enough, I'd better let him do the talking.*

It turned out that Mr. G. was a better salesman than I was. He started to sell me on the merits of the fashion world, describing how *exciting, challenging and creative it was.* "And," he added "there is a lot of room for advancement, and later, the opportunity for travel—"

"Stop," I interrupted. "You got me on 'challenging,' *the* magic word. When do I start?"

I could not believe that I would find the retail fashion business interesting after my five-year stint as a professional singer, but I was wrong. It *was* challenging but in an easier, less-stressful way. Having worked so long and hard for a little recognition in the show-biz world, all of a sudden I received a paycheck every week for just showing up and using my God-given brains mixed with a touch of common sense—in other words, doing things naturally. For example, the retail experience I'd had up to that time worked well in combination with the core values I had learned and utilized in selling my talent.

The entertainment business is, in many ways, a very "giving" business. When you are alone on stage, you work hard at trying to give the audience something positive to take away with them—a feel-good sentiment, which you are sometimes lucky enough to arouse by singing the right song on the right night. Here, on the third floor in the Better Dresses office at Eaton's, Queen Street, I had an opportunity to do the same thing. I discovered that when you are able to give a client something good back to them, you are giving them a gift—whether it is by way of an improved self-image or a more flattering exterior. I implemented this philosophy into my selling technique and soon found out that it not only worked, but I was able to surpass my own expectations and the clients' too. The idea was to talk about everything but the price; once they were sold on a new self image, the rest was easy.

On my very first day at Eaton's, I struck up an acquaintance with one of the cleaning staff and he remained helpful and friendly until the day I left. What I didn't realize was that there's a hierarchy in a large store, exactly the same as in the corporate world. By befriending the cleaning guy, unbeknownst to me, I was already breaking rules. Happily, I didn't know any better. The same thing happened with the sales clerks. They were all older than me and, as an assistant to their manager/buyer, I was also their boss. But having been plucked off the street to fill a position that required more experience than I possessed at that point, I didn't feel like anyone's boss. I remember smiling to myself a lot, as though I were playing a trick: *I'd better work hard and learn fast, so that they (the higher-ups) won't clue in to the idea that they'd hired a fraud.* Well, fraud or not, I fell in love with the job as naturally as I'd fallen in love with singing. In the latter, it took a little talent, one good note, B flat above middle C, and a lot of hard work. In a way the same thing happened at Eaton's: I worked hard, learned through hands-on experience and before long I was on my way to what would become a successful twenty-year fashion career.

The First Week

From the start I loved my job as assistant buyer. First of all, it helped that my direct boss, Doreen Maxwell (a pseudonym), was an alcoholic. I know that sounds like a terrible thing to say, but from my first day I discovered a capacity in myself to be efficient in an effortless way that had, until then, been hidden. I always returned phone calls and, being naturally friendly, the suppliers and managers of the other Eaton stores were cooperative in return. Because of Miss Maxwell's lunch-time drinking habit, she started trusting me within two days of my tenure by relinquishing some of her decision-making power and deferring to me in a way that forced me to learn my job quickly.

At the outset I didn't really understand the extent of Miss Maxwell's drinking. I noticed that she came back from her extended lunch hour, usually at two-thirty, in a giddy mood. Having been around nightclubs a lot, I could easily detect the gin/vermouth combination. Although I suspected she drank most, if not *all* of her lunch, it was of no direct concern to me at the time. There was a set routine: by mid-afternoon, around three o'clock, she'd start to droop, near four o'clock she'd get cranky, and by four-thirty, she'd remark that she had a headache and was going home—dipsomania at work.

"Here's a list of things I'd like you to look into, Miss Steele, before you leave today."

Her list usually coincided with the one I'd written for myself, but it was always longer because many of her items had already been addressed while she was absent for her two-hour lunch. From the start, I felt Miss Maxwell liked me because she had finally found a person who was dependable, self-directed and capable of problem solving without her chronic attention. And I liked her. I liked the way she trusted me. It made me feel good about myself, a feeling that had been missing since the New York fiasco.

For many months in the beginning, I would forego my lunch hour altogether. Later, I would bring a sandwich from home, eat it at the desk then work past the store closing hour until five-thirty or six o'clock. I never talked to Miss Maxwell about this overtime until well into the job, maybe five months later, after Craig came to live with me. I was so excited about having a real job and a regular pay check that I didn't mind what Miss Maxwell did—as long as she didn't fire me.

Our Eaton's Better Dress department had ten stores to look after strung across Ontario: Queen, College, Yorkdale, London, Hamilton, Don Mills, Oshawa, Shoppers' World, Cloverdale and Sherway Gardens. Better Dresses consisted of medium to high-priced dresses, including classic wedding gowns. In the mid 1960's, Eaton's better dresses retailed from forty-nine dollars to one hundred and twenty-nine for designer styles. Wedding gowns were priced between one hundred and two hundred and fifty dollars—the latter, in pure imported silk. To place our orders, we would visit the Toronto market centered around the garment district on Spadina Avenue, south of College. During the major buying season, four times a year, Miss Maxwell would travel to the Montreal market and stay over to place orders with the Quebec manufacturers and their salesmen. This last situation was why I was sent out to buy wedding dresses on Spadina Avenue, *alone,* on the third day of my first week on the job!

Luckily I knew a little about finer fabrics. Silk: raw or shantung, satin finish or chiffon. Rayon: flat weave or slub finish in combinations with polyester, linen and occasionally cotton. I knew that the quality of the fabric and degree of lace on wedding gowns helped determine the cost, and as far as colors went, well, there are only so many shades of white. Most of what I knew had been learned at my Grandma's knee beside her ever active sewing machine, or bargain-hunting with her in Eaton's basement, searching for fabrics to sew our everyday clothes and ornate fabric for the priests' robes.

On the day of my inauguration into buying wedding gowns, I was known in the market-place as "Miss Maxwell's New Assistant." Clutching my beloved music case, now transformed into a business briefcase full of blank Eaton's order forms, I was as surprised as the suppliers that the "new assistant" was being sent out solo to buy expensive wedding gowns on her third day on the job. Unabashedly green, I apparently asked all the right questions because the suppliers were very polite in their answers. They seemed to like me in my new role. Later I found out that some of them had heard me sing when I was performing at the Royal York Hotel the past year. Soon I realized that part of their respect shown to me was because of Miss Maxwell's exalted rank among the manufacturers due to Eaton's extensive buying power.

After the relative success of those first few days, we silently worked out a mutual agreement: I would do double my work so that Miss Maxwell could cut hers by half. No problem. I was young, keen and anxious to earn my pay check, which chronically amazed me by showing up on time, every two weeks. I was never again put into a compromising position regarding my rent or car payments. For the first time in years I was financially independent, and it was a truly freeing experience!

During the buying seasons, four times a year, Miss Maxwell made side trips to the big fashion shows in New York. At the start, I wasn't involved in those trips—they came about six months later when I became a bona-fide buyer on my own. That too was a fluke.

Suede, Leather and Good Luck

"What do you know about suede and leather?" Mr. Graham asked me one morning, as he sauntered past my desk on his way to the cafeteria for his coffee.

Not much," I answered. "Why?" my 'enquiring mind' called out, but he was already on the elevator. *Well, what do I know about suede and leather,* I thought. *I know that you can't wear suede out in the rain because it will spot, or if drenched, it will dry very marked and very stiff. Why?* I wondered. *After all, some animal lived outdoors for years in inclement weather before being skinned and styled into a collar, coat or cuff, so why does suede have trouble surviving ice, rain and snow?* By now my interest was piqued; I wanted answers.

"So ... Miss Steele, what *do* you know about suede and leather?" Mr. G. threw out at me again the next day as he ambled past my desk on the way back from his morning coffee.

"What I don't know now, I'll know by Monday morning," I retorted, without missing a beat or even looking up. *All it will take is a trip to the library on Saturday,* I thought. *I'll leave work a little early.*

Miss Maxwell won't be here; she doesn't work Saturdays now that she has me as her assistant. And that's how I got my first promotion—being my natural curious self. Six months under Miss Maxwell's guidance and soon after Mr. Graham's approach, I was asked to open the first Suede and Leather Shop in Eaton's large Queen Street store.

See Sinc, curiosity did not kill this cat or even skin me alive! All it got me was a great promotion and a raise!

All in the Past

During market week near the end of my six-month's training with Miss Maxwell, we headed out to the Royal York Hotel, where the imported lines, Gucci, Missoni of Italy and Diane Von Furstenberg of New York, all represented by the Brodkin Brothers of Montreal, were set up for viewing. Arriving at the hotel by taxi, we were greeted with conversation, coffee and croissants and then shown the new lines on the rack. If a sample dress or suit was appealing, the house models would be called upon to show it. This was an eerie experience for me, having been one of those house models in Montreal not so long ago. I remembered working for those same suppliers, but if they knew me, they didn't let on. *Just as well,* I thought. *It's all in the past anyway.* But on that particular buying trip with Miss Maxwell to the Royal York Hotel, in Toronto "the past" did not stay *past*.

Stepping off the elevator on the ground level of the hotel, I saw that we were standing next to the Black Knight Room where I'd performed so successfully a year earlier. Directly in front of me was a large glass marquee displaying photos of former entertainers and those still to come. Surprisingly, my photo was still there. It jumped out at me. Slick and sultry in a full-length New York glossy print, all curves, hair piled high, eyes weighted heavily by dark eye-shadow and thick mascara, I presented a sophisticated, almost haughty demeanor: "Come hither," those eyes seemed to say—and I did. Wrapped in surprise, discordant as Christmas in July, my past invaded my present. In an eye's shift I felt myself in an earlier time last year, upstairs in my Royal York hotel room, knitting, while putting in the hours between the early and late shows:

Flashback

Whoa, it's almost midnight, time for my second show. I throw down my knitting, wiggle into my royal blue and silver gown, apply fresh lipstick, and head into the empty corridor. Walking constrictively in my sculpted gown, I catch a side-glance of myself in a wall mirror. *Hmm,* I think, *I look okay, almost as good as my expensive New York picture in the marquee downstairs next to the Black Night Room—all curves, but wait ... what's that bulge on my backside? Is that the Montreal couturier's foam derriere?* Since Craig's birth, now that I'm walking tall and straight again, I realize it looks ridiculous. I had forgotten all about it, sewn as it is into the lining of my gown. *Ha! Mom will get a good laugh out of this one,* I thought. *But it's too late to worry about it now ... it's show time!*

With my stomach knotted in nerves, as usual, I step off the elevator into the corridor that melts into the smoky shadows of the toney Black Knight Room—its patrons barely visible as I enter. Standing in darkness behind a pink spotlight, I wait for the clatter of dishes and the chatter of patrons to stop. While waiting, I take a deep breath and exhale slowly, studying the audience, their heads drifting beneath haloes of smoke as they murmur to each other behind their glowing cigarettes. Scanning the room, I shape the scene and pull them towards me ... *okay, they're ready.*

I give a nod for the opening chord, and, starting at the bridge of "Just in Time" I sing out a full *a cappella* on B flat above middle C—a safe note to awaken my voice and the audience— "Now you're here.…." *Okay, here comes the chorus, they'll all recognize it and stop* talking. The piano, joined by the bass and drums, establishes an easy tempo, a lazy 4/4, and we all relax, my butterflies included, as the crowd settles into the familiar tune, happily bringing forth their own fond memories of how they met. *This opening feels just right. It's going to be a good show,* I thought, as I worked the room.

∞ ∞ ∞

Feeling a nudge, I am startled out of my nightclub reverie into the sharp fluorescent presence of my boss, Miss Maxwell, standing beside me at the marquee next to the Black Knight Room in the Royal York lower lobby. *Whoa, how long, have I been daydreaming,* I wonder.

Turning to Miss Maxwell, seeing her looking at me with concern, I soon realize that she doesn't recognize me in the marquee.

"Miss Steele, are you alright? Do you want some water, or something?" Still in a daze, I indicate "no" and try to concentrate on concrete reality as we head for the revolving door.

"So sorry," I murmur as we step out into the haziness of a September sun and the busyness of Bay Street at lunch hour. "I guess I was just day-dreaming."

Secretly, I was annoyed with myself. I thought I was done with those feelings—the excitement of performing finally surrendered to the past, replaced by new hope and promise, but apparently not. Just seeing my New York glossy in the marquee triggered a strong reaction, an emotional truth I'd long been hiding from. Feeling my present so readily dissolve into my past I finally realized the capricious nature of memory. It seems it is ready, on the slightest whim, to invade the heart and awaken old dreams—as alive this day as yesteryear. I thought I was doing fine, in my new present, by leaving old disappointments behind, striving towards a high future, but no, memory decides to barge in. Obviously, old passions are as close as my heart. *What to do?* I guess I'll have to grapple with my singing memories, move them into inaccessible shadows where they will finally rest in peace, or, barring that, grab hold and strangle them to death. But, is either of these choices possible?

No, answers Sinc, succinctly. *Accept the fact that forty years from now, these memories will be alive as ever—and move on. That's all you can do.*

Sinc was right.

Star for a Week

After the strange experience at the Royal York Hotel with Miss Maxwell, I rushed home to my apartment on Jarvis Street, vowing to re-read the *Canadian Weekly* interview before retiring it *and* my singing addiction into the mammoth box kept for treasures and memories, flippantly labeled: "Lives Past: Do Not Open on Penalty of Death."

Anxiously, I unfold the magazine, its cover bold in the brightest of reds, and study the close-up of me reclining on a pillow, talking on the telephone in a low-cut black dress. Everything false is in place: wig, eyelashes and bosom.

CANADIAN WEEKLY:

Singer Elaine Steele reveals: WHY I QUIT THE MERRY-GO-ROUND.

Published by TORONTO STAR LIMITED
FOR **STAR WEEKLY, TORONTO,**
WEEK OF MAY, 8-14: 1965.

"After years of singing in night clubs, Elaine Steele of Winnipeg, in this candid interview, tells why she finally said: '**Stop the Merry-Go-Round, I Want to Get Off.**'"

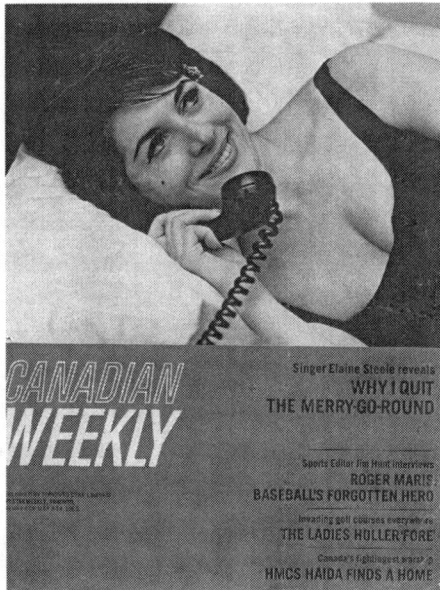

Canadian Weekly cover page, May 8-14, 1965

"Little Elaine Sawchuk, a minister's daughter who grew up in the north end of Winnipeg with a need for attention and a love for singing, could see only the magic in show business. She pursued it after becoming an X-ray technician, she pursued it after becoming a wife and a mother. And as Elaine Steele, one of the best supper club singers in Canada, she got as much of it as she had a right to expect. [*What does he mean: I got as much of it as I had a right to expect? Just who sets the limitations?*] But Elaine had to pay a high price for the little bit of glamour and those moments of applause which didn't always come. She became used to rejecting the mashers and learned to accept the audition failures and the lonely hotel rooms. She could even forfeit her marriage. But, when it came to forsaking her baby, however, the magic ran out for Elaine Steele. [*That part is perfectly true.*]

"In this frank interview with Peter Sypnowich, a staff writer of *The Canadian Weekly*, recorded in her hotel room during her last engagement, Elaine tells her story:"

Q: You've been quoted as saying "As long as I can keep singing, I'll be happy." Is this still true?

Elaine: Some of my happiest, happiest moments have been while I'm singing. I don't think I'll ever stop singing, but now things have taken a different turn. My values have changed.

Q: What's wrong? Here you are, appearing in the Oak Room of the King Edward Hotel in Toronto; presumably you have more bookings....

Elaine: This is my last supper club engagement. I've cancelled all the rest. [*Yes! Upon re-reading this, I take great pleasure in my independence and integrity displayed so many years ago.*]

Q: What's wrong?

Elaine: For me, it's just not enough. The career is at a standstill, and has been for a year. You can't just keep playing the same rooms over and over. When I first started five years ago, it was all so terribly exciting. Now I realize there are certain prices you have to pay. You have to travel and you have to accept bookings out of town; like I had been living out of a suitcase for a year. I want to put down the suitcase, my arm is tired. [*This is a succinct explanation, to be sure.*]

Q: What did you hope for when you started your professional career?

Elaine: (Sighing) Well you secretly dream things, but your heart's desire is not very quickly disclosed.

Q: Do you get much pleasure out of the bright lights and the introductions, your name in print, having strangers recognize you? [*It doesn't happen often. Have you seen me sans makeup?*]

Elaine: No. What means more is to make an appearance and walk away, saying to yourself: "I've reached these people, I've entertained them. That's exciting." [*Absolutely.*]

Q: *Variety*, which is usually called the bible of show business, has said that you are 'a looker and nicely built,' and that you have 'top quality pipes and plenty of chirp savvy.' What have you lacked to become a really top star? [*One needs money and a helpful Canadian mentor.*]

Elaine: What's talent? I went to New York four times, and I made some contacts, and I auditioned for some top people in the business. Did they really feel there was talent there? Or was it a come-on? Because they're so expensive to work with, these people, these arrangers, you know. You even have to doubt someone's opinion as to whether you've got enough talent to bother going on. There's a well-known arranger there who was very interested in me, felt I had some talent, who said it would require just a little more work before he presented me in New York. But he wanted a $500 retainer before he even started to work with me. Talent will out, yes, but to do it on your own, to have constantly to come up with your own material, I mean if you haven't even been able to afford the best creative people, well, it's frustrating. All the people who have become stars have had this help. [*I've had very little personal help except for that one year in Montreal. Johnny Gallant was great.*]

The Canadian Attitude:

Q: You haven't been able to find help in Canada?

Elaine: The few agents there are in Canada are doing what they can. But there are no star-makers. Is it not an indication of the Canadian attitude? Time and again a couple will come up to me and say, "Miss Steele, we really enjoyed your singing very much. Where are you from? And you say, "Well, I'm Canadian." And they say, "Oh really? We thought you were American." It's as if a Canadian performer can't be good.

Q: What's your favorite town?

Elaine: I adore Toronto. I think Toronto is *the* city of Canada, [*Yes, when it was still known as 'Toronto the Good!'*]

Q: What about New York?

Elaine: New York is very, very exciting for a person in this business. If you make it in New York, like everyone considers, that's it—you've made it. But it's impossible. It's so expensive. To exist, you've got to live like a gipsy. And you have to live there to do the rounds, and make the contacts—every day you've got to get up with the pain in your stomach, and face the music, literally. I never really considered taking up residence in New York.

Q: What kind of upbringing did you have?

Elaine: I'm one of eight children to start with. Okay? Now, I'm the second youngest. It was a very full, full house, always, because there were grandparents, and extra people living upstairs. [*Yes, the priests in the attic, let's not forget them!*]

Q: Your father was a minister, wasn't he?

Elaine: Yes. He still is. Well, he's the Dean of St. Andrew's College on the campus of the University of Manitoba. My father is a very intelligent, well-read, educated man, and like most parents, he wanted his children to be, you know, outstanding enough. It was always very important to me to be of some significance in my father's eyes. It was a great day when I finally felt that he really did have some sort of respect for me as, say as a performer.

Q: What is your parents' attitude toward you and your career?

Elaine: They feel I've worked very hard. I think my mother wants to say, in essence, "Stop, dear, just now take a rest." People have said to me, "Your father is a minister, and what does he think of you singing in supper clubs?" Well, I've never appeared in low-down clubs, so I've never worried about it, and I don't think he has either. [*Dad's different, an unusual man and father.*]

Q: What made you become a singer?

Elaine: I always loved to sing, I always loved it, that's all. [*And who am I to fight against love?*]

∞ ∞ ∞

Reading the interview, I am happy with my attitude and honesty. As Mom once said, "You've always made a fuss on the way *out*, but 'better late than never!'" *True again.*

Whoops, there's the telephone, civilization's weapon against reverie. I guess I'll have to finish reading this article later. I pick up the phone and say "Hello."

Chapter 10

No Games, No Guile

Within us, still within us, always within us, childhood is a state of mind.... We find this state of mind in our reveries; it comes to help us put our being to rest.
—Gaston Bachelard, *Poetics of Reverie*

Joanne Small and Craig Steele, 1965

Don't Worry About a Thing

"Hi there, it's Alan. How are you doing?" Jolted out of reading my Star review, I am startled but excited to hear Alan Small's rich broadcaster's voice again.

"I'm okay, I guess, and how about you?" I ask, trying to sound casual.

"I'm good and getting better" he chuckles. "Anyway, I'm calling to ask you out."

"But you already have—it's a week this Friday. Have you forgotten?"

"No, but I don't want to wait. How about we go out *this* Friday? What do you say?"

"I can't. I'm picking up my son, Craig, from Scarborough; he's going to be with me for the weekend, maybe longer. Anyway, I don't have a babysitter—nothing's arranged yet."

Surprised, yet pleased, I thought: *this guy sounds interested; I think I like him, even though we've talked on the phone only once—for over an hour!*

"Don't worry about a thing," Al continued, "I found out from my accountant Marty that his mother lives in your building on Jarvis and she babysits. I've already talked to her, and she's available. She said, 'any friend of Marty's etc' ... So?"

"Gee, I don't know. It may be kind of confusing for Craig. He's only been here once before, and a new babysitter and all..." I trailed off. I was thinking: *I haven't been out on a date in four months, not since starting at Eaton's—it might be good for me. Also, Alan's been a widower for over a year, with a little girl just nine months older than Craig, so she would be near to four. He's been through a lot, losing his wife so early in life, and I'm sure he's more practical and serious than others his age. I sort of trust him already.*

"Don't worry about a thing," Al repeated comfortingly. "If the sitter doesn't work out, we'll order in. I've made reservations at the Royal York for dinner and dancing. What do you think?"

I *thought* the whole thing sounded wonderful, amazingly well-planned. What I *said* was:

"Well, maybe ..."

"Aha, sounds like a yes—yes?" he queried. By now I was smiling.

"Yes, okay, well maybe, but I'll let you know tomorrow, for sure," I said, still smiling.

"Well, in case it's 'for sure,' then how about seven o'clock on Friday?" he persisted.

Hmm, I thought, *I like this one's perseverance; sharp and refreshing, yet somehow innocent—no games, no guile.* "Okay, if it turns out to be *for sure* then I say 'sure' too," and now we were both laughing.

∞ ∞ ∞

Al was on time. At seven sharp he was at my door—beaming, looking flushed and excited carrying, in one hand, a gold-wrapped box of chocolates, and in the other hand, pink miniature roses.

"Hi. How nice of you. See? The roses match my dress perfectly and Craig will love the chocolates."

Okay, I thought, *so far everything's great—except he's the wrong guy!* Earlier that week, I'd checked with my cousin who worked at CFRB Radio; it was she who had given Al my phone number, and Eleanore had described Alan Small to me in a way that conjured up altogether another face and body. In fact, I mistook her description for another broadcaster whom I'd met when I was there for an interview with Betty Kennedy of TV's *What's My Line* fame. I well remember my surprise when I opened my apartment door on that first date.

"Hi," I'd repeated, then added "but, where's Al?"

Not that I was unhappy with the big guy standing in front of me wearing an off-white flannel suit and a smile wider than Missouri—I was just surprised. Happily he must have thought I was joking. Not quite ready, I invited him in and introduced him to Craig who was emptying his makeshift toy box; then I headed back to my bedroom to finish getting ready. When the accountant's mother, the babysitter, knocked, Al let her in and all hell broke loose; Craig started bawling and ran away from her. I still don't understand what started it, but I remember thinking: *Great. Craig doesn't like her, so that's that.* There I was, trying to finish my makeup in spite of Craig's crying, rushing around in my pink linen shoes, still wet, hoping they would dry out in the breezy June air. I'd colored them pink with a toothbrush dipped in Rit fabric dye, because, of course, they had to match my Jeanne Scotte silk dress purchased that day for ten dollars from our Eaton's "high fashion" discount rack. Getting more nervous by the minute, I wondered why I didn't just give up and stop trying so hard. *The shoes don't have to be perfect and you don't have to be perfect either!* I chided myself.

That's right, interrupted my censor, Sinc. *Don't do your best, do your worst. In your case, it will probably be good enough.*

Oh sure, I thought, *here's my censor giving me advice again, just what I need. And wouldn't it be easy to simply stop wanting, stop trying and stop dreaming. Just give in, lie down and let fate's truck roll over you. Great....* But Sinc persisted.

Just a minute; this guy likes you. You can see that. Give him a chance!

I'd noticed Craig's crying had stopped. Peeking out the door I could see Al playing and joking with him: they were both down on their haunches, pushing those little metal Dinky toy-cars around. They seemed comfortable, easy with each other, and that's when it hit me—this one *is* special. He doesn't look like your usual "hit and run" guy. No, if he really likes me, he looks like he might hang around for a while—maybe a year or even two—and wouldn't that be nice.

Al proposed to me that very night in the Imperial Room at the Royal York hotel and despite an untenable wall of domestic strife and pressure, he hung in and waited two-and-a half years for me to be granted a divorce so that we could get married. But what a time we had in between! Madly in love, our two kids, Joanne and Craig, were a big part of our life together. We wrapped ourselves around them, clinging tightly, ensnaring all of us in a mutual net of love. When we'd first met, Craig was my focus and Joanne, almost four years old, was the diamond in Alan's eye. Because her mother had died of cancer two years previously, I took Jo on as my own. For me, it was love at first sight.

∞ ∞ ∞

On a balmy Sunday afternoon in late May, after attending Timothy Eaton Church just west of CFRB on St. Clair Avenue, I met up with Al at Fran's Restaurant across the street for lunch. Following a quick bite, he announced that we were heading to Willowdale, in North Toronto to meet his mother and daughter. "It's time, definitely," he'd said.

Although we'd only been dating a couple of weeks, we both knew we were in love. Al had proposed marriage to me on our first date, and so, although it seemed too early in the game to meet the family, I went along with his plan. One of the things I loved about Al was his inclination to take the lead. I needed this. I was exhausted from years of planning, wanting—always working from a fixed fulcrum of need which inevitably spread into an infinite field of lack. *Wanting*, such a hungry word with so many derivatives—*lack* and *need* weighing in equally; burdened words too heavy to go the distance, and sometimes, through *lack*, grabbing onto wanting and catching *wanton* instead—"a romantic interest without serious intent." Through garbled semantics the path of love is easily diverted, as wanton and need combine to elude the eye of love—the watchful parent of both. *Beware*, I remind myself. *You've been here before.*

I felt a little nervous as we pulled up to Al's modest split-level home in Willowdale. I was wearing a white cotton dress splashed with purple violets and a matching jacket that I'd slipped off in the convertible as a way of cooling down. With my dark hair styled simply in a Sassoon cut and a modicum of light make-up (no false eyelashes!), I felt young and pretty—and why not? I was deeply in love. I tried to relax as we walked towards the front door. Al called out as we entered and a short middle-aged woman, pretty, with a round face and reddish hair, appeared in the kitchen doorway carrying a frosty glass of beer in one hand and a lit cigarette in the other. Heading toward us with a friendly smile, she asked,

"And would you two like some beer?" in a broad Yorkshire accent.

"Absolutely," I answered —though I rarely drank beer, and never in the afternoon. After his mother came back from the kitchen, Al performed the formal introductions, and while we were swapping small talk and sipping beer, I could feel myself starting to relax.

"And where's Joanne?" I wondered out loud, more to myself than anyone else. Then I heard the giggle.

"Come out, come out, wherever you are," cajoled Dad, by now into his third beer and hovering just outside his homeland's Yorkshire dialect—the broadcaster's mid-Atlantic neutrality cast aside. Tentatively, with a chubby hand raising the cloth, Joanne appeared from under the dining room table, a blond butterball with the face of an angel dressed in a Sunday-best sailor outfit with a red silky tie and pointy red Mary Jane shoes, which she later referred to as her

"Dorothy" shoes from *The Wizard of Oz*. Smiling shyly, she walked directly towards me, and without a word climbed unto my lap.

∞ ∞ ∞

After that meeting we included Joanne and Craig in most of our activities. In the spring, we took them on fishing trips up north, and later, in the summer, out to the vast sandy beaches off Lake Ontario—Sandbanks Provincial Park near Picton—where we would stay overnight or longer, depending on when we had to have Craig back home with Mike. And then there were those long hot summer nights of barbecue parties around the swimming pool in Al's backyard with lots of friends popping in, many from CFRB. In winter, we'd head up to Hidden Valley to ski for the day, Joanne and Craig in tow, the three of us wobbly and willing participants while Al, perched high above on an open deck enjoyed the panoramic view and us over the rim of a rum and coke.

Looking back, my copious photo albums show proof of many happy days, but there were troubled times too. We all seemed to be waiting: me, for the day when Craig would be with us full time; Al, for the day when we could finally get married and all live together; and the kids, Joanne and Craig, only nine months apart, just waiting and trying to make sense of it all. In Timothy Eaton Church, sitting on each of my knees, they'd argue: "She's my mother—no, she's mine," trying to figure it all out while looking for some order in their lives. Sensing their confusion, I would hug them closer, murmuring, "Of course I'm your mother, both of you." Rejoicing in their need of me, I was plunged into a well of love so intense, that now, in reverie, those same feelings surface—as vibrant today as decades ago. But in between the good times and the loving there were disagreements and disputes, some serious.

Once, while sleeping over, a noisy tiff started up between Craig and Joanne, who were ensconced in separate sleeping bags on the bedroom floor. Al and I came running in to tearful shouts of "Mummy, she hit me" ... "Daddy, he choked me," and, as the wailing accusations continued, a quarrel ensued between us over who was really at fault. Sensing an unjust attitude in Al, something I never expected, I gathered Craig up and drove him back to his dad's house, both of us in tears. That night, the first arrow of single parental loyalty had been hurled—and it hurt.

Looking back to when our kids were little, I see them tangled up with our intense love and need, Al's and mine, in a way that they formed an integral part of what was essentially a love triangle. As such, I soon discovered that apprehensions with the kids soon translated into problems between us; but, despite the troubles looming—my desperate fight to prove my motherhood and gain custody of Craig—I still felt that a "normal" family life was possible.

We had Craig with us every second weekend. Al was always fair and generous with him, and Jo, who still had her Grandma Small and now her darling Uncle Brian from England living with them, saw Craig as her brother. All in all, I was convinced that we had a real chance as a family.

∞ ∞ ∞

Early on in our relationship, Craig's dad, Mike, was perfectly willing to agree to a divorce on the grounds of adultery—in the sixties, the only sure route: "The adultery would be on *your* part, of course," Michael had stated, "and only if you are willing to *sign* Craig over to me." Furious with his offer, I refused on both counts, knowing that anything less would threaten my chances of ever getting Craig back. I was adamant in my reply:

"No!" I exclaimed. "You go too far. I will never comply with your suggestions. A son cannot be signed away, negotiated over and traded off, like a holding—a chattel. It's ridiculous of you to suggest this. I'm Craig's mother; I'm here for him—always will be. My career absences during the past two years are over and done with. Just read the *Canadian Weekly* interview!"

By now I knew that a husband could be expunged—one could learn to live without him—but not a son. Once a son or daughter takes up residence in your heart, they cannot be evicted; their possessory rights hold true through sickness, health and death. At that time, I felt all of this instinctively. Now, forty years later, I have proved myself right; a son or daughter *is* forever.

∞ ∞ ∞

I surprised myself when I suggested to Michael that he read the *Canadian Weekly* interview. I realized after I said it that I had not finished reading it myself. Something had interrupted me. Oh yes, it was that second phone call from Alan when we arranged our first date. The Star was still sitting open on my coffee table under some unread magazines. After the upsetting conversation with Michael regarding the divorce and custody of Craig, I decided to take time off to find out the rest of the story. Earlier, when I was first reading the Star article I'd left off where the interviewer, Peter Sypnowich, asked me, "What made you become a singer?"

I picked it up from there, and in doing so, as on the last reading, I had some reactions. *These are in italics.*

Canadian Weekly:

Elaine: I always loved to sing. I always loved it, that's all.... After I worked at my first job as an x-ray technician for a couple of years in Edmonton, I applied to the Banff School of Fine Arts where I met Dr. Ernesto Vinci from the Royal Conservatory of Music in Toronto. After studying at the conservatory for four years, I said, to myself, "If you want to perform publicly, you can't do it as a classical singer. You're not a Teresa Stratas (who eventually became a well-known opera star worldwide) and you never will be." Around this time I got married to Michael Steele. We met at a singing audition in Buffalo at which we both failed. We went out west, where we were going to make a home for ourselves in Winnipeg. I did some radio work, appeared in the summer theatre, and had the beginnings of a television series; then my husband went to Montreal because he had a chance to get into television production. I followed, and in Montreal I met a wonderful vocal coach by the name of Johnny Gallant, who had been a musician there for twelve years; he trained and developed me for a year, and I made my supper club debut at the Ritz Carlton Café in Montreal at $550 a week. It was an undreamed of amount. This was the high point of my life because less than a month before that my son Craig was born. (*This is certainly a succinct synopsis of seven traumatic years! I was, I believe, very fair to Michael in my comments. This was good for what followed.)*

Q: What happened to your marriage?

Elaine: I've been separated from my husband for the past year. My marriage was, I think, affected by my show business career—my absences. I was trying to be a successful singer and trying to combine that with the role of a wife and mother, and unfortunately my strength sort of gave out. My career wasn't lucrative enough to allow us a full-time housekeeper.

Q: How much are you making? (*How bold are these next questions in today's world?*)

Elaine: My average weekly salary when I was working was $300 to $350 a week for an average of 10 weeks a year. But by the time you subtract all of the expenses—you've got to put out thousands on gowns, even your everyday wardrobe, than there are musical arrangements and photographs, and agent's fees. It's incredible. You write off at least half of what you earn.

Q: Where is your son now?

Elaine: He's in town, he's with relatives. I can't say more than that, because this is a very touchy thing, I mean, you know, I'm working toward something in this relationship with my son.

Q: Where's your husband?

Elaine: He's here in Toronto. He's a floor director in television. He too has his own ambition. That's another thing—when you get two people together and they're both very ambitious, it's like the paths start veering. Trouble starts. (*This is not something one plans, for sure.*)

Q: Did your husband ever ask you to give up your career?

Elaine: Never.

Q: Did you ever consider it?

Elaine: Not until now.

Q: What was the straw that broke the camel's back?

Elaine: What triggered it was that I appeared in a club in Akron, Ohio, over the Christmas season. The job came up through a New York agent, and I took it and I was away from my son and I didn't see his ... I wasn't there to see his eyes when he got the hobby horse I bought for him. I telephoned him and I sort of, well, completely broke down, because he said, "You don't go away no more, Mommy," and, "I want *you*." Well, there I was, in my gown, you know, Madam Glamour-puss, and I just wanted to be with him. And you know what I did? I took a taxi out to a woolens shop and bought some wool to knit Craig Anthony a sweater. I sat there in my room for the whole two weeks, knitting and crying—there was a tear in every stitch. (*This sounds dramatic, but it's all so true.*)

Q: Is it true to say that up to now you've put your career ahead of everything else?

Elaine: I imagine I sort of did. And you know what? You can have the gown on, you can have the false eyelashes on and you're ready to step out to the club, and the child has a dirty diaper and is crying—and that is very real; you are faced with a choice. There's an unbelievable conflict, such a constant conflict. And very recently it came to me, "This is a means to what end?" To completely forfeit my motherhood, my friends—so you say, "It's a merry-go-round, it's a merry-go-round, and I must stop." I mean, stardom, it's such a nebulous thing. Really, what *is* it? Motherhood is one of the strongest drives, and you ask yourself, "What is this other need, this force that has taken hold, so that I need the excitement and that applause?" You begin to wonder about yourself. You really do. (*I doubt that this self-query is universal among entertainers, but I've always been one to question myself.*)

Q: Exactly what is this need, this drive? Do all entertainers have it?

Elaine: Don't we all stand up there and say, "Love me. Admire me. Admire me and love me because I'm not so sure I love myself." Our needs are just that great. And your ego takes a terrific battering. Every time you stand up and perform, you are leaving yourself wide open, my dear. You are asking for approval, but you don't always get it. (*At this point in the article I stop reading to ponder my last statement.*)

Do any of us really change? Do we ever stop seeking approval? Maybe this is a good thing ... maybe this gives us an edge. I know that I was very interested in the approval factor in my new fashion career that fell out of the sky through fortune's (prayer's) smile, after the Star article above came out. As to my self-approval rating—at Eaton's, it soared.

The New Assistant

As my ardent romance with Alan progressed, so did my job with Eaton's. While working with Miss Maxwell, and, until Craig came to live with me in the Jarvis Street apartment, I didn't have any problems keeping up. With my first buying experience at the Royal York Hotel, when a couple of the suppliers suggested that they "knew me from somewhere," Miss Maxwell ignored them and brusquely reminded them that we should be getting down to business. She always introduced me as her "new assistant, Miss Steele," and I liked it. Miss Maxwell made me feel as though I belonged somewhere important (in the sixties, Eaton's was a huge retail entity); her act of recognition and approval significantly enlarged a persona dwarfed by years of self-abnegation. I was finally able to stand tall and cast my own significant shadow of being in the *real* world—no longer driven to perform in a make-believe world of fantasy. More importantly, through an act of faith, I had a new career in progress.

∞ ∞ ∞

Sitting in the showroom at one of the long desks (pattern-cutting tables) as Miss Maxwell's *new assistant*, I would write up our chosen styles on Eaton's wide order forms, the ten Ontario store names strung across the top. The styles being shown were usually "knock-offs," modified designs of originals that had been shown that fashion season in New York and Europe. With ten stores and a full line of sizes in at least two colors, these orders involved many thousands of dollars—a significant sum in the economy of the sixties. Miss Maxwell was in a position of power with these suppliers, and she knew it. After I'd been with her for maybe a couple of weeks, Miss Maxwell would turn to me and say: "Well, what do you think, Miss Steele?" Without a moment's hesitation, I would give her my opinion, drawing upon information stored about fabric quality, style, pattern and customer appeal—information I'd first garnered at my grandmother's knee. Added to this cumulative information, I learned to watch for signs of coming trends becoming familiar with them in scanning the fashion magazines, which I certainly couldn't afford to buy, at the news-stands near the subway. All in all, the job of selection depended on a few merchandising rules such as cost, mark-up, color, size suitability and, most importantly, the value and wear-ability of the current trends as perceived by the client. All of these were practical decisions that were easy for me to implement as I had learned a good style sense from my four older sisters and our gorgeous Aunt Mary—in her youth, a fashion plate of Winnipeg. Earlier, as a teenager and young adult, I was unable to afford ready-made clothes, so I sewed my own. Now the possibility of becoming a full-fledged buyer in a department store like Eaton's, with personal access to wholesale prices, seemed like a job opportunity made in heaven. And at that point in my faith life, it was.

Maybe

I loved my job, and I was excited about Craig finally coming to live with me. Now that I had an apartment, a car and a new job, I had the confidence to request that he stay with me for a while. No firm custody settlement was in place, and, until there was a divorce granted without the demands previously made—an adultery and custody sign-off—the best I could do was keep my relationship with Craig as close as possible for as long as possible. I thought my troubles were over, but in retrospect they were just beginning; how could I have known what lay ahead?

Craig, just past three years of age, was a smart, good-looking boy, but his physical health had always been a challenge. After his bouts of colic in Montreal, he developed some allergies that were asthmatic in nature, and after he moved out of Scarborough into my apartment, these symptoms, exacerbated by the smog and air quality in downtown Toronto, returned.

"He can't breathe properly in this city, just look at him," the doctor said. I looked, and my heart fell. He had developed the allergy-sufferer's dark-circled eyes and sniffle-salute, and this combined with a sporadic night cough resulted in chronic sleep-deprivation for both of us. As Craig's health deteriorated, my stressful migraines increased. How would we manage?

Meanwhile, in another stroke of answered prayer, I'd discovered a pre-kindergarten school up the street, the Red Feather, subsidized by the government with a tuition fee of six dollars a week. I had no idea what the name meant, but I envisioned it on a Robin Hood cap, a badge of honor, its red color exuding radiant energy in its mandate for justice and freedom of the underprivileged, children and parents alike—or maybe it was just a meager government's social imagination at work. I didn't bother to ask, I was too grateful for the opportunity presented. Now that Craig could attend nursery school, maybe I would be able to keep him with me for longer intervals and hopefully, one day, permanently—a futuristic dream for me. But in its capricious nature, enhanced by my own naivety, this dream shaped itself into a long drawn-out *maybe*.

Our mornings were hectic: fussing with Craig, feeding him and getting him ready for play-school while trying to look good for my fashion job was a challenge. In the sixties we wore false eye-lashes, hair-pieces, hats and even wigs to work. In that era, as today, there was enormous competitiveness in the fashion world and one always had to keep up appearances; moreover there was little interest or sympathy for a single working mom. Looking untidy or being late on Craig's account was not an option. And it was hard. I don't remember any government assistance programs aside from the six-dollar baby bonus allotted monthly, just enough to pay for one week at the Red Feather School. As Craig's father did not think I was entitled to help, I found it a real struggle to keep up. Eighty-five dollars a week before taxes barely covered our monthly rent, school, food, clothes and Craig's allergy medicine; but aside from the finances, my greatest challenge was the lack of *time*—there just wasn't enough of it!

The administrators at the Red Feather School on Jarvis were not allowed to dispense medications of any kind to the children. Since I didn't have any immediate family in Toronto (they were all in Winnipeg or out west), I had to find a way to administer Craig's noon-time allergy medicine myself, and this took some creative time juggling. I remember how stressful it was to fit this chore into the middle of a business day.

At lunch time, I'd take the subway north from downtown Queen up to Bloor Street; there I'd wait impatiently, stomach knotted, for the Bloor bus to come. Sometimes, if I'd just missed the bus, I'd start walking—fast at first, then jogging, then running, and finally galloping east along Bloor Street, darting around pedestrians to arrive at the school panting and disheveled—the teachers indifferent to, if not amused, by my plight. One time, when I simply could not get away from work at five PM, they locked up and left Craig, just three years old, standing alone in front of the school and told him to wait for me! Yet another abandonment issue is born. Luckily, in those days, it was still "Toronto the Good"—but what a worry.

Every noon hour, I'd search Craig out, give him his allergy dose, a quick hug and then turn around and head back to Eaton's, hopefully within my allotted lunch hour. Sometimes in the morning, I would have time to make a cheese sandwich, which I would eat on the run, and if not, then I would resort to a cinnamon "sticky bun," available on the fly at Eaton's main entrance from the subway. While trying to juggle my career and my personal time between Al, to whom I was at this time formally engaged, and Craig and Joanne, I found myself in a constant state of fatigue, fighting migraines that lasted for days, even weeks. Still, in between time constraints and migraines, there was a driving force, a euphoria fed by manic energy and a belief that, as an ambitious and capable young woman of the sixties, I could "have it all." *The current rules of convention, be dammed*, I thought; *all that's required is unlimited energy, creative time management, no sleep and innovative cooking skills.*

White Spaghetti—No!

One day, coming home late from work, tired and hungry, I found that there was nothing in the apartment to cook but one small package of spaghetti. Remembering my childhood and how I hated plain white spaghetti, I scrounged around for something, anything, to mix a sauce that had color as well as taste. I finally came up with a single package of dehydrated onion soup that cost ten cents in those days, and, taking a page from my Babka's depression-era cookbook, I mixed the onion soup with a quarter cup of boiling water. Then I added a heaping tablespoon of ketchup to make a quite acceptable spaghetti sauce. Craig says he remembers this; I say maybe. All I know is that he survived quite nicely, growing up to be a sturdy good-looking man, six feet, three inches tall. But it was not always so; as a toddler Craig had health issues, and consequently, so did I.

Chapter 11

Show Me the Way

I waited patiently for the Lord.
He turned to me and heard my cry.
—NIV Bible: Psalm 40:1

Craig Steele at three

The Hard-lots

Just before I met Alan Small, my son Craig, three years old, came to live with me. By this time, legally separated from Craig's father, Michael, I was living alone on the main floor of an apartment building across from the CBC (The Canadian Broadcasting Company) on Jarvis Street, next to the Four Seasons Hotel in Toronto. I mention this location because it helps to explain the bizarre circumstances of what happened while living there.

A few weeks after Craig moved in we were informed by the young superintendent that there was a formal complaint lodged against us: in essence, we were being told that we would probably have to move out of the apartment. I'd lived there almost a year with no problems, so I was shocked and confused by this notice. Apparently the gist of the complaint from the ladies in the apartment next door centered on "that bratty kid who moved in next to us; he never stops coughing and crying all night long so that we can't sleep, and we're too tired to go to work in the morning." I was baffled.

Yes, at times Craig cried at night, the way of most three-year-olds. Yes, he did have a croupy allergy cough and sometimes he yelled out in frustration, apparently nightmares—"normal for a boy in the midst of a change of environment," the doctor said. But aside from these minor problems, the rent was always paid on time and we were never rowdy, so how could we simply be thrown out? That night I gave Craig an extra dollop of Benadryl for his cough; it helped him get to sleep, but I remained sleepless, listening for the ladies to come home, to see what would happen next. Sure enough, around midnight, I could hear them whispering in the hall, accompanied by a low-keyed male voice urging them to "hurry, *please*." Peeking out, I saw a familiar-looking man, nervously crowding, almost pushing the two youngish women who were erratically swaying and nudging each other while giggling and rattling their keys. Finally, the door opened and they all fell in—then, silence. Happily, Craig was still asleep; a light snore accompanied his congested breathing, but otherwise he seemed okay. Tucking him in, I crumpled into my own bed exhausted. With no interest in reliving my day I was soon fast asleep.

The next morning, I called my dear friend Roger, a CBC choreographer who lived nearby, to tell him what had happened. He was my best friend and I wanted his advice. He was succinct. Sounds like you're living next door to a couple of 'ladies of the night'—harlots, or *hard-lots*," he expressed in his Aussie vernacular. "Check them out with the hotel next door; you'll see that I am right." *Dearest Roger*, I thought as I put down the phone, *so sweet yet so wise*.

That same morning, as we were leaving for Craig's nursery school, I'd noticed a white envelope peeking in from under our door. Not one to put off bad news, I ripped it open and stared at the scrawling words written with a thick black pen, almost illegible, complaining about "that boy next door who cries all night." We would have to leave. I was angry, frightened.

What will we do? Where will we go? Aah, but I can't deal with this now; we're going to be late for school and work. "C'mon sweetie," I murmured, "we have to go."

By the time I returned home from work that day, my fear had given away to a burning anger now followed by action: I rapped sharply on the building superintendent's door: "Of course, the harlots are tired!" I exclaimed to the disheveled young man who appeared. Seeing him blink at me in confusion, I thought, *he's far too young to be a building super—he should still be in school, and he's definitely too young to be married with the responsibility of two little girls. He looks uptight, probably in the middle of feeding the kids their supper; I know his wife works a night shift cleaning a building downtown. I guess it is bad timing on my part.*

"Sorry to bother you, but I have to get this settled," I said, holding out the eviction notice. "Did you sign this?" Without taking the note, the super glanced at his watch then looked over to the sofa where his little girls, close in age, were huddled together giggling and playing with their Barbies. Stepping closer, I realized that he was the same fellow I'd seen with "the ladies" next door, last night, around midnight. Now I was annoyed. *What's going on here? Don't tell me he's fooling around with those "hard-lots" while his wife's working all night cleaning buildings! Maybe they're blackmailing him into this!* Here, my musing was interrupted.

"Sorry about the notice," he muttered, looking genuinely distressed, "but I have no choice. When you first moved in, you didn't say anything about your kid coming to live with you; it might have been okay since you were already a tenant, but a formal complaint was sent to the management office and they've told me that you and your son have to move out. There's nothing I—"

"Just a minute," I interrupted angrily, "since receiving the harlots' complaint I've done a bit of sleuthing around the Four Seasons Hotel next door, and when I asked the night clerk about the ladies living beside me, he'd bluntly stated,

"I'll tell you what's keeping those harlots awake; it's their 'night work,' *not* your son." Hearing this, the super's face turned dark.

"I'm sorry," he muttered, turning away. "There's nothing I can do—I have my orders."

"But, don't you see there's something terribly wrong here?" I limply protested as he moved back to close the door. But by now I could see that my explanations had failed to make an impression on the young super, who obviously had his own problems and interests at heart. Glancing briefly at the eviction notice in my hand, he said that since it was dated yesterday, we'd have to be out by the first of the month, "which is, by the way, this Saturday"—and with that he closed the door. I could see I didn't stand a chance.

Almost forty-five years ago, when this took place, there was no Tenancy Protection Act as we know it today; no sixty-day notice to be in place before you could even begin to evict a tenant. And so, on the following Saturday, around noon, a bewildered Craig and I found ourselves out on the street in front of our building, staring across at the CBC where last year I had performed successfully so many times. Exiled and homeless, I stood on the pavement, shaking in the raw light of my new reality. Dispossessed of a home through circumstances beyond my control, I'd been jolted out of every aspect of that make-believe world across the street, realizing for the first time the true experience of poverty—the plight of those who find themselves imbedded in a society ready to turn its face. Evicted from a downtown building where children are not welcome, surrounded by suitcases and brown cardboard boxes hastily packed, Craig and I were as orphans—victims of a culture who preferred prostitutes to parents. With Craig tugging at my sleeve, I garnered my faith and did the one thing I knew how to do. I prayed.

A Contrite Heart

I'd had no time to do any research on apartment vacancies (in the mid-sixties, the Saturday *Star* want ads provided the only handy source of information), and when we were served that final notice on Thursday to be out by Saturday, I'd started packing at 6 p.m. and halfway through that night and the next in an effort to get ready. Early Saturday morning, while in the communal laundry room, I'd overheard some ladies talking about a similar apartment building to ours up the street, on Jarvis near Isabella; apparently there was a vacancy sign in the window. Yes, I was eavesdropping, but by now I had trained myself to listen for answers to ongoing prayer. Since my St. Patrick's Cathedral visitation and consequent spiritual experience, I discovered that not only my own spirit, but that of strangers could provide prayer answers anywhere at any time. The answers come unexpectedly, in many guises, through the comments of friends, the muted conversations of strangers, or personal intuitions and verbal thoughts. One must *listen* ... to hear. Having overheard the conversation in the laundry room, I accepted that divine providence had made a suggestion for my ears only, and, contrary to my former doubting ways, I would act on it.

My dear friend and confidant, Roger, was to come and tend Craig, the luggage, and the boxes at curb side, so that I could head up Jarvis Street to see about the other apartment. As we waited, I continued to pray. Broken and homeless, my hair unkempt, my eyes red-rimmed I stood on Jarvis Street with little Craig, who, bewildered, forlorn, and pulling at my sleeve whined, "Mummy, what's wrong? Mummy, don't cry." That's all I could do. *Show me the way,* I whispered through tears, over and over again ... and by the time Roger came bouncing up, we both felt better.

"How are you doing, luv?" he asked, in his friendly Australian manner. Hugging Craig, he murmured, "There, there, my dear, don't worry, we'll fix things up." Then he turned to me and said, "Now, off you go, Mum, we'll be fine here. And keep smiling."

Walking fast towards Bloor, I stopped smiling and started praying: *Show me the way, Lord, show me the way,* I repeated in tandem with my steps while tears welled. Thoughts came—*be humble, be contrite.* Yes, that's it. It's Psalm 51:17. How does it go? Oh yes: *The sacrifices of God are a broken spirit; a broken and contrite heart, O God, you will not despise.*

"Do not despise me," I mumbled to myself, as I headed for the apartment building's main entrance.

∞ ∞ ∞

"Oh, I see ... the other place is too small? How unfortunate," the manager murmured. "Well, let me see what I can do for you. Oh, there are two of you? Fine; and you work at Eaton's in the position of an assistant manager? Good. Eaton's is a fine store. Well, you seem fine to me, but I'll have you fill out this form while I find out whether the tenant, George, hmm, what's his last name"—

"Murray?" I interjected.

"Yes, that's it. Lovely man, George, he sings with the CBC you know."

"Yes, I *do* know ... and I know *him*."

"You do? Fine, well then, why don't you fill out this form and we'll settle the apartment lease right now."

"Fine," I echoed, and that's exactly what we did. The tenant, George who had once been married to Shirley Harmer, a very popular singer at the CBC in the '60's, had already moved out. The super gave me the keys to that fine apartment, and next thing I knew I was walking back south on the fine street of Jarvis—giving thanks for my faith, fine-tuned and strengthened that day through constant prayer. When I got back to my former building, after smiles and hugs from Roger and Craig, I called my cousin Eleanore who had promised to bring her 1958 Nash Metropolitan over to help us move our stuff. She did, and soon enough we were all seated on the carpeted floor of the new apartment, laughing, sipping beer and talking about those awful *hard-lot* ladies and "how lucky" I was to find an apartment just up the street.

"Just a minute," Eleanore interjected. "How *did* you manage to sneak Craig into this building? Isn't there a sign on the outside door saying *Adults Only?* "

"Could be, but luckily I didn't notice it. Besides, the lease application asked for the number of tenants, and I truthfully stated 'two.' What can I say?"

"What *I* can say is, that as usual, you were *very* lucky," offered Eleanore.

"And very *contrite*," added Roger, with a sly smile.

Elevated Status and Good Times

I lived in the second Jarvis Street apartment for two years. It took that long to reach an agreement on the divorce. Michael, Craig's dad, was in the driver's seat. I had adamantly refused his request to "sign Craig away," and it was not until a divorce would satisfy his own interests that he finally agreed to one. Meanwhile, in some ways, those two years of waiting were the best of times for us—"the good old days." Alan was in top form, getting lots of air time with CFRB and many voice-over commercials including Ford of Canada, which paid our mortgage for years to come. "Get a Mustang!" a rock-style soprano screamed out hourly on the television and radio shows for years …and eventually I did.

In Toronto, there were great nights out with the likes of Jack Jones, Tony Bennett and other stars who were performing at the Imperial Room of the Royal York Hotel from where Moxie Whitney's dance band, hosted by Alan Small of CFRB, was broadcast. And, there were great dinners out with local friends: "All You Can Eat Lobster," every Tuesday night at the Silver Rail Restaurant downtown on Yonge Street across from Eaton's for seven dollars and ninety-five cents. Alan always managed to get through at least three lobsters at one sitting. Then there were the succulent steak dinners from Carman's Steak House, still in business today after fifty years at 26 Alexander Street, two blocks north of College Avenue near my former apartment. This was a weekly treat with lots of drinks—in the sixties, it was always hard liquor, not just wine. And of course, there was the well-established Chalet Barbeque Chicken at Yonge and Eglinton, the *original* Toronto "Chalet" restaurant, with the kids every Sunday after church. In those days the white quarter chicken dinner cost one dollar and sixty-five cents, as delicious then as now. I also remember attending the very first ACTRA awards formal dinner and later that same year, a fancy opening-night preview of the new movie, *Dr. Zhivago,* to which I wore a glittery turquoise blue gown, long white gloves, my silver fox shoulder shrug and a faux diamond tiara! (I have the picture.) Those were good times, and for a while, I seemed to have everything—but I didn't have Craig.

∞ ∞ ∞

Earlier on, when Craig first moved into the second apartment on Jarvis Street, the one near Bloor Street, things didn't go too well. There was the chronic worry over his deteriorating health. His allergies and cough were getting worse; the black circles under his eyes and habitual sniffle had turned him into a Dickens' waif, a victim of our modern industrial revolution and Toronto's poor air quality. Seeing him look so poorly, I felt awful—guilty as the good warden's conscience on execution day. Between my guilt and the added responsibilities at work my nerves were frayed, worn bone-dry. Whenever the phone rang I jumped; consequently, so did Craig.

The phone rang ... we jumped.

"Hello, hello, Olanna?"

"Hi Dad; yes, yes, it's me."

"I'm here in Toronto," my father announced, "at the Royal York Hotel. I'm busy tomorrow, meetings you know, but today I thought I'd jump on the subway and come up to see you. What do you think?"

"That's great, Dad. I'd love to see you—Craig would too."

I hadn't seen Dad in two and a half years, not since I'd taken Craig to Winnipeg for a visit when he was six months old. When Dad arrived at the apartment, I was surprised to see how good he looked. Mum told me he'd impatiently pushed aside his seventieth birthday, bidding it curtly to "be on its way" as though minor defiance could blot out a natural apprehension over such a watershed birthday. *And keep me safe from harm, oh Lord just for today*, echoed Dad's favorite song, first heard while I was in the crib, now drawn up in memory just seeing him again. That prayer had served him well; although he appeared a little shorter and a bit stooped, Dad still possessed the enthusiastic humor of his youth:

"I was just passing by," he stated as I opened the apartment door (this said after a subway trip *and* a bus ride to reach our apartment). As soon as Dad entered, I felt his energy filling our sparse apartment, the same as when I was a little kid. As soon as he'd walk into our big manse in Winnipeg, Mum would sing out, "Daddy's home," and the house would come alive. Later on, as an adult, I witnessed the same energy whenever my father entered any room, even if it was filled with strangers. *Nothing's changed*, I thought. *He still has that*

147

distinct aura, a positive outlook infused with humor and hope—that's why everybody loves him.

Bending down to eye level with Craig, Dad gravely shook his hand and solemnly announced that he was his grandpa, and that he'd just flown all the way from Winnipeg to see him, and now his arms were tired, so could he please have a cup of tea? Craig probably didn't remember Grandpa, but still, I could tell that he liked him and caught on to his humor too.

"Next time, Grandpa, take a plane. Here, I'll show you," and he ran to his toy box to get one. When he came back with his plane, Craig asked Grandpa: "Would you like a cookie with your tea?" but before Grandpa could answer, he mischievously added "I hope not, 'cause I just ate the last one." At this point Dad was smiling, his big smile that shows up when he's charmed. Craig was being *cute* with Dad, and I didn't have to wonder where that came from; I did the same thing myself when I was a little girl. Being charming with Dad was my game.

∞ ∞ ∞

Back in my father's house, as the youngest of seven, "cute" was my forte. I don't remember how I fit in with Dad's priorities, there were so many of us, but somehow he managed to squeeze me in. Whenever anyone hears that I am one of eight children, they always ask me if I ever felt left out—deprived.

"No, not exactly," I'd answer, "except for the time I hid in the furnace room in the big house at St. John's Avenue for half a day waiting to see if anyone would miss me or come looking ... they didn't." Although I was only six at the time, I remember that incident as being a positive lesson for the future. When I finally got hungry enough, I came out, having learned an early life lesson. If I play it right, that is, not bother anyone, get good marks and stay out of trouble at school, I'll be able to do whatever I want. No one worries about the wheel that doesn't squeak. It worked well then, and with minor modifications still works today. Show up for work on time, do your best and smile a lot. After that, pay your bills and practice faith. That's it. Everything else will come.

As the seventh child in line, on the plus side, I was the first kid in our house and in grade school to have braces on my teeth—that was really unusual back then. Braces were innovative and expensive, but Dad managed to pay for them from grade six through to grade nine—an amazing feat on a minister's stipend. Unfortunately, I lost an upper eye tooth in grade ten and the other teeth anxiously moved over to fill the space; hence the speedy return of my toothy overbite. Added to my braces, there were many other family expenses: eyeglasses galore (almost everyone in our family was myopic), extensive dentist bills, dance classes for the girls and piano lessons for all—the list is endless. In spite of these chronic expenses, I remember getting nice 'prizes' at Christmas: new hand-knit mittens, a glossy hard-covered book, a small box of chocolates of my very own—so how was I deprived?

A Course in Commerce

Recently, through my older sisters, I've found out that during the late-thirties depression and World War II years, we were poor. I didn't know this because of Dad's gentlemanly behavior regarding money: when we were young, he rarely said no to anything he considered of value (education topped that list). If we were going to bother Daddy for money or anything personal, we'd have to run it past Mom first. If it was a *need*, not just a *want*, we'd get permission to take it further up the ecclesiastical ladder to Dad. That's what happened with my "need" of a bicycle: I planned my case carefully, well in advance.

I had already learned that to get past Dad's resistance to a *want* and convert it to a *need*, I would have to attain top grades. At this time I was in grade six, doing okay, but I knew this wouldn't be good enough; so I worked hard and pulled up from fourth place in class to first out of forty-one students. Good. Having reached that goal, I advanced to stage two: sell myself.

"Dad, you know how you have all of those letters to mail every day, and you know how you are always sending me off to the Main Street post office to pick up or drop stuff off? Well, if I had a—"

"Okay Olanna, tell me what you want." *Great*, I thought, *he's using my Ukrainian name, so he's in a good mood.*

"No, no Dad, it's not a want, it's a *need*," I explained patiently. "You see, this family *need*s for me to get a bike, because of all the errands I run. Remember that time when I was little, how upset I got when I fell into the ditch and broke one of the eggs and I offered to pay back one penny for the damage? And remember how I cried that time when I slipped in the mud and the quarter you gave me to buy rye bread [my favorite] at Oscar's Deli fell out of my hand and rolled away into the ditch, but I searched and searched until I found it, and remember—"

"Okay, of course I remember," Dad interrupted, smiling to convince me he was still listening. "But before you go on, let's move out of the past into the present. Why don't I look at your report card. Alright, it's not too bad; I see you got "excellent" in most subjects except geography—that was just 'very good.' But wait, here's a comment about 'talking too much in class.' What do you have to say about that?"

"I can't help it, Dad, I guess I'm just like you—too many friends. I suppose I'll have to drop some of them."

"Well, it looks like you've passed stage one," he said, laughing. "Now tell me about what you *need*."

"A bike, Dad, I need a bike, with a basket. Then I can *ride* all of the errands instead of running them. I'm only going to charge two cents a run—for Babka and Mama when they need flour for baking; for Dido when his leg is sore and he can't walk but he needs tobacco and paper to roll his cigarettes; and for you, when you need all of those letters mailed—okay, I'll do your first trip free—and for Snowy, when she needs that scarlet red nail polish for her toes, and...."

In the middle of June, the bicycle arrived. To me it was beautiful, even though it was a used boy's bike and too big for me (that bar *hurt*). Dad had painted it smooth with shiny green paint over the chipped wheel guards (almost a perfect match), and best of all, he'd attached a new silver basket to the front handle bars, "...to start out your new business properly," he said, beaming with pleasure at my obvious ecstasy.

And what a business it was! Not long ago, my brother Leo reminded me that I was the *only* one in the family that ever had any money to lend him. "Okay, okay," I said, "but was I smart enough to charge interest?"

"Of course," he snorted "that's *why* you always had money!" And that was the start of my business acumen. At age eleven, I learned the value of financial independence—with it, anything is possible. Work for what you "need" and you'll soon be able to afford what you "want" became my credo, and it's carried me through at least five successful business careers to date. In retrospect, I credit Dad with my personal financial stability—all due to stringent monetary values established early on, under his watch.

A Man of Influence

Within us, still within us, always within us, childhood is a state of mind.... We find this state of mind in our reveries; it comes to help us put our being to rest.
—Gaston Bachelard, *Poetics of Reverie*

As a kid, I always knew Dad liked me. Maybe he saw something of his own boldness in me. Maybe he saw something of Mama's looks in me. Maybe he liked me because I tried to be like him: open, friendly and ready for a laugh, I don't know. In reverie, going back to my early years with Dad, I remember most fondly the family holidays at the beach—fantastic summers at beautiful Grand Beach, outside of Winnipeg on Lake Manitoba.

In the white July heat, the sandbanks burning too hot for a baby's feet, Daddy would scoop me up and march out into the cool shallows and sandy shoals, holding me wet and slippery in his arms so tightly that I could feel his heart beat. I remember getting deliciously excited as he lowered me into deep water, announcing: "It's time for you to learn to swim." Loosening his hold as though to let go, he'd wait for my ready shriek then grab me back, laughing as he held me tightly against his sun-warmed chest—at that time, my universe of safety and comfort. Today, this last memory remains the most durable image of my childhood.

In reverie, I always draw strength and courage from that one particular day at the beach, when I felt so loved, so secure and safe in Daddy's arms. But, who was this man? This man of influence, who was so able to turn my child's world into a place of safety and comfort one day, then be distanced and preoccupied in a complex world of church politics and priests on the next?

A Man of the Cloth

Dad loved kung-fu movies and murder mysteries. Perhaps this could be seen as too liberal a quirk in a "man of the cloth," but then Dad was never ordinary in any sense, including that of being a minister. As one of the founders of the independent Ukrainian Greek Orthodox Church of Canada, formed in 1918, he fought the idea of being bourgeois, of accepting the status quo. For example, not only was he was the first in Canada to translate the common prayer book into English from Ukrainian, but he was also "daring" enough to perform the first mixed marriages between the offspring of Ukrainian immigrants and those of English society. Many saw him as a visionary, and today, considering some of the battles he fought against the conventional church standards of that day, I believe he was. But, where did this "visionary" come from? Who was he? As a young child, I never really knew.

Born into humble circumstances, my father was one of a minority group of Ukrainian immigrants who came to Canada from the province of Bukovinia in south western Ukraine (Galecia) in 1899. Dad, the youngest of three brothers and a sister, along with his father and mother, Mataya and Varvara Sawchuk and other extended family, took a homestead and settled into farming near Mountain Road in Manitoba. The next quotation from Joseph R. Romanow's book, *The Coming Together of Four Ukrainian Pioneer Families in Canada*, gives a very brief but succinct history of my father's work:

> *When Vavara and Matay Sawchuk emigrated from Galecia [Ukraine] to Canada in 1899, they could not know that in their four year old son, Semen [Sam] they were bringing a Ukrainian Martin Luther to the new world. In his paper, "The Reverend Semen Sawchuk and the Ukrainian Greek Orthodox Church of Canada," printed in the scholarly Journal of Ukrainian Studies, Professor Oleh Gerus of the History Department, St. Andrews's College, the University of Manitoba states: "The Very Reverend Dr. Seman Wolodymyr Sawchuk was not only the Church's chief architect, but also its driving force for over three decades." This well-*

researched paper, supported by sixty five documentary references in its bibliography describes the Roman Catholic Church's early twentieth century attempts to cater to Ukrainian pioneers, its cultural and language shortfalls and the consequent creation of a dissident, independent Ukrainian Greek Orthodox Church of Canada. It then records the struggles, guidance and leadership ... which Seman [Sam] provided to the new church from its origin until his semi-retirement at age sixty-seven [1963]. That was when he concentrated on building and running the large, new St. Andrew's Ukrainian College on the University of Manitoba campus.

In its early decade, 1920 onwards, due to a shortage in the priesthood, the church growth was very slow. But in 1934, a large church residence at 7 St. John's Avenue in Winnipeg was purchased and designated as the home and office of the consistory of the Ukrainian Greek Orthodox Church of Canada (UGOCC). Due to a shortage of space and money, my father established a seminary for training and teaching student priests on the fourth floor of our church mansion, which was also our home. As such, the priests who lived in the attic were a visible presence throughout my childhood. It was at our manse, a veritable hive of activity, that I first experienced my father's tireless efforts in his role as manager of the UGOCC— his dedicated vision in shaping and establishing the first Ukrainian Orthodox Church in Canada.

As administrator of the new church, Dad became exposed to an array of confrontations based on the loyalties of congregations in Ukraine to either eastern or western attitudes. Dad favored the western, as the eastern primate was not, in his words, "legitimately consecrated." Disputes within the factions of the Ukrainian Greek Orthodox Church in Canada were primarily based on canonical legitimacy. Here, Dad's early talent as a debater was brought to the fore and proved useful in negotiating compromises favorable to his prime intent of preserving the independence of the church. According to the comments of his contemporaries, Dad was considered to be "staid, sincere and principled," and, as such, in an open and bitter struggle with opposing forces for control, the formal council backed him. The fight between the two factions, which caused some personal bitterness between their leaders, was eventually settled in 1940 by the Supreme Court of Canada in favor of the new church, the UGOCC.

During World War II, Dad brought the Church into the Ukrainian Canadian Committee, an organization initiated by the federal government to coordinate all Ukrainian churches and associations, except the communists, in an initiative toward the war effort. He then served in WW II as the principal Ukrainian Orthodox army chaplain, fulfilling military duties in Canada and England with a Captain's rank. Later, after serving as chairman of the executive of the consistory (council) for a number of years (1955-63) Dad shifted his focus on to St. Andrew's College. Serving as its rector, St. Andrew's became an associate college of the University of Manitoba. In the words of Professor Gerus, of St. Andrews College, Winnipeg:

"The UGOC ... needed a dedicated, strong-willed and yet pragmatic leader with a sharp sense of humor to overcome its growing pains and turn it into a major ecclesiastic body. Ukrainian-born and Canadian-educated, Sawchuk proved to be such a dynamic and resourceful leader."

Although Dad's pecuniary bequest of one thousand dollars, the amount left to each of his eight children was appreciated, it's impossible to tally up the aggregate force of my father's presence in my life. For me, Dad is recognized as *the* architect and driving force of my young and adult years. Although this year marks the twenty-seventh anniversary of his death, I feel him here beside me right now. Anything I've accomplished before and since Dad's passing, I credit to his inspirational influence on me as a young child and now, as a senior, writing this book. These pages, written within my perspective and emotional truth, fill in some little-known details of Reverend Dr. S. W. Sawchuk's life as a loving husband and loving father—as seen here through the eyes of his youngest daughter.

Chapter 12

Turbulent Times

Whether you turn to the right or to the left, your ears will hear
a voice behind you, saying, 'This is the way; walk in it.
                                    —NIV Bible: Isaiah 30:21

Kevin Small, at two years.

Father Knows Best

When Dad visited me in the second Jarvis Street apartment, he had just turned seventy; still energetic of mind and body he was, as always, willing to listen to me. Dad took one look at Craig and me and later said "he knew we were in trouble." I don't know what gave us away; maybe it was the allergy circles under Craig's eyes or the fact that later that day I fell asleep halfway through a replay of the seminal movie, *Bridge on the River Kwai*—a popular box office hit a few years earlier. Dad had good reason to be concerned.

Aside from the joy of having Craig with me for several months on Jarvis Street, what I remember most is the feeling of being tired *all* the time. I was bone weary, physically debilitated by a lifestyle that centered on Craig, work, Alan and Joanne—not always in that order but always with a goodly amount of hurry and worry in between. Then there were the migraine headaches.

I'd been plagued with headaches since age thirteen, due to "teen-age disrupted hormones," the doctor advised my mother. For years afterward, I thought every female teenager felt as though she had a permanent paring knife buried in her head—no wonder we were *disruptive*! When I was not quite eighteen, and had started my x-ray training at the Winnipeg General Hospital, I was finally diagnosed with "cluster headaches"—a variety of migraine associated with diet, stress, and the release of histamine. In my late teens, the headaches had seemed connected to food, specifically chocolate bars, then later, as an adult, most varieties of cheese as well as wine, particularly red. It took me a while to connect the diet dots, but as a busy working mother I couldn't seem to control the stress; so the headaches persisted, often lasting a couple of days, or even weeks.

Between my chronic fatigue and persistent headaches, I was a mess; when Dad visited us, I guess he could see that. Wanting to give me a break, to treat me to a night out, Dad called our accountant's mother (through her persistence, she had been finally deemed "acceptable" by Craig,) and asked her to babysit. My father's idea for my treat was slightly calculated, in that he'd missed the *Bridge on the River Kwai* movie when it first came out in 1957. Apparently it was now being reissued at a Toronto film festival down the street, and, having served in WW II, he was anxious to see it. For my part, I was delighted with the idea of a "date with Dad." He suggested that we go to dinner first, probably the Chalet Barbeque, and then take in the movie.

"Sounds great," I said, tricking myself into believing that I could pull off this family date after last night's prolonged beer and lobster-fest with Al at the Silver Rail. This always used to lead to crustacean-induced ardor, but not in these days—now sleep is the priority. Despite my generic fatigue and to not disappoint Dad, I was fully determined to go to the movie.

Although I remember enjoying the first part of the film, it was not long before I was surreptitiously nodding off at Dad's side. After being awakened by the collision of my chin on my chest for the third time, I shook myself into consciousness and looked over to see if Dad had noticed. I think he did, but he was too polite to comment. Embarrassed, more than anything, I thought that some water might revive me so I excused myself, muttering something about "the powder room," and left. Fine plan ... but Dad never saw me until the film was over. He later admitted that he was so engrossed with the movie that he'd lost track of time *and* me.

At first exasperated, then worried after thoroughly searching the lobby, Dad headed toward the ladies' powder room, the last place I'd mentioned before I left him. I don't know how long he looked but he finally did find me, almost by accident.

Because the movie was so long, a large group of women, more anxious than usual, crowded the open door to the ladies' room trying to get in—but something was holding up the procession. Dad, curious by nature like me, managed, by standing tall and craning his neck, to see over the crowd; apparently what he saw was pretty shocking. I and another woman were crawling around the black and white tile floor on all fours, groping for something—with me, sporadically shouting into the crowd, "Whatever you do, don't move." Of course Dad wouldn't call out to me; he knew that would be embarrassing for both of us, so he just stood off to the side and watched. Finally, a resounding "Here it is!" was shouted out by both of us, and with a combined rumble of relief, the line proceeded forward.

Exiting gleefully, catching sight of Dad off to the side, I could see he was confused and more than a little annoyed, "What happened?" he queried. "Where were you? You missed the whole movie. Are you okay?" Dad's impatient at the best of times and since it was close to midnight he was probably very tired, so I thought I'd better explain, and fast. *Just keep it simple.*

"I'm so sorry I upset you, Daddy, but you see that's how exhausted I am: I loved the movie but I was embarrassed because I kept falling asleep. I didn't want you to see me because then you would say we'd

157

better go home, but I didn't want you to miss any of the movie, so I thought a drink of water would wake me up, but when I went into the ladies' powder room, it's huge you know, I saw a comfy sofa and I just couldn't resist lying down ... *aah, this feels so good, just for ten minutes*, I thought, already half asleep, but the way I feel these days ten hours wouldn't be enough and—"

"Take a breath, Olanna."

"Okay, okay, sorry. Anyway, when the ladies started chattering outside the door, I woke up with such a start that one of my contact lenses, they're made of hard plastic you know, jumped right out of my left eye—that's my bad eye, the one that they had so much trouble fitting—and of course I got upset. That's why we, the nice lady and I were crawling around the floor. We couldn't let anyone in because the lens is so small and so expensive and it would have been crushed. I don't even own *real* glasses anymore and you know how blind I am. I was praying the whole time, and yes, by a miracle we found it! But I'm so sorry that you were worried. By the way, how *was* the movie?"

Lucky for me, Dad's a good listener, and by the time I was finished my convoluted story, he was laughing. "Okay, my dear," he said in Ukrainian, while gallantly offering me his arm. "Let's go home. If you don't mind, we'll walk ... I have to talk to you." And talk he did.

Legal Limbo

In one short simple statement, Dad changed the course of my life and Craig's too. When he finally said what he had to say on our midnight walk home from the movies, I came to a dead stop. First, to accommodate the stab of pain that followed his declaration, then, to fully absorb his words.

We'd been walking north on Jarvis Street from Carlton Avenue. It had been raining, and the strong street lights on the glistening pavement caused our elongated shadows to appear giant-like, surreal, as they swallowed us up with each step. Even in high heels, my shadow stretched short of Dad's, and it reminded me of those early years when I was a little kid and had to run full stride to keep up with him. There was a soft evening breeze; the late lilacs, still in bloom, were beaded with rain and gave off a heavy sweetness, a pungent scent, whose essence so filled the moment as to lock it permanently in memory. Each spring thereafter, that same scent reopened the hard the key of truth in Dad's simple statement:

"You can't go on this way; you have to give Craig back to his grandma and his father."

I knew Dad's words were laden with truth born of love for me and Craig. I knew this, and because I trusted him implicitly, my every instinct told me that he was right ... but the reality broke my heart. The plan I'd worked so hard for, giving up my singing in the hope of rebuilding my life to include Craig every day, was dashed with Dad's perceptive but painful observation.

One week later, Craig was back in Scarborough with his father and Nanny Steele. And how did I cope with my loss? I'll explain it this way.

Forgetting

After I agreed to return Craig to his paternal Grandma, I tried to forget ... but no, despair prevailed. Although in my mind I knew I'd made the right decision on Craig's behalf, in the deepest place of my mother's heart, there remained a spurious guilt underpinned by a self-loathing that would not let go. As impractical and unrealistic as my hope had been, to keep Craig with me under any circumstances, there was a lack of support of every kind—financially and personally (in the sixties a single mother was an anomaly abhorred by the government), and my family was too far away to help out. By now, my cousin Eleanore had moved back to Saskatchewan, where she married Roy Romanow, who was elected and successfully remained, for many years, the Premier of that province.

At the time, my minimal wages were barely enough for food and rent and since there was no financial help from Craig's father (he himself was struggling), I simply had to give Craig up—temporarily, I'd hoped. For the next years I suffered a barrage of guilt, underlined by despair that no amount of work and intrepid busyness could allay. I felt I had failed, and badly.

Abandonment issues took hold on both Craig's and my part that could not, *would* not, be reversed. And so, under recurring nightmares and migraines, I privately suffered various shades of remorse relieved only by my loving relationship with Al and Joanne—both a source of immeasurable joy. All of my requests to Michael for a divorce were denied, unless I would agree to his request for *permanent custody* of Craig. Time lumbered on without a backward glance, healing no wounds, leaving in its wake two long years lost in a legal limbo of delayed expectations. Meanwhile, I was saved from a deep depression by that great panacea, the cure-all for most human conditions—work.

After successfully completing Eaton's merchandising program, with Fred Eaton himself in attendance, I stealthily maneuvered the corporate ladder to become, within a year, a full-fledged buyer in charge of Eaton's first Suede and Leather Shop in Ontario. Travelling to Montreal and New York with other buyers, seeing all the fashion shows and fitting in a full itinerary of buying appointments, I got a different view of "The Big 'Bad' Apple," which by now, for me, was just *big*. As fashion buyers, we were treated well. Booked into the top hotels, with a credible daily expense account, New York took on a different hue—still exciting and energizing, but now with a lightness of mood that somewhat obliterated the darkness of my experiences the first time around with the show-biz czars. All of these pleasures, however, were tainted with a mother's guilt.

Since custody had not been settled at the legal separation (an unusual decision by the judge and one that I believed was an answer to much prayer on my part), I was advised by my lawyer that I should "prove my worthiness as a mother by providing a respectable home environment." In the lingo of the sixties, that meant, getting married before pursuing my case for custody. And so we waited, held hostage by Michael's refusal of a divorce unless I would "sign my son away." Yes, I saw Craig consistently during those two years of waiting, and yes, we have happy memories of our family times together on our bimonthly visits, summer weekends at the Sandbanks beach in Picton, Ontario, and winter weekends skiing up north in Collingwood and Mt. St. Louis. We have these memories, but it seems Craig's are blurred. Today, he tells me that much of that time of separation was too painful to retain.

∞ ∞ ∞

In early summer of 1967, without warning, I received a phone call from Craig's Dad. He was "interested" in a divorce; would I like to proceed?

"Under what conditions" I asked, suspiciously.

"Mutually agreeable," was his perfunctory reply. Apparently Michael had met someone he was interested in marrying, and now it suited him to seek a divorce. And so it was that two weeks after my divorce, Al and I exchanged wedding vows in the presence of my mother, my Aunt Mary, my brother-in-law Brian, my good friend Pam, a few other close friends and some of Alan's CFRB listeners who unexpectedly showed up at the chapel at Timothy Eaton Memorial Church in Toronto. Many of my own family members were absent, including two people close to my heart—Craig, because of a conscientious decision on my part not to further confuse his already splintered loyalties, and my own father, because of a work conflict.

A short time later, Michael re-married and moved with his new wife and Craig to West Hill, an eastern suburb of Toronto. Up to this point, I'd been struggling to gain permanent custody of Craig. Now "properly married," I felt I stood a better chance, but by the time I was able to marry Al and be in the right position to fight for full custody, Craig had left his babyhood behind. Living under the care of his Grandma Steele and his father in a small house in Scarborough, Craig had clean air to breathe, a new dog to play with and a large grassy yard in which to chase the puppy around. His allergies had settled down, and, now being established in kindergarten at the local public school, Craig seemed happy—but I had never stopped pining for him or wanting him back. In a reverie of those stressful years waiting for Michael to agree to a divorce, I've dubbed those long days "The Kid-Napping Daze"—a ready clue to our sad, sorry shenanigans.

The Kidnap Caper

There were desperate moves on both sides. On one occasion in Toronto, Michael picked Craig up early and took him to Montreal for a full week without notice; this move was against the separation agreement. After they came back, by now frenzied, I kidnapped Craig and "hid" him for the weekend with Al and his mother in Willowdale, while I attended my brother Buck's wedding in Winnipeg. At this point, Michael retaliated by kidnapping him back again. And so it went ... two desperadoes tossing Craig back and forth like a hot grenade, seeking to overpower each other while putting him in the danger zone of a furious custody battle. In retrospect, this was so sad for Craig, and shame on us, his parents, for this "all too human" bad behavior.

Today, when I talk to Craig as a grown man, I try to lighten things up by referring to those insensitive acts as the "napping-kid capers" because they usually took place at night when he was sleeping. In some small way, I'm trying to assure him that he was intensely loved by both of us, his Mom and Dad equally.

After my marriage to Al, when I was finally in a position to bring Craig back home to us on a permanent basis, it was too late. By now he was fully immersed in a new life, and I knew in my mother's heart that to disturb the situation would not serve his best interests. Throughout his youth and early teens, Craig was with us on a regular basis, and, when possible, he stayed over for special holidays in the winter and extra weeks in the summer. We were definitely a *family* at those times, as my daughter Joanne attests (in contrast to Craig, she remembers *everything*). Craig now agrees that Alan was always generous with his time and love. Many years later, just before Craig attended university, he lived for a while with Kevin and me—we three were on our own. The other day we were talking about those times when we lived together for six months at 3435 Yonge Street, north of Lawrence, above my second fashion store, Alaynes II.

"Don't you remember, Mom? You used to mix the milk with that skim powdered stuff. We didn't like it, but we drank it anyway," Kev reminded me.

"Well, guys, you know I hadn't sold the building yet and we were skimping. What could I do? You drank three quarts of milk every day between the two of you! We were on a strict budget—twenty-five dollars a week—but we managed, right? And we had lots of fun that summer, didn't we?"

Then the boys would roll their eyes, and sing out in unison: "Yes Mom, we know, 'those were the good old days.'" And in many ways they were. As a teen, Craig had a good relationship with me that eventually grew into a fine one. But those early separations when he was little were never easy—for either one of us.

A Tear in Every Stitch

After giving Craig up, concurrent with my Dad's advice and my own belief of what had to be done at the time, I suffered years of chronic headaches—at that point a recipe for my way of life:

"Take some wracking pains of remorse and mix in generous dollops of guilt; now fold in a mother's ultimate sacrifice—the honorable gesture of giving up her child in love—mix thoroughly, roll flat, sprinkle lightly with tears (not too many, you will upset the appearance), then smile bravely as you present your culinary feat, your latest self to the world: reshaped, re-styled and re-invented."

To relieve the pain of sacrifice there was always my censor-self, Sinc, reminding me: *There was no other way—you had no choice. You can make a new life. You'll have him back. You'll see; he'll be with you one day. What did the Star article say? A tear in every stitch; but these tears will dry, and you'll be whole. Trust me....*

But the tears didn't stop, not one of them dried, and I did not become "whole." The pain of our separation surfaced *every* time I dropped Craig off, even when he was a teenager, at his dad's. After each visit, I would drive away from his house in tears and by the time I reached the highway I'd be howling. But, as has happened to me before, in midst of my longing, relief came through a miracle of faith. And what was this miracle?

A beautiful baby boy, Kevin Alan Joseph Small, was bestowed upon us graciously, reverently. Just as I'd given up trying to fill the vacuum that Craig's absence created, after all of those seasons of grief, along came Kev. And just look at him! What a miracle of love and new life he is—a wondrous promise of renewal, yes, and a restoration of hope. But will he be a replacement of the firstborn son? Never, *Nor should he be,* adds Sinc. But a mother's heart grows to suit its needs. It is malleable; it regenerates. Through my yearning, that place of wanting and desire that holds the potentiality of love, a miracle was born:

"Hi sweetheart," I whisper, leaning down over Kevin's crib after a sleepless night of worry over his fever and rising temperature. Looking down at his six-month growth of fuzzy blond hair, his wide-open eyes so stunningly blue and his sweet baby smile, two lower teeth gleaming, I marvel at his beauty. In the fullness of my love, I coo, "I knew you'd be feeling better today. I prayed you'd be fine this morning, and you are. You know, God answers prayer; he surely did when he sent you to us. He loves you as much as I do, maybe more," I whisper, in gratitude for this beautiful son, given to us, September 1ˢᵗ, 1968. Yes, motherhood came easy, but my new lifestyle in the suburbs did not. The first year was tough.

Suburban Blues

Two weeks after our wedding, July 15, 1967, I'd packed up my Jarvis Street apartment and headed up to Willowdale, in North Toronto, to live with Al and Joanne—leaving Eaton's and my flourishing career behind.

Aah, I thought, *finally, a "normal" life—a change of venue away from the unstable heartbeat of the city to the calculated confines of suburbia.* Although this style of designed domesticity was foreign to my past, how difficult could it be? ... I found out.

I thought I understood something of a married woman's suburban lifestyle. I'd watched my friends play at it for years, and I had no doubt that I would easily slip into their well-heeled matronly shoes. Ensconced in suburbia, finally free from financial anxiety, I would trot off to the morning coffee klatches; then, unmindful of the clock, I'd happily stroll through the outdoor markets, carefully picking out the best of everything: plump, organically grown tomatoes; the darkest of green romaine lettuce; and thick, finely marbled sirloin steaks.

"Only the best will do," Al would remind me, while searing the steaks on the barbeque. Then, of course, there was the mandatory stop at the liquor store for a super-sized bottle of Smirnoff's vodka and a very small bottle of Schweppes tonic:

"Whoa, the less of that stuff, the better," Al would say, as he downed his third pre-dinner vodka and tonic.

That first summer, just before I moved into Al's Willowdale house, he'd put in an expensive in-ground swimming pool replete with an extended deck and change room. And what a time we had! Decadent days of outrageous swimming parties: one tipsy guest swam lengths of the pool with such a powerful stroke that he managed to break his prominent nose on the third turn. Then there were the after-golf parties—near-strangers wandering to the back pool area looking for a beer and burger or whatever else on the go. "Happy Al" the Barbeque King looked after that part while I scurried out for more supplies, thinking: *So ... this scintillating severance of civility is what suburbia is all about? Maybe Sinc was right:* "Beware of what you pray for," he'd warned. But it was not all booze and banality.

There were poignant weekends at the Sandbanks invoking memories of my own summers at Grand Beach, my dad protecting my baby feet from the burning white sand. Now Joanne experienced the same joy with her dad as he scooped her up squealing with excitement before plunging her in and out of the cool shallows, hugging her tightly in between dips. Those were our glory days that would never end—but of course, they did.

What's the Buzz?

From the start, I felt a negative omnipresence in the house in Willowdale. I blamed this feeling on the buzzing of the high-voltage power lines that populated the lengthy green belt stretching behind our house. Swimming in our pool, staring up at the black poles pointing skyward, I'd imagine them as depraved messengers of doom, hissing their signals through electrostatic discharges that could, at will, reach down and zap me out of existence. I felt singularly vulnerable: *Just how dangerous is this? Whoa, I'd better get out of the water!*

Of course, everyone thought I was mad, but after investigating the therapeutic powers of magnetic therapy for healing back problems, and, in tandem, having discovered the potential danger of electronic discharges from hydro poles like those hovering behind our house, I was led into further inquiry.

My research into "ionization through high energy radiation" indicated an ongoing controversy between two schools of thought—both holding positive and negative views regarding health hazards.

This information coupled with my own earlier experience while training with roentgen rays (x-rays) in the Winnipeg General Hospital—where the leakage prevalent in their out dated equipment proved hazardous to our health—convinced me that our home environment could be dangerous. I went so far as to be suspicious of the power lines for the cancer diagnosis of Alan's mother just before she left the house with my brother-in-law Brian to live in the apartment down the street. She passed away two years later.

In light of these and other circumstances, we sold the house, and soon after, a neighbor informed me that the new owner had also come down with cancer. A couple of years later, Alan did too—a coincidence? Perhaps; although in many ways I consider myself a risk-taker, in matters of health I prefer to err on the side of safety. I was, however, not always so prudent in matters concerning my personal life. In 1968, in Toronto, and Canada in general, many social changes were taking place and my curious self, my pragmatic self, wanted to be in on the action.

Chapter 13

Chaotic Moral Dismay

*Brief were my days among you, and briefer still the words I have
spoken....
And if this day is not a fulfillment of your needs and my love,
then let it be a promise 'till another day.*
                                        —Kahil Gibran, *The Prophet*

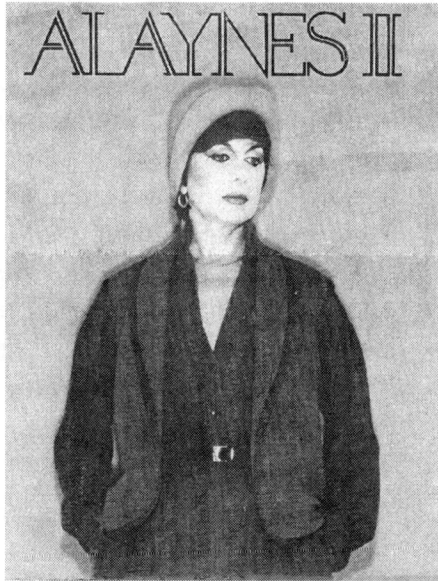

Alaynes Fashions, 3435 Yonge St, Toronto

Two Dynamic Decades

The sixties were the age of youth, as 70 million US children from
the post-war baby boom became teenagers and young adults. The
movement away from the conservative fifties continued and eventually
resulted in revolutionary ways of thinking and real change in the
cultural fabric of these lives. Content no longer to be images of the

generation ahead of them, young people everywhere wanted change. An estimated 850,000 "war baby" freshmen entered US colleges; emergency living quarters were set up in dorm lounges, hotels and trailer camps. These days of rebellion were spawned by the likes of American writers, Jack Kerouac (*On the Road*), a leading figure of the beat generation and Allen Ginsberg, who spearheaded the early poetic expressions of the counter cultural movement with his poem *Howl*, followed later by Bob Dylan, who created distinctive protest music eventually applauded by millions worldwide. His song, *Blowin' in the Wind*, became the anthem for the civil rights movement.

Here in Toronto, Canada, we experienced similar changes as our own counter-cultural movement, centered in Rochdale College, off Bloor Street, took up permanent residence in a small retail section flanked by Avenue Road to the west, Yonge Street to the east, Cumberland and Bloor to the north and south respectively. Yorkville Avenue, contained within this sphere, became a prime example of overcrowding rebels and revolutionary actions. Here, the Canadian youth of the sixties were inspired by innovative artists and musicians who encouraged them "to do their own thing," which many of them did, through drugs and undisciplined living, much to the consternation of the governing bodies of the colleges, universities and surrounding population (all those over thirty were suspect, could not be trusted and were *too old* to *understand*). As for me, being on the outer cusp of this movement, I found the new attitudes outrageous and energizing, at the same time.

The uptown core of Toronto, Yorkville, became the Mecca of the hippie movement; coffee houses sprang up three on a corner encouraging poets and musicians (*everyone* owned a guitar) to declare their position. These were the early days of Canadian luminaries such as Neil Young, Judy Collins, Joni Mitchell and Leonard Cohen—a consummate poet (*Beautiful Losers*) and subsequent song writer (*Bird on the Wire*), today, still performing to avid audiences, aging Boomers and Zoomers alike. American influences such as Carol King's songs and Janis Joplin's radical line from *Me and Bobby McGee*: "Freedom's just another word for nothing left to lose," echoed their way into the early seventies through scenes of protest as innovative fashion statements were paraded daily by the baby boomers—the "me" generation in full bloom. I watched all of this from the confines of suburbia in a fascinated wistful mood—feeling sad, lonely and very much "out of the loop."

Camelot

In America, the Civil Rights movement made great changes in society. President Kennedy's Inaugural parade, which took place on Friday, January 20, 1961, in Washington DC was televised for the first time in color when NBC news covered it following the black-and-white swearing-in ceremony and the inaugural address at the capital. This heralded the start of the fabled *Camelot* years in the US that ended abruptly on November 26, 1963, with the tragic shooting of President John F. Kennedy. Even today, just to indicate the extent of our enmeshment in all things American, any Canadian asked where they were and what they were doing when they heard of the John F. Kennedy assassination can relate those happenings in explicit detail. For example, I was with Michael Steele, Craig's father, driving up Bay Street in Toronto towards Bloor Street, when we heard the news on the radio. Like many others, we headed directly home where we remained fixed to the TV for hours, even days. Every detail of the American tragedy was minutely absorbed by our Canadian hybrid consciousness. It's hard to describe the affect of the assassination to those who were not part of it; as a kindred nation our sorrow knew no bounds. Then, five and a half years later, just as the US had gathered en masse and risen out of its emotional slump, sorrow returned with the assassination of Dr. Martin Luther King, in April of 1968. This tragedy, soon followed by the shooting death of J.F.K's brother, Senator Bobby Kennedy, in that same year, left the Americans numb. As stalwart Canadians, while we walked an empathetic path with our southern cousins, we were still searching the horizon for a hero of our own—and in that year of tragedy, in Canada, hope was reborn.

Canada's "PET"

In 1968, Pierre Elliot Trudeau, began his first sixteen years as Prime Minister of Canada. The country's new leader excited Canadians more than any other politician ever had. P.E. Trudeau wanted a "just society" in Canada, and in this sense of equality he protected the rights of the disadvantaged and of minorities. With his dynamic personality, Trudeau's youthful image appealed to Canadians. Everyone supported the new leader, who, in 1971, at age fifty two, married Margaret Sinclair, a beautiful young woman, who was thirty years his junior; thus initiating our own Canadian version of *Camelot*—furthering the "Trudeau mania," which had spread in a wildfire of emotion. In his years in office, Trudeau tried to make Canada less dependent on the United States by strengthening its own culture, economy and institutions. But America's influence on our pop culture was still strong.

Leading its desire to move into the future, which the space age seemed to forecast, the new name of the century in pop-art was an American, Andy Warhol, who produced paintings and silk-screen prints of commonplace images such as soup cans and photographs of celebrities.

Although we were on the cusp of the sixties movement age-wise, we found ourselves directly involved and personally affected by the rapid changes in values, lifestyles, laws, earnings and entertainment practiced by our southern neighbors. Statistics show that while the average salary in Ontario was around $4,700, at that time the average teacher's salary was slightly higher, around $5,200 per annum. The minimum wage was around $1.00 per hour, and the life expectancy for males was 66.6 years, and 73.1 years for women. As I recall, after I quit my singing career in the mid-sixties, my first "real job" (an assistant buyer with Eaton's) paid $85.00 a week, which translates into $4,420 a year. Some women, me included, took advantage of changes devolved by the radical cultural and social movement away from the mores of the day: We found a way to break out of the late fifties-early sixties ethos of "love, marriage and a baby carriage," but it wasn't easy. Leading us "early protestors" and encouraging us was the radical feminist literature that emerged.

By the mid-sixties, literature in America and also in Canada reflected what was happening in the political and social arenas. Women's books—Sylvia Plath's *The Bell Jar* and Mary McCarthy's *The Group*—spoke of women's roles outside of those of the "happy wife and mother" of the fifties. American feminists and writers like Betty Friedan, *The Feminine Mystic*, and Gloria Steinem, founding editor

(1972) of *Ms.* Magazine, led the way for radical change in women's perceptions of their place in a male-dominated society. In Canada, Bulgarian-born French linguist Julia Kristeva led Quebec interests in radical feminism, ranging from social theory to psychoanalysis. By the sixties, the women's movement brought new possibilities for social change, including women's roles as wage earners, women's control of their sexuality through birth control pills and an end to violence against women. In the mid-sixties, when the US brought in a ratification of the Equal Rights Amendment, which spoke of socio-economic, political and equal rights for all women equal to those of men, I, for one, was listening.

Here in Canada, the women's movement met in consciousness-raising groups—in women's centers, rape-crisis centers and homeless shelters where they demanded change. Although I was not an *active* member of the movement, still, in those early sixties, I was "walking the walk"—contributing to and supporting these groups in my own lifestyle. Inadvertently breaking through wage barriers, I always asked for, and received, more than was offered; I instinctively wore boxing gloves when dealing with male bank managers. How else would an unemployed, nearly homeless woman extricate a $1000 loan from a bank manager in the early sixties in order to purchase a used yellow Toyota? Also, birth control, already in place in the late fifties was opted by me and included in a mindset that would not tolerate physical violence, against me or anyone else near me ... and this was in the *early* sixties. In Canada, in 1967, Prime Minister Pearson's government appointed a Royal Commission on the Status of Women to look into the real position of women in society. For six months in 1968, public hearings were held across Canada; and at the turn of the decade they published a 500-page report dealing with the following topics: equal pay, maternity leave, day care, family law, the Indian Act, educational opportunities and other topics of great importance to women. Formal changes in the status of women accelerated once they started, but for me it had been a long wait. I'd been thinking on these issues forever—actually, from the age of eleven.

Where's the Power?

While living at home, in the manse at #7 St. John's Avenue in Winnipeg, I witnessed firsthand what I considered an inequity in the quantity and quality of work that was expected of women, as compared to men, in the thirties-fifties era. Here, my father is absolved in the sphere of *quantity* (he worked many all-nighters in his office), but I was always envious of the *quality* of his work: writing, speaking at conferences, preaching, listening to confessions and attending banquets (which occasionally included Mom) were interspersed with travel to Ukraine, inter-provincial parishes, overnights to district churches within the diocese, late-night business meetings at our house and a modicum of family household work, mostly gardening, in just about that order.

At my young age, Dad's work seemed far superior to Mom's and Babka's endless tasks of childcare and housework. The latter included cleaning and polishing four levels of hardwood floors, laundry and ironing for twelve, shopping, preserving and cooking for that same number plus the sewing of clothing for all the family, including robes for the priests in the attic—to name just a few of the necessary chores that Mom and Babka were responsible for. Upon leaving the house in the mid fifties, I was all for any movement that could bring about new possibilities for social change, particularly for women. Though at the time, I did not consider myself a "women's libber," still, looking back, I can see that I was perfect fodder for their precepts—raw material for their revolutionary ideas which began in the late fifties and are still evolving today. Manpower, a generic term denoting "the power of human strength" to men in a literal way deemed women *powerless*—and in many ways we were. My recollections of how early on I considered the inequities within my own family denotes how quickly the exchange of ideas and roles seeped in and then flooded a social structure ready for change. New attitudes rendered a dramatic alteration in the nuclear family as laws radically changed and divorces were no longer as difficult to obtain.

My own long-awaited divorce, achieved in 1967, finally came about when legal separations were accepted on the basis of marriage breakdown rather than a formal count of adultery. Unfortunately, the attitude of government social workers did not readily follow along with the changes. In my own experience, I was shunned by them, criticized for leaving a "perfectly good husband"—yes, Michael could be very charming—and striking out on my own. The nuclear family became a thing of the past, as increased divorce rates introduced society to single-parent households and more women entered the work force. Again, I was a little ahead of my time. Moving against established traditions seemed to be my way of life, but there were certain modern trends I shunned.

Don't Lose Your Key

In the late sixties and early seventies, alcohol was the drug of choice for the thirty-something group: everyone drank, everyone smoked cigarettes and *almost* everyone attended *key* parties—a coming trend in suburbia that gained popularity and lasted into the seventies. These parties were rarely talked about openly; only if you were a willing participant did you get to hear about them. Luckily, our own street was recently constructed and our neighbors were fresh newlyweds like ourselves, so the notion of picking out a neighbor's key for a temporary dalliance in an exchange of partners did not enter our sphere of interest. But this idea, destined to continue well into the next decade, gave fair warning of the general marital discontent brewing in the "burbs."

In 1970, away from the work force for over two years, I had to admit that life in the suburbs was less than enough for me. Feeling isolated, left out of the "real" world, I grew increasingly annoyed with my situation and myself. Here I was, living in a folkloric society that refused to grow up *or* grow old, with everyone drinking too much, myself included, but I didn't know how to get out. Separated from my downtown friends and the daily excitement of work, feeling increasingly left out as the parade passed me by, I continued to live my white lie as a "normal" housewife, but my *true*, other self, kept nagging at me and would not back down.

Divine Providence, seeing well past my purported desire for "normalcy at any cost," turned its gaze away, no longer willing to tolerate my naive illusion, that one day, if I really tried, I could force myself into *feeling* normal. Then, happily, I'd be like everyone else. *Be careful what you pray for,* my censor, Sinc, echoed. But short of tolerance and long of memory, ingenious fate allowed my hapless prayer to filter through, and for a little while longer I was able to extend my dalliance in delusion. I really believed that my other self, my singing, soaring self, could slow down its dervish dance to a two-step and take the well-travelled path born of suburban homilies to achieve wisdom. Not so; sounds great in theory, but Destiny, who knew me better, had other plans—and trading my key or even losing it wasn't one of them.

∞ ∞ ∞

In Canada, the chaotic events of the late sixties—advances in civil rights, the increased influence of the women's movement, a heightened concern for the environment and a growing disillusionment of government—left everything open for change. The post-war baby boomers were becoming young adults and, as the validity of the Viet Nam war was being challenged by American youth, our established convictions and beliefs in Canada were also being questioned. This attitude opened the way to a free-will life based on personal choices, from multiple career opportunities to soft drugs, hard liquor and opportunistic sex—everything was a "go."

As the radical ideas of the late sixties gained wider acceptance, they were mainstreamed into the new decade. By the mid seventies, my adopted city, Toronto, literally grew up with the unveiling of the CN Tower in June of 1976—to that date, the world's tallest building. Amid war, social realignment and presidential impeachment proceedings, and while American sentiment was running low, our Canadian dollar was peaking high, at $1.05 US. At this point, the average annual salary of the early seventies had increased to $7,300 and as our culture flourished, following in the steps of the Americans, the events of the time became the inspiration for much of the music, literature, entertainment, and fashion of the decade.

The hippies' influence of the sixties was mainstreamed into the fashion statement of the seventies. Men sported shoulder-length hair. Women's hair was either very short, or long and lank and non-traditional clothing became the rage as bellbottom pants, hip huggers, gypsy dresses, shawls, platform shoes, earth shoes and clogs surfaced in the thirty-something crowd. Knits, denims and non-creasing synthetics were the fabrics of choice; men's leisure suits, the two-piece polo style great for backyard barbeques, watching football and jogging, were the rage. Polyester dress suits for men became commonplace while fashionable women wore everything from ankle-length dresses to micro-mini skirts and "hot pants."

∞ ∞ ∞

With time to pore over the newspapers, glossies and *Vogue* magazines, I felt increasingly isolated and envious that the fashion universe had gathered for a worldwide revolution to which I had not been invited. Why? I had erased my name from the guest list when I left Eaton's in the midst of my fortuitous career as a buyer. In the heady haze of July, 1967, when the divorce from Craig's dad finally came through and I was able to marry Al, I *knew* that I was not ready to give up my fashion job at Eaton's. I felt I had no choice, so I made the decision to do the "right thing"—retire to the suburbs as a full-time wife, mother and housekeeper.

At first, the newness of married life as a young Willowdale matron was slightly interesting. I tried to adjust to a suburban lifestyle through exercise classes, reading clubs, meditation classes and finally, even golf. The truth is, golf made me angry; I just couldn't accept the idea that a still-young talented guy like Alan would want to spend so much time and money at the Summit golf club, a fair drive north in Richmond Hill. He was in his mid-forties, and that was a pretty young age to retire—albeit in a part-time manner. Since I was already a "golf widow," I decided to join the club, to see what I was missing; as it turned out … not much.

"I just can't see the point of leaving Kevin with a babysitter while I waste money, time and energy chasing a pesky little ball on its devious course," I exclaimed to Al. He wasn't listening. He was having a bad-golf day. After a badly hooked drive, I watched incredulously as he wrapped his driver around a thick maple tree then stomped away in a rage. I lost my rag:

"I've had it! This game is the devil's device, and it looks like he's reeled you in, hook, line and *stinker*! (Al loves to fish). Calling after him, I shouted, "You know what? I think I'll leave golf for my old age, after *you've* grown up!" With that, I organized my cart and trundled off to the clubhouse to pick up my stuff. That was it; I gave up golf. Ironically, today, it is one of my favorite addictions.

Back, in the summer of 1968, looking for loftier goals, I'd applied to York University as a "mature student"—anyone over twenty-five—and was thrilled to be accepted. Going back to school was scary, but wonderful. I started back the summer I was pregnant with Kevin, just one course to start with, but later, as a philosophy major sitting in seminars with a young TA, Sam Mallin, who later became the Philosophy Director at York, discussing Heidegger, Hegel and Kant, I found that I was an excellent student, better than when I was younger. I loved learning—it was as simple as that. My insatiable curiosity had discovered a bountiful banquet in the likes of philosophy, ancient and modern alike, and that's when I realized I'd have to follow my natural inclination to keep studying, not just for the love of learning but also to reach an understanding of my own fundamental philosophy and beliefs. This determination, practiced for six years of part-time studies sandwiched in-between life's daily challenges of love, labor and loss, was temporarily dropped to be picked up later, in 1996, when I joyfully discovered that "the best was yet to come." This time around, I attended York University full time, which meant sitting in day classes with delightful students younger than my children. In five years I completed an honors degree in English and picked up a second degree, an MA in English, in 2001.

See, Sinc? Curiosity did not kill *this* cat! In fact, I count those senior years at York as another career—my most successful one to date. But, almost three decades prior, in the early 1970s, depressed and bored while attempting to play out my role as a happy suburban housewife, I soon realized I wanted to return to my profession, the creative fashion world of the surreal seventies. I needed to get involved, get back in the game—but how and with whom?

American and foreign designers, from whom I had bought when I was with Eaton's just two years ago, were creating fantastic styles and futuristic designs in the fashion world; I missed them and the work. In the suburbs, out of the mainstream, I felt stylistically dead and obsolete. Every morning, staring out my front window and watching my neighbors leave for work followed by their bigger kids heading off to school and the little kids trundling off to kindergarten, it struck me hard that *everyone* but me, had somewhere to go. For twelve years I'd been steadily involved in interesting careers, and now I felt useless. *But you should be happy,* Sinc reminded me. *This is what you wanted; domesticity, peace, tranquility.*

"Okay, but I'm not dead! I'm not finished!" I hurled back. "There's lots of stuff going on in downtown Toronto, lots of opportunities. The fashion world's gone crazy, flying off in all directions, heading for the moon and I want to go along for the ride!" *Then stop whining and do it,* Sinc murmured—just loud enough for me to hear.

Doctor's Orders

On September 1ˢᵗ, 1969, a year to the day after Kevin was born, I took him in for his annual checkup.

"Well, the doctor commented, "The baby looks fine, but what's wrong with you?"

"You mean I don't look fine, too?" my performance-ego countered.

"Well, let's put it this way, I've seen you look better. What's the matter?"

"Nothing, and everything," I sighed.

"Well then, let's start with 'everything,'" the doctor kindly suggested.

"Okay. I admit that I should be ecstatically happy with Alan, our gorgeous baby, Kevin, darling Joanne, Craig on weekends, and the house in Willowdale—suburban bliss, I know—but something's wrong and I can't put my finger on it," I finished lamely, tears now welling.

"I can," the doctor said, handing me a Kleenex.

"Okay, what is it?" I asked, bracing myself for the worst. "What should I do?"

"It's simple. Go back to work," was the doctor's sage advice.

I was excited. I'd been given permission to go back to work. But where should I start?

In answer, I recalled something I'd once read: "Just start where you are." *Okay, I can do that* I thought, as I picked up the telephone (my best friend in suburbia) to call my best friend in downtown Toronto.

Hi, Pam, it's Elaine," I said, again admiring the pleasant quality of her voice on the message machine. "Give us a call as soon as you get the chance, Okay?"

I didn't really expect to find Pam at home in the middle of the day, but I wanted to send out the alarm anyway—we were close friends. Pam was a graduate of Ryerson's Radio and Television Program. I'd met her some years ago through Michael, Craig's dad, when they had both worked for CFTO television. After my divorce, she was my matron of honor when I married Al, and a year later, she threw a delightful baby shower for me the night before I unexpectedly gave birth to Kevin—two weeks early. Affectionate with my kids and a frequent guest at our table, in the past ten years we had been through a lot together—including a few of her romances. In other words, Pam was my best friend. Still single, she was a very busy gal, fully involved in the performance arts, primarily as a singer. At this time, she was singing with the popular folk group, "The Travellers," but she was also heavily involved with other work: ads on television ("Speedy Muffler" was her biggie at the time), jingles, stage work and dating. Pam was very popular and everybody loved her, including me.

Not only was Pam good looking, with her short mop of golden curls, sparkling blue eyes and stylish size eight figure, but she had a great personality too. She knew a *lot* of interesting people: singers, actors, broadcasters in television and radio, fashion designers and a shop owner on Cumberland Avenue, located in the heart of the Yorkville district—in the early seventies, the Toronto Mecca of fashion and tourism. The name of the shop at the time was The Cat's Meow, and it specialized in couture fabrics, fashionable accessories and personalized dress designs. In her efficient manner, Pam made a call to her friend, the shop's proprietor, and a few days later I was back in the fashion world ... sort of.

The Cat's Meow

Arriving at my new job on time for work was not easy. I found I was out of practice, and I had a lot to contend with even before leaving the house every morning, but I managed. It was wonderful being back in the mainstream of downtown Toronto (actually Bloor Street was considered *mid*-town in the early seventies). I loved the *idea* of being back at work, but I didn't love the work. It was too confining, and after six weeks, I was feeling frustrated. My talents as a trained buyer were not being utilized: in truth, I was a glorified salesperson at best and a *gofer* at worst. It wasn't too bad being sent out of the store to pick up buttons, bows and oddities; I enjoyed the air, but about six weeks into the job, my already battered ego was further tested.

"And don't forget the toilet paper," the owner/manager sang out to me as the bell attached to the door tinkled behind me. Startled, surprised and finally irritated at the request, my first thought was *Oh, how the mighty have fallen.* Increasingly annoyed, walking too quickly, my face burning in anger, I inadvertently made a wrong turn to find myself on Bloor Street fighting the noonday crowd. Just as I made the turn, I heard Sinc impatiently announce: *Okay, lady, this it. It's time for a change. Enough is enough—do something!* By now, I had learned to listen to my critic's voice. His urging usually had merit and although he could be brutally honest, even harsh, I trusted him. At this point, my feet seemed to take on their own agenda; without warning, they made an abrupt turn to the right and stopped dead in front of the elegant glass and copper-plated front door of Holt Renfrew—an exclusive department store managed out of Montreal with branches in all of the major western cities. Without any idea of what I was doing, I entered.

Seduced by the inviting smell of moneyed accessories, pure leather handbags and kid gloves, and surrounded by the intoxicating scents of expensive perfumes and colognes, I felt quite giddy. Striding through the fragrance department, in an effort to boost my self-confidence, I inadvertently squirted myself with Paco Rabanne—a popular cologne of the day, for *men*. Never mind, I thought, it makes me feel good—aggressive. Enjoying my positive mood, and guided by some invisible force, I headed for the main elevator. It appeared that there were only four floors in the building and by now, with a vague idea of what was urging me on, I proceeded to the top, assuming that the employment offices would be housed there. Stepping off the elevator, I spotted a desk nearby. As I approached it, a pleasant-looking woman looked up from her typing and obligingly smiled. I returned her smile and in a pseudo-calm voice asked: "Would you mind directing me to the employment office?" (No fancy "human resource" offices in those days.)

I can probably help you," she smiled back.

"I hope so," I said, then went on to explain: "I am a trained fashion buyer; I've been with Eaton's for two and a half years, but I left to get married, and now I'm back in the work force."

"I see," she said, still smiling. "Why don't I get you an application form?"

At that point I noticed an attractive man, in his mid-forties, with reddish-brown hair and horn-rimmed glasses looking at me through the open door of the office beside me. Smiling at him briefly, I turned back to the desk and asked if this was indeed the store manager's office. As the secretary nodded in affirmation, I casually added, "You know, I don't really do application forms. I'd much prefer a personal interview. Is this possible?"

"I suppose so," she said, her smile quickly fading at my effrontery. I was tempted to explain: "Please don't blame me, I'm being *led*," but decided that would further exacerbate her obvious annoyance with me. Smile gone, she passed me a yellow note pad. As I wrote down my name and phone number for The Cat's Meow, I noticed the store manager watching us again. Flashing a wide smile, I picked up my handbag and left—in a hurry to buy buttons, bows and toilet paper. Five minutes after I got back to the shop, the phone rang.

"It's for you," the proprietor said. My heart jumped.

∞ ∞ ∞

"Lucky again," said Al, when I told him about my upcoming interview at Holt's. "I guess we'll see even less of you now, what with your classes at York, your typing course and your church stuff. Well, never mind, we'll manage." I could sense the sarcastic strain in his voice, and it should have given me fair warning, but at the time I was too excited to think about it. *What if*, I thought, *what if I'm lucky enough to get my foot through the buying door at Holt Renfrew? Maybe, just maybe, I could work my way into the same buying position I had with Eaton's. After all, the present buyer at Holt's has been with them over twenty-five years; surely she's getting ready to retire. Stop it*, Sinc interrupted. *Get the job first, and then start planning. You've got plenty on your plate right now. Take a closer look, before you leap.*

Okay, okay, I thought, *Sinc is right.* Just then, Kevin, with his long blond hair still damp (I couldn't bring myself to cut it), cuddly-clean from his bath and so cute in his yellow sleepers, came bouncing into our bedroom for his good night visit. Just two years old, already walking and talking (well, *I* could understand his every word and whim), he was pure delight in every way.

Kev had been an easy baby from the start. When he came along, we spread our collective arms wide to welcome him. Joanne, seven years old by then, was excited about her new baby brother.

"And don't forget the diapers, Mum," she'd remind me on my way out the door to work. Craig seemed happy about his arrival too, and Al was thrilled to have a son. As for me, I could hardly take Kev in, I found him so special and precious; he was sweet, independent, non-demanding, and, in the way of second integrated marriages, the heartbeat of our family.

Reconstructing the early love we all felt for each other and the beautiful new baby, I now believe that in some profound universal sense, a circle of love was created that was being nurtured, and, despite the later troubles in our family, it would all prove worthwhile. In retrospect, whether we understood it then or not, those definitely were "the good old days."

Escaping Reality

Escaping suburbia's humdrum reality and rejoining the faux existence of the fashion world at Holt Renfrew was just what the doctor ordered, except that by now, I was *too* busy. I'd joined a running club near our house and a health club downtown—in those days everyone did aerobics. Also, I'd enrolled in a typing course (missed it in high school, took German instead), in order to do the papers for my night courses at York University. By now I had finished my first year mandatory subjects and I could select my major, philosophy, in which I was soon immersed. All of this activity took place while I was working and looking after the practical domesticity of the house, the kids and Alan; after all he needed *some* attention in between his work and the daily golf games with his cronies.

"What about some dinner? Who's cooking?" I'd hear, upon entering the house in the evening after a tedious drive home from work—an hour or more in traffic. Aside from Colonel Saunders' Chicken and McDonald's, there were very few takeouts in the seventies; at least twice a week, around five AM, I'd stagger downstairs to prepare my "specialties." These consisted of a variety of ground beef dishes: hamburgers, meat loaf, meat balls with sauce, and spaghetti with sauce, all frozen individually in an early version of TV dinners.

Recently, when I reminded Kev of those days, he started laughing: "Mom, I don't know why you bothered making that beef stuff into all those different shapes. When I closed my eyes, they all tasted the same. You could have saved yourself the trouble."

"Oh? Well, maybe you should have kept your eyes *open*. They might have tasted better! Remember Dad's words: 'Only the best is good enough?' Well, at five AM, that was my best."

"It's okay Mom," Kev countered. "We all survived. And look, we all admit that your lasagna was absolutely the best—whenever you found time to make it!"

When I first went back to work, Kevin was just a year old. The mornings' hassles reminded me of those early days with Craig on Jarvis Street, but this time it was easier because Al was around. His classical music radio show, "Starlight Serenade," went on the air in the evenings, so he had loads of time to play his beloved golf in the early afternoons, while Mrs. Parks, our day-sitter, was there. Looking back, I remember having fearful nightmares over the loss of "Parks" (as Kev called her) as a babysitter, wondering how I would manage without her, even for a day. In the seventies, a married woman's working life was still tenuous: problems at home or even a child's illness were never an acceptable excuse for missing work or being late.

Although the rise in feminism in the seventies brought more women to the work force, it is important to note that women's rights were still far from equal. In 1971, women were earning only 58 percent of what men earned doing the same job. Although I personally witnessed the attitudes of society become more amenable to working wives and mothers from the early seventies through to the nineties, generally, in the middle class today, nothing much has changed. As tough as it was for working mothers then, in some ways it's even tougher now.

Observing our working mothers today, I see them juggling as many tasks as we did, and then some. For one thing, I don't remember having to ferry kids back and forth to their activities, because they just weren't involved in as many after-school pursuits as young people today. Also, everything was community driven and closer to home. Many of today's career-mothers must seek fulltime live-in help, which many have done successfully with the influx of Filipinos who came over to Canada as domestic help during the early nineties. Other stress factors for career mothers today are the triple roles they must take on as "sandwich" caretakers—those with young children on one side and aging parents on the other—leading to their increased work hours at home as well as to competitive full-time jobs outside. Once the children approach their college years, the added financial burdens for those women who followed the trend of starting their families late, in their thirties, will probably lead to prolonging their work life. Rather than the much-touted early or even regular retirement, they may be forced to work far longer than anticipated or desired. There's nothing new in these observations, but what bothers me is the lack of self-recognition on the part of these women: over-worked, over-burdened, they end up satisfying the needs of everyone but themselves, and this in turn leads to stress related illnesses.

In my view, our modern, tech-oriented culture is getting ready to self-destruct. Today, everyone and everything is ultra-competitive. One must be superior at every turn or be left behind. I see this in adults and children as young as six. Even at that young age, there is no time for them to contemplate nature or their own thoughts. From dawn till dusk they are off running at top speed in a world that's propelling them forward—to what? With no time to engage in their birthright—their opportunity to be kids when they *are* kids—later, as teens, they seek pleasure in material acquisitions, computer toys and early sex. These produce temporary satisfaction but provide nothing for their spiritual well-being. But kids are not the only victims of today's harassed society.

Working mothers have no time for themselves and little time to control their families, especially teenagers. In subtle ways, today's mothers are not reaping the benefits of our pioneer feminists. Everything has turned around: it's a kid's world; their "wants" come first and they don't even have to earn them—they have "rights." The Privacy Act, lately passed, has severely curtailed parents' control over teenagers from the age of fourteen on, even though these kids are living under their parents' roof, totally dependent on them for food, clothing and designer jeans. Parents, grandparents and teachers, watch out. These kids are out of control—they're taking over! But I'll stop right here. In the words of songwriter Paul Simon, "Who am I to blow against the wind?"

It's *Not* About the Money

In the beginning, my position with Holt Renfrew was as tedious as the job at The Cat's Meow. Although the manager, Mr. Boyd, appreciated my buying experience and background with Eaton's, he felt it would be best if I started off in sales in order to learn the ropes. "Then we'll see," was his comment. It turned out that "learning the ropes" meant literally stepping into a boxing ring of competitive sales without gloves—one sales mishap and you were down and out of the game. Selling was the name of the game, and if you weren't trained, you were "maimed."

At Holt's, as at Eaton's, most of the saleswomen were older than me and being thrust into a den of top-notch women selling on commission was a radical experience. The only other place I'd felt more competition was in the New York Broadway auditions, where, in comparison, stabbing in the back was a minor offence. Here they went for the jugular, and then casually stepped over the body to be first in line as the elevator doors opened to unload the unprepared victims—the customers. Dressed in regimental black, the punitive garb of the upper class saleslady, they would pounce, albeit gracefully, onto the unsuspecting clients, and then cajole each into a strategically placed armchair where they would offer them tea or coffee before their onslaught of sales patter. If the client had unwisely not called in advance, they would parade their own choices before them—everything from pale silk afternoon-tea garden suits (very few of our clients were working women) through to the prevalent late-day cocktail dresses (yes, the cocktail hour was still popular in the seventies). If the client asked for a special occasion dress, they'd be offered our one-of-a-kind gowns, newly available in Toronto, just in from Balenciaga or the House of Dior—Holt's held the exclusive rights for Dior across Canada. This matter of exclusivity was of paramount importance to Holt's clients. I learned this on my first day:

"It just wouldn't do to run into myself at one of our social functions, you *do* understand?"

"Yes, of course," I'd murmur, smothering a wry smile. "Then how about one of our classic designer gowns just in from Zurich? They're quite different you know, and again, these styles are Holt's exclusively." After an hour or so of showings, we would review the picks, and with hard-won luck, score a win, so that by noon we may have been lucky enough to sell one-half of our day's quota. If so, the old-fashioned cash register would loudly sing out announcing victory like a referee's bell at nine rounds. During this performance, the "clientless" salesgirls would move about, feigning busyness (standing still was *verboten)*, arranging, then rearranging the racks of dresses and suits while Mrs. Mezzner, the senior saleswoman in charge of Better Sportswear, eyed their movements with *faux* detachment from her desk.

Known amongst the sales girls as the "sergeant," this twenty-five-year veteran was acknowledged as the chief hawker at large and not to be messed with. Her thick, black horn-rimmed glasses, longish grey side-swept hair and black Reebok-styled leather shoes—a fashion leader on both counts—made Mrs. Mezzner an imposing figure worthy of the others' deferential regard. As for me, I was fascinated by her selling style—an unusual combination of nonchalance and arrogance sprinkled with sardonic humor delivered in a matter-of-fact way, with no hint of the rancor that was the under-text of her character if anyone dared come near her clients. Everyone, including the Montreal management, was afraid of Mrs. Mezzner. Her controlling asset was her wealthy clientele that ran the gamut from Rosedale west up to Forest Hill, east along the fringe of Lawrence Park and south again to Bloor. This territory was hers exclusively. Two decades had been devoted to this cause, and as such, the iconic Mrs. Mezzner produced an enviable sales record valued at several thousands of dollars per week—a formidable amount of money in the early seventies!

First thing each morning, Mrs. Mezzner would be on the telephone calling her regular clients, describing the latest in the Missoni knits, the stunning Gucci silks, the latest Oleg Cassini and Louis Scherrer suits. Talking fast, laughing, joking, her effusive personality would sporadically heighten in stimulation by her own fashion chatter which, in turn, would ignite her clients whom she called on a rotating basis. She'd set up her appointments and before daylight had dwindled, she'd be tops in sales again—artisanship at work.

As for the rest of us, the elevator crowd, we were on double-duty alert. Wary of appearing too anxious to the clients or each other, we'd casually strive to be first in the line of attack. Truthfully, at the end of each day I would be quite exhausted from my own internal pressure in coping within such a competitive environment while trying not to rouse resentment from the established old-timers. Discouraged at least once a day, I would call my dear friend, Frankie whom I first met when Pam brought her to Kevin's baby shower. To me, Frankie was the one woman in our group who I considered movie-star beautiful. A tall slim redhead, in looks and figure a combination of Ann-Margaret and Racquel Welch, she was a professional singer who sang with big bands that often included her husband, Al. He was an excellent trumpet player, known in jazz terms as a "screecher" (proficient in the high notes), who had just finished a stint with Paul Anka. At that time, Frankie was also a professional hairdresser, writer, artist, mother, wife and friend. But in her heart she was a gypsy and in her spirit, a soothsayer. Our group of girlfriends considered Frankie our own personal fortune teller, and in her amenable way she went along with us, as we looked to her for encouragement and futuristic advice:

"Frankie! Hi. I'm calling from the store. I can't talk loud. How are you doing? Good. So tell me, what do you see that's new? You know, regarding my future here at Holt's?" I'd whisper. "Do you see anything good coming down the pike? I'm going crazy; I don't know how much longer I can last. I'm ready to throw in the towel. Sooh, what do *you* think?"

"I think you should listen to the tea leaves and the cards. Just hang in with the towel. Don't you remember what I read in your leaves the other day? Something great is going to happen at work—and soon. On your way home tonight, drop in and we'll have a cup of tea and do a re-read. Then, on Saturday night, we'll get together with Pam and the others to do some serious tarot-talk. Okay? But, for now, do *nothing*."

In retrospect, this last message, which I vividly recall, seems silly, naive and somewhat desperate. I never believed in the tea leaves and the cards—what I really needed was Frankie's positive attitude. That's what I loved about her. As a group, we were close and we supported each other's endeavors. All working, some married, some not, we were an eclectic bunch. There were six of us: two singer/actors, two in PR, one dancer and myself in fashion.

Frankie was right. There *was* something coming down the pike. It was exciting and new, and, as at Eaton's, I was in the right place at the right time. Just one week from the Friday when I called her for moral support, I was told I would be leaving the "elevator brigade." I'd been asked to move down one floor to open the new Holt Renfrew "au Courant" fashion department. I was being promoted to the status of buyer, and as such I would be travelling to Montreal and New York. I'd have the good fortune to be working with a strikingly attractive woman, Patricia, who was opening the same department in the Montreal store. Pat, close to six feet tall, had a well-sculpted face with sweeping cheekbones and a voluptuous smile that entitled her to wear her auburn hair pulled straight back, tied in a low chignon that flattered her face, her demeanor, and added a chic sophistication to her already startling presence.

The story goes that one evening, probably a little tipsy, Patricia was seen walking *barefoot* downtown on Sherbrooke Street wearing a lipstick-red Halston dress and her trademark wide-brimmed cream Stetson hat. As tall and attractive as she was, barefoot and all, she sauntered along with such sophisticated aplomb as to literally stop traffic, creating a rapid string of front and rear-enders as everyone stopped to ogle. As a result of this scene, Pat became known as Montreal's "pixilated princess of pizzazz." She didn't mind the title except for the pixilated part, which in time became a problem. We got along extremely well, both personally and within our respective departments, but unfortunately, when the next promotion came along, Patricia was passed over. It seems the Montreal fashion world was small—too small for the likes of a *pixilated princess*.

∞ ∞ ∞

My new job with Holt Renfrew, as a buyer, was to start one week Monday. There was a slight raise in salary, nothing startling, but at that time, "working at Holt's was never about the money, it was all about the prestige"—well, that was management's attitude, and at that point I wasn't going to quibble. Here's the gist of my conversation when I phoned Frankie to tell her my exciting news:

"Frankie. Hi! I had to tell you first. It's so amazing what happened today, and the *way* it happened: from The Cat's Meow to—"

Frankie interrupted by finishing, "to God's ear." (She thought I'd said "from The Cat's *Mouth* …") I started laughing and so did she. We were always in tune.

"No, no, I said: 'From *your* mouth to God's ear.'"

"Okay," Frankie agreed, still laughing. Have it your way. We'll talk about that at the celebration party; so, where's it going to be?"

"Right here, at our house, Saturday night."

"Great!" she announced, then broke into a version of the Hank Williams Jr. song, *Jambalaya*. "'Son of a gun, we'll have good fun, at *your* party.' See you there!"

Take a Mulligan

Mulligan: A golf shot not tallied against the score—granted in informal play after a poor shot, especially from the tee.
—American Heritage Dictionary

Al seemed to take the news of my new buying job at Holt's very well. Frankly, I was worried. I well remember his crack: "Well, now we'll see you even less," when I first mentioned that I was going back to work in accordance with the doctor's orders. Now, with this new position at Holt's, he understood that there would be travelling involved, but still, he seemed to accept my promotion with uncharacteristic equanimity. I could hear the warning bells sounding off, but I couldn't find the fire. All kinds of thoughts ran through my head: *Maybe he's found someone else at the club? There are lots of good-looking single women running around there. Or maybe he's happy with his life: he has his work, very nice pay for very few hours; he's getting to play golf with his buddies every day and he has lots of time to spend with the kids. Maybe he just wants me to be happy.* Whatever fear I felt, I was afraid to take it up with Al. In a way, it was a selfish decision. Our relationship had hit the seven-year mark; Alan was in his mid- forties, already "over the hill" in the heady *youth-ism* of the seventies. I'd read enough to understand the pitfalls of that age in a man, and although the male menopause was not openly recognized or discussed, I could tell that his machismo monitor had dropped near to zero. At this point our conjugal communication had rolled into a supine position, one that didn't require too much effort by way of expectation or energy, and this *seemed* to be working out fine for both of us—but was it? I was afraid to ask. I didn't want to disturb the status quo.

By now, Al had left CFRB to devote himself to his commercial work and his new successful television show, *Untamed World*, with which he was involved from its inception. Other than this, his lifeline stretched between the house and the Summit golf club. At that time, I never really appreciated Al's obsession with golf, but now, in my present-day experience with the game, I see it differently.

A golf club and the game itself can mean different things to individual members and players. Here I speak from my own current experience as a golfer and also from my personal observation of the etiquette and attitudes intrinsic to better golf clubs. For me, the game, aside from the club, can be a place of refuge, an escape from reality, a return to nature, a way of re-connecting with myself within the nourishment of quietness. For Al, the social aspect of the club expanded his self-identity: being within a perceived society of wealth provided a comfortable haven in which to drink with the boys—a daily focus and succor for a bruised ego after a too early retirement. If anyone asked me, "How's Alan?" I'd always say, "Oh, he's fine. He's doing very well. Now he's a 'golf every afternoon' kind of guy." But really, how well *was* he doing?

I'd first heard the term *mulligan* years ago when I started playing golf with Al. "Well, what does it mean?" I demanded. I had earlier made up my mind that I wasn't going to like golf. I only started it up with Al because I wanted to find out what the huge attraction was. I could feel us drifting apart, and I wasn't sure who or what to blame—him, myself or golf.

"It means, the last shot doesn't count, you can take it over again," Al explained.

"But isn't that cheating? I mean, aren't you supposed to count *every* stroke?"

"Yes, but it is okay if you're among friends and they agree, or just don't care ... get it?"

"Sort of, so it sounds like you're supposed to get *permission*—but from whom?" I asked.

"Those you're playing with. But who cares? Remember, it's just a game," Al countered.

Well, it's taken me over thirty years to understand the attraction and addictive power of golf. For any number of reasons it is a *feel-good* game. But right there, that puts it into the category of an addiction. Like any other "feel-good" drug, you can *never* get enough. Here's an example of Al's golf-addicted dialogue:

"That wood shot should have been straighter, longer; the birdie should have been an eagle: the putt, a half inch off the hole should have dropped; I was robbed. And look at this lousy tee shot—what a hook. Whoa Nellie, stop! It's gone in the water. Okay, how about a mulligan?"

"Sure, why not?" I'd say. "It's only a game; besides, who's counting?" ... *me,* said a small still voice. I strained but could hear nothing more—just dead air. I've always felt that "taking a mulligan" is a form of cheating. Golf, even in informal play, is a game of honor and since you are essentially playing against yourself, trying to improve, not only are you taking advantage of your partners but you are including them in your self-deception. And that's exactly the way I came to feel about Al's drinking.

Every time he drank too much, he would get rude and verbally abusive ... then, when I reacted, I was of course the miserable creature that brought about his bad mood. First, I would get angry and then, I would feel great disappointment. Al's self-deception—his inability to see that taking a mulligan, taking advantage, was not the way to improve a golf game or a marriage. As far as I was concerned, he was cheating himself and me by his denial in both realms.

Covert doubt on my part and mistrust on Al's was creeping into our lives, corroding our relationship and in turn creating problems for me at work. The process of erosion, insidious but determined, took place over seven years and although our mutual disappointments took on different addictions—Alan's manifested as an alcoholic and mine as a workaholic—today I see them as equally destructive.

The workaholic syndrome, manifested through its miserly attention bestowed upon those who sorely need it, is insidious in its damaging effect because it is masked in overt respectability and positively affirmed in a world driven by materialism. And an alcoholic's need to obliterate his bereft ego through over-drinking, today medically described as a "dis-ease," can be, in its prolonged state, likened to a death wish—equally damaging to the drinker *and* the enabler, who at this point, also requires therapy. And so the years of our marriage passed, in a circular dance of disagreement and broken trust between disappointed partners in need. Both desiring love—unable to stay, unable to go—we slow-danced to our own rhythms, marched to our own beat, while time ignored our delusions and resolutely passed us by....

Chapter 14

Memories, Legends and Longing

I will lead the blind by ways they have not known,
along unfamiliar paths
I will guide them; I will turn the darkness into light before them
and make the rough places smooth.
—NIV Bible: Isaiah 42:16

Westminster Abbey, 1971

"Caged"

"I know, but this is my work," I protest to Al. "It's important to me. This is a great opportunity. I'll always be sorry if I give it up." This was on a Thursday in late March 1971. Alan and I were having another one of our arguments, this time about my latest promotion at Holt Renfrew. Leonard Cohen's album, *Songs from a Room* was playing. Reluctantly, I shut off the record player. *Lenny shouldn't have to compete with us*, I thought, following Al out of the room, while explaining:

"You know, this promotion has come out of the blue, unexpectedly—that's what makes it so special. The head buyer of Better Suits and Dresses, where I worked when I first started at Holt's is retiring as the European buyer for Toronto and the Western stores, which include Winnipeg, Edmonton, Calgary and Vancouver. Shockingly, the assistant buyer, after twenty-five years of service, has been passed over. And now, surprisingly, the position has been offered to me!"

Yesterday, when Mr. Boyd called me up to his office, I thought it was to discuss last month's sales figures for the *au Courant* boutique I'd set up six months ago, but no, it was not that at all. When he finally told me what he had in mind for me, I must admit that I was truly surprised—no, shocked:

"Well, Mrs. Small, you've done a fine job with our second floor boutique, *au Courant*. Now in confidence, I will tell you that after twenty-five successful years, our head buyer on the third floor is retiring, and after substantial discussions, I've convinced Mr. Samson, our president in Montreal, that you are the right person for the job. If you accept, you'll be starting Monday. [This was Thursday!] As you probably know, this new position will require you to travel to Europe for the spring showings that start this April 6, in Florence, Italy. Not much time, I know, but if you are interested in the position, you would have to let us know by Saturday, that's the day after tomorrow; then you would have to make arrangements to leave for Europe one week from this coming Wednesday. The general itinerary is Florence, Paris, Zurich and London, each for a week, which adds up to being away for a full month. By the way, have you ever been to Europe? No? Me neither. Well, I should think that the first thing you want to work on is your passport—make sure that it's in order." *Passport, what passport?* I thought.

After Al listened to my story, I could tell that even he was surprised: "What kind of company is this? I've never heard of such a thing. It sounds crazy to me; what's the rush? They offer you a fancy job and you've got one day to think about it? It sounds fishy, to me."

"Well, they're not a huge company. Probably they're rushing their decision because the present buyer can't, or is unable, to go to Europe—maybe she's sick or something. Anyway, I think it's a fantastic opportunity. You know, I would really like your blessing on this."

"I can't give you that, but I won't stop you from going either. Anyway, it sounds as though you've already made up your mind."

"Not exactly," I mumbled, fighting back tears. *Why is everything so hard?* I wondered. *Why do I always have to fight so hard for whatever I want?* I went up to our bedroom, taking the new Leonard Cohen album with me. Listening to Lenny's gritty, audacious growl of a voice I was brought close to tears. Such unusual lyrics; so different, so intimate—a modern day troubadour defining a new era in an old world:

> *And a pretty woman leaning in her darkened door,*
> *she cried to me 'Hey, why not ask for more?'*
> *Oh, like a bird on the wire, like a drunk in a midnight choir,*
> *I have tried in my way to be free.*
> —Leonard Cohen: *Bird on the Wire.*

The words haunt me. Maybe I *do* ask for too much—maybe not enough. Maybe I should just stop wanting … but oh, how that last line resonates with me. I *have* tried in my way to be free. But how many have I hurt in the trying? In answer, Kevy came bouncing in for his bedtime visit—synchronicity in full play. I switched Lenny off.

Gathering Kevin close, cradling his warm body, I rock him back and forth. He is almost three, not a baby anymore, but he still likes to be held. Looking at his perfect face, I wondered how much more love I could hold. Can a child, so loved, be left for a whole month? What can I do? What *should* I do? Distraught, I clutch Kevin closer and reach for my bible. It opens at Psalm 55:22. "Cast your cares upon the Lord and he will sustain you; he will never let the righteous fall."

"I will try," I murmur in response. "I will try."

The Art of Prayer

The next day I am still mired in ambivalence: To go, or not to go; that is the question. In a Shakespearian turn of mind, I wrestle with the problem of taking on the European buyer's job. Saturday is looming and that is the final day for my decision. What to do.... Unlike Hamlet, I am not looking "to take up arms against a sea of troubles," rather I am trying to stem the tide that would push me further into that sea—oh, would that "outrageous fortune" had not placed this choice before me once again. A beautiful son must be left, if only for a month. Will I once again be accused of abandonment? I turn back to the Psalms:

"I will remember the deeds of the Lord; yes, I will remember your miracles of long ago. I will meditate on all your works, and consider all your mighty deeds." (Psalms, 77: 11-12)

"That's it," I declare out loud as I close the book. *I will be shown the answer. Just stay calm and listen for a word....*

Almost instantly a word comes—and from an unlikely source:

Okay, that's enough! Stop worrying, Sinc chides, barging in on my thoughts. *Lots of working wives go on business trips. This is the seventies! Get over your guilt! Besides, Kevin will be perfectly safe at home with his dad, Carminda and Joanne.*

Well, that last part is certainly true, I thought.

At eleven, Jo was already an embodiment of the care-giving archetype (later, a natural-born mother who would give birth to her fifth child before she was twenty-seven years). As I wrestle with my indecision, some other words of Leonard Cohen's signature song *Bird on the Wire* return: "If I, if I have been untrue. I hope you know it was never to you." On this last phrase, my mind rests:

I always knew that underneath Al's drinking and bravado there were deep-seated problems; for some of these he passed blame onto me, but he had no reason to doubt my fidelity. Although I'd honorably navigated my marital vows for years, Alan's fears of my unfaithfulness persisted: the idea of me journeying through Europe for a month was more than his fractured ego could bear. In spite of the problems within our marriage, I had never been untrue; I may have had a transitory flirtation here and there, but never one that had any serious intent. Still, Alan was worried about Italy—he even wrote a satirical poem about it. And then, of course, there was Paris, London and Zurich on the itinerary, a week's stopover in each. In retrospect, I'm sure that these were places he wanted to visit, but at the time, I reasoned that his feeling of jealousy was a natural reaction to my leaving home for such an extended time. Still, I didn't fully appreciate his reluctance. I needed to get him to understand my position. I was being offered an opportunity to do something special at a time when I had given up the idea of ever having a real career again. I certainly didn't want to jeopardize my marriage; but on the other hand, I didn't want to pass up an offer that included a promotion, a pay raise and the opportunity to see Europe.

I would have to find a way to satisfy Al's concerns, convince him not to worry. Later that afternoon, I set it up:

"Let's go out," I suggested. "It's Friday night, and we haven't been dancing in ages. Isn't there something going on at the club?" I was pleasantly surprised when Alan willingly concurred. I should have been suspicious, but I was already upstairs calling the babysitter and deciding what to wear.

We had a great time dancing and drinking, with no time in between to worry about the immediate future. Our best friends happened to be there, and at one point, they casually announced that they were going back home to Yorkshire, England, for a visit. Then, even more casually, they suggested: "Why doesn't Al come along? He could pick you up in London after your work is done, and then the two of you could bop around, see the sights and even visit his home town of Hull. What do you think?" they asked.

"I think the three of you have been cooking something up, and it sounds pretty good to me," I replied. What I was *thinking* was that this was indeed an answer to prayer. As I've stated before, I've learned to listen and remain open in order to *hear* prayer answers. They are always creative and original, far beyond anything I could possibly dream up—that's the exciting part. All you have to do is *believe* that your prayers are answered. Of course, this may sound too easy, but in a way it's that simple.

What I do first is *practice* believing—this is true of every skill that is acquired through training or experience. I practice by openly sending out a prayer request to God, my Highest Power. When you have acquired the faculty to believe in the *power* of prayer (this is an innate capability that we are all born with, but rarely use), you have to be willing to recognize the prayer as having been answered—not necessarily in your desired or planned way. This, for me, is the most important part. My prayer answers are often "off the wall," even bizarre, and can consist of a door being loudly slammed while a window is quietly opened. In any case, I listen, and *hear,* sometimes without understanding and other times in a state of peaceful calm. And ever since I have learned to trust and believe in prayer's power, I heed the call. In this case, I started the path of *cause*—an agent that permits the occurrence of an *effect*—then faith enabled that power to produce an unusual and satisfying outcome. I believe that prayer is like any other skill. It requires practice.

After all of the fuss and flurry of preparing for my first trip abroad, it was finally time to depart. For two reasons, I remember the leave-taking very well. First of all, there was the pain of leaving Kevin. Standing in the driveway with Alan, Joanne and Carminda (our *au pair* from Portugal), Kev didn't seem too concerned. I guess he thought I was going to work, not the airport. Joanne, in her eleven-year-old motherly fashion told me "not to worry" and Alan, by now into his cups, gave me a big smile with an *arrivederci* salute to send me on my way. As for me, even while pulling out of the driveway, I could feel the sharp waves of a migraine coming on—a result of the stress, excitement and arm-loads of guilt I'd been carrying around over the past week. On the way to the airport, I tried to relax, but the waves kept coming. I knew, then, that this was going to be a bad attack; I reached for a blue and white Fiornal capsule, gathered some spit and swallowed hard.

Firenze Fever

Over-medicated and over-tired from the twelve-hour flight, I was still very excited when our entourage disembarked in Italy. Often called "the paradise of travelers," Italy greeted me with a cacophony of sights and sounds in a way that can never be erased: here was a brilliant azure sky dotted with puffy white clouds that appeared to be painted in place. Although it was early April, the sun had already taken up permanent residence as it smiled benignly on us that day and all through the coming week. Added to my pleasure was the excitement of hearing Italian spoken out loud for the first time: ephemeral voices announcing arrivals and departures amid clamorous shouts by taxi drivers, excited conversations and joyous bear hugs between newly arrived visitors punctuated by bursts of laughter followed by tears of joy. What a scene!

I was filled with wonder at actually being in Italy to hear and see this marvel of humanity at work. As their heady language sang out to me, those emotions of my first touchdown in Europe, the sights, smells and sounds were etched in remembrance so powerfully, that today, in reverie, I can call up that same immediacy of awe and wonder at will. As is my practice in writing, I am led to my passions through music, and although I don't speak Italian, the intensity of their language in song can still move me to tears.

While at the Toronto Conservatory, I'd only ever sung in Italian by memorizing the words and general meaning, but I'd fallen in love with the rhythm of the language with my first Mozart aria from *The Marriage of Figaro*, *"Voi Che Sapeta"*…. "Say, ye who borrow Love's witching spell, what is this sorrow naught can dispel"—the words so much more appealing in Italian!

My first attempt at singing in a foreign language took place under the patient tutelage of Madame Rublev, my beloved accompanist and friend from my conservatory days, who happily developed my B flat above middle C to its full potential. At that same time there was that soulful romantic interlude with my erstwhile Italian baritone: *Dio, comme te amo*, "Oh God how much I love you …he earnestly sang." There, I'm in tears again.

On that first flight to Italy, I travelled with Madame Roxwell and Mr. Dixon. Mrs. R. had been Holt's Montreal overseas buyer for many years, and as such, she was far beyond my excitement level—in fact she seemed quite bored by my enthusiasm. But, that I was a-twitter with excitement at being in Europe, particularly in Italy, did not go unnoticed by Mr. Dixon. He seemed to get pleasure out of my obvious delight at being in Rome for the first time.

"Wait until you see Firenze … that's Florence," he added.

"Oh yes, I know Firenze, the home of the river Arno and the famous Ponte Vecchio, both familiar to me through Giacomo Puccini's opera, *Gianni Schicci*." Mr. Dixon seemed impressed.

Reverie's Gift

In the late fifties, when I'd first studied voice at the Royal Conservatory, Maria Callas (1923-1977), the American coloratura known for her newly acquired slim figure and dramatic intensity, appeared at the Maple Leaf Gardens to a sell-out crowd. Of course, as poor starving students, we could only afford seats high up "in the gods," but I well remember the thrill of Callas' performance. Although her notable operatic role was in Bellini's *Norma*, I always associate her with the famous aria, "Oh Mio Babbino Caro" from Puccini's opera, *Gianni Schicci*—an aria that every studying soprano, myself included, had in her repertoire.

Legend has it that near the end of her career, the only concert aria Callas was capable of performing consistently, in good form, was *O Mio Babbino Caro*, "Oh my beloved father." This was up to 1975, before she was closeted in Paris in the throes of depression after the death of her former lover, Aristotle Onassis—the Greek shipping magnate who, much to Callas' chagrin, had married the former US First Lady, Jacqueline Bouvier Kennedy, in 1968. Pundits have suggested that Callas' affinity for this aria was due to the accessibility of her voice to Puccini's hauntingly beautiful music and also to the lyrics themselves—which in their own way expressed her dependency and obsessive love for Aristotle Onassis, her senior by many years. On September 16, 1977, two years after Onassis' death, Maria Callas died, at age 54, having spent her last years alone as a virtual recluse in a Paris hotel. The cause of her death (a broken heart?) still remains unclear.

Here I pause. Can any of us know the pain of another's suffering? Should we even try? Listen to the poignant words of longing in Puccini's aria: *O mio babbino caro:* Oh my dear papa; *Mi piace, è bello, bello.* I like him; he is handsome, handsome.... And if my love were in vain, I would go to the Ponte Vecchio, and throw myself in the Arno!"

∞ ∞ ∞

Now, as I write this, I am in awe of the nostalgia evoked by Puccini's celestial aria and his reference to the Ponte Vecchio over the river Arno—directly across from the palazzo where I first stayed in Firenze, almost forty years ago. Today, hearing this beautiful aria sung, wrapped as it is around my early music studies and my first trip to Europe, I am lost in a powerful reverie—a kind of joyful mourning: a sublime combination of loss and joy for my past youth, my music, my first love and the heady excitement of those early days at the Toronto Conservatory, so many decades ago. Fascinated by the immediacy of this reverie, astounded by the wealth of emotion aroused as measured against the span of time, I turn to my muse and mentor, Gaston Bachelard, for understanding. In *Poetics of Reverie* he describes the reverie *process*:

> *The reverie is going to be born naturally, in awareness without tension, in an easy cogito [meditation].... The imagining consciousness holds its object (such images as it imagines) in an absolute immediacy.*
> —"Cogito of the Dreamer."

In recording my life, I have found this "immediacy of images" to be a timely blessing, a benefit bestowed on the creative writing process in so many ways. Even though, on the surface, my feelings appear to be a non-sequitur of the original image—in this case Maria Callas, the river Arno and the Ponte Vecchio—my meditation upon this image triggers a reverie which engages my past in such "absolute immediacy" that the emotional truth of who I was then is not only accessed but the same range of feelings is experienced now. Time simply falls away, and I am again in the fullness of my youth, all the pain and joy relived.

Today I am as enthralled with music as I was in my youth—no less passionate ... organically one and the same. As such, reverie's "emotional truth process" informs me of the language and creative method to be employed in writing my stories—a precious gift. In revealing the passionate love of my early musical experience and my youth in general, yesterday's timelessness allows me to savor these emotions again as I relive my first trip to Italy.

Looking for David

"Where's 'the David?'" I asked Madame Roxwell, while we were driving to the fashion showings at the Palazzo Pitti on our first day out in Firenze. She gave me a blank stare.... "You know," I continued, "the famous statue, Michelangelo's 'David.'"

Another stare ... this one shadowed by consternation and a teacherly tone.

"I'll tell you, my dear, we're here to work. This is not a holiday to run about looking at art and statues. I know this is your first trip over, but you will find that, because of the language problems, the work is much more demanding here than at home. As you know, we have to work through an interpreter—in fact we're on our way to pick her up now."

"Okay, but don't we *ever* get a day off?" I queried, deciding to play the naive game so as to satisfy her obvious need for superiority and control.

I'd felt uncomfortable with Mrs. R. from the moment we met. Obviously she wasn't happy with Mr. Boyd's choice of me as the new Toronto overseas buyer. Maybe I was too young, an upstart in a company where everyone in management was older than I was. Maybe she was upset about the assistant buyer, her long-time friend, being passed over after twenty-five years of service. I couldn't blame her for that. Being asked to tidy your desk and leave at closing time on a Saturday afternoon, the same day as your replacement accepts your job, is a harsh way of handling things—unconscionable, even in 1971, when good faith was temporarily out of style. Also, as I found out later, added to Mrs. Roxwell's uncertainty about me was her annoyance with my *parvenu*, "upstart" wardrobe followed by the issue of smoking.

Back in the early seventies, almost everyone smoked, in restaurants, at the store, even at our desks. Everyone smoked except Mr. Dixon and Madame Roxwell. Apparently Mr. D. was allergic to smoke, and whatever bothered him, bothered Mrs. R. Today, almost forty years later, it may seem like an oddity that everyone smoked whenever and wherever they pleased. For example, there was smoking in the group seminars and night classes at York University; also smoking was allowed in the movie theatres, in the back eight rows. And yes, smoking was allowed in *all* of the restaurants, no matter how expensive. In the divided cubicles of large business offices, smoke would waft over from one section to the next, claiming unsuspecting victims on its flight. The truth is, we weren't duly informed of the dangers, and if we were, we weren't listening.

Meanwhile, on my first buying trip to Florence with Madame Roxwell, my established three-day migraine took umbrage at what should have been considered a minor personality clash; deciding to stay on it grew in strength, pulsating its way from the back cranial area over the frontal sinuses into the maxillary area where it settled deeply into the upper bones of my jaw. Eventually my whole head was numb with pain—even my teeth ached. A full week later, after many blue bombs (Fiornals), there was still no sign of relief. Collapsing with fatigue every night, I'd wake up exhausted after a fitful sleep to be greeted with the "jaws of death" well in place, firmly clamped around my wobbly head. Grabbing a blue pill, or two, depending on the severity, I'd struggle to get dressed for the seven AM breakfast meeting where the day's plans would be discussed. Throughout the day, obstinately gaining in strength, the narcissistic presence would drum out its demands to be fed—a pain-killer every five hours, one starting at seven in the morning, another at noon and by late afternoon, tea-time, the second-last blue bomb of the day would be swallowed. I'd then get dressed for dinner, keeping Mrs. R., the designated fashion cop, in mind as I bravely soldiered on—by now half silly with the drugged-down pain.

Little did I know that the fabulous array of exotic cheeses and ruby red local Chianti offered at every meal was providing my sensitive migraine with enormous sustenance by way of additives found in ripened cheese, rare steak and the tannic acids present in wine. Once my food allergy came to dine, it held on and feasted for days, while, in reaction, my stomach went on an acid strike. After dinner, upon returning to my hotel room, exacerbating this already stressful depletion, there were the phone calls. Alan started calling the hotel on my third night in Florence; the gist of the conversations was always the same. It was two A.M.:

He's lonely. He's missing me. He didn't stop to figure out the time. He's so sorry to hear that I still have the headache. He's missing me. What am I doing? Do I miss him? Kevin misses me. Joanne misses me. Have I been going to the wild Italian discos? Am I behaving myself? He's missing me.

Well, I knew Madame Roxwell was an insomniac, and I was sure she was awake in the adjoining room. I spoke softly. "I'm fine. Really, I'm okay. I'm sure this headache will soon go. This isn't helping ... I just got to sleep. No, there are no discos. We work all day taking notes at the shows, than write up the orders that night after dinner, often working well past midnight. Yes, the food is great, but everyone serves red wine and there's always cheese in everything—probably that's what is causing these dreadful headaches. All I know is if I don't get some sleep, I'll never make the morning meeting. Then I'll really be in trouble ... Mrs. R.? Oh, she's okay, as long as she's the boss. Sure, I get to make my own selections style-wise. Toronto is different from Montreal—more reserved in their taste. Yes, I love you too. Give the kids a big hug. You mustn't call at this hour. The phones here have a very loud ring and the walls are thin. I'm sure Mrs. R.'s awake and can hear every word. Yes, yes, I'm now in tears. What do you expect? I'm under enough stress as it is. Now I have to worry about you, too. No, no, please don't bang down. If you do, I'll never get back to sleep. Listen, it's only been a few days. In a couple of weeks you'll be leaving on your trip over here, to London. It won't be long. Okay? Love you too. 'Bye."

The next morning at breakfast, Mr. Dixon asked Madame Roxwell how she had slept. "Not too well," she stated, giving me a side-long glance. *Oh, no,* I thought. *I'm in trouble. She probably heard every word last night.* After breakfast, on our way to the Pitti Palace for the fashion showings, I tried again to be friendly: "You know, Madame Roxwell, I have to admit that I'm very excited to be here in Florence. There are so many wonderful archaeological museums and art galleries. I know you told me before that 'we are not here to play,' but are you saying that there are *no* days off? I mean, will there be a little time left over for me to see some sights?" Tentatively, I added, "By the way, just where *is* the famous statue, *David*, by Michelangelo?"

"The original is in the Galleria dell Accademia," Mrs. R. stated off handedly, "but don't worry, you'll be able to see the modern *copy* of it at the Palazzo Vecchio—it's there to the left of the entrance. I'm sure we'll be driving by on our way to the showings before we leave Florence."

With my headache getting worse, by now in a stupefied state, I boldly asked: "You mean, in all your years of coming here, you've never seen Michelangelo's *original* David?"

"No, but don't worry" she said, patting my knee; "I'm sure the copy will do you fine."

Leaning back in the cab, I sighed to myself. *This is crazy. Not anything the way I thought it would be. Here I am, my first time in Europe and I'm working night and day, with no time to see anything, including 'the David!' When we leave for Paris, very early tomorrow, we're meant to have our Florence orders ready to hand over, sized, priced and tallied up, with a final total of budget dollars spent to date. There are so many stores for me to write up—double those of Mrs. R.—all of the Toronto stores and the western provinces too. That means working all night! Dear Lord, I hope Alan doesn't call again.* He did.

∞ ∞ ∞

The subject of Al and his late-night phone calls was brought up on our morning flight to Paris. I was sitting beside Mr. Dixon: "Well, Mrs. Small," he asked, "How are you feeling about your first trip to Europe?"

"Fine, but I didn't get to see Michelangelo's *David*. Not even the *faux* copy." I was trying to distract him by going on the offence, from what I intuited was coming.

"Yes, I heard about that. Well, maybe next time." *If there is a next time,* I thought.

"Now, I've also heard that you are having a little trouble on the home front. Do you want to tell me about it?" *Not really,* I thought. *This is ridiculous! Now Madame R. is a spy?*

"It's just that my husband misses me. (I didn't dare mention the children. In business, in 1971, they didn't exist.) I'm sure he'll get over it. He's going to meet me in London for a couple of days. I want to make sure that's okay with you? I have a little holiday time coming."

"Yes, yes, that's fine. But on the subject of your husband, I hear from Mr. Boyd that he's opened a shop on Markham Street, behind Ed Mirvish's store on Bloor Street. Apparently he's planning to import some fashions with a friend of his, a supplier of ours—a Ken Vernon. What's going on?"

"Well, they've been talking about it for a while. I guess they've gone ahead with their plan. Is this a problem?"

"Indeed it is. Our president, Mr. Samson, considers it a direct conflict of interest. You'll have to speak to your husband about this. Also speak to him about the late-night phone calls. We can't have you dragging yourself around in an exhausted state. There's too much money at stake. I'm sure you understand?"

I understood, only too well. I knew, and my migraine knew, that the real wrath would come when I returned home. As such, we both settled in for a long, painful wait.

Out of This World

Is it possible to feel joy when your head is numb? Oh yes, especially if this is your first visit to Paris, France. My prime memory of Paris is that of my beautiful and expensive room at the Hotel Plaza Athenèe and the experience I had there. The room was not large, but it had an authentic old-world elegance. The double bed looked so cozy with its high double mattress and gold feathered comforter that I decided to stretch out and test it. As I sank into its depths, I could feel my body relaxing … letting go.

Sighing in relief I closed my eyes, and, with my thoughts free-floating, I drifted towards sleep. Warm and snug in my bed, I felt my troubled past in Florence lifting and leaving a calm harmony in its wake. Peaceful, almost asleep, I took in a long deep breath, and upon release I felt a soothing sense of relief—a lightness of spirit, as though the weight of my body was leaving me, being raised into another sphere. Cocooned in my bed in the softest of silk, I watched my spirit, my other self as it took on bodily form and floated upwards toward the ceiling. I saw myself hovering there, suspended in mid-air, while at the same moment I looked down and viewed myself fast asleep. Floating above, watching from below, I saw myself being drawn by a compelling force towards a lighted tunnel which took on the form of a huge halo. Once inside this circle of white light, I was bathed in such an encompassing peace that I remember wishing I could stay in that infinity of love forever.

When I woke up the throbbing migraine had gone, and a dull ache remained in its place—a bruised memory overshadowed by joy. The wrenching headache that had plagued me for over a week was replaced by calmness and a peaceful promise of a solution to all my fears. I contemplated the strange happening, as it etched itself into memory; so that now, many years later, I still recall with enduring gratitude the comfort of that other-worldly experience and its numinous healing. Today, I strongly believe that I was lifted out of my body and out of this world for a brief insight into the ethereal timelessness of God. As such, the rapture accompanying that experience has fused my belief with an enduring faith; today I am suspended in the certainty that, although my corporal body was sorely wounded, divine intervention *can,* and often *does* bring physical healing.

Joie de Vivre

By now, Paris has completely exhausted any superlatives that can reasonably be applied to the city by natives and tourists alike.

"Yes, yes, I've been there. Oh, the River Seine; Notre Dame; the Eiffel Tower; I have seen them at sunrise, and at sunset. C'est *magnifique!*"

Everyone loves Paris. In the words of Cole Porter, "I love Paris in the springtime ... I love Paris in the fall...." In *my* words, I loved Paris just because I was there. Yes, that first time, it was in the spring, and yes, I *did* see the Eiffel Tower at sunset and indeed it *was* magnificent.

Alone at last; after my epiphany in the hotel room and relieved to be rid of my numbing nemesis, the headache from hell, I decided to forego dinner with "the gang" to do a little sight-seeing on my own. It's true, there are no superlatives left to describe the grand magic of strolling along the avenues of Paris on a balmy spring evening in April. Even the public buildings are impressive in their *Belle Époque* grandeur, and seeing the platinum shops lining the rue du *Faubourg St. Honore* for the first time was exhilarating: Lanvin, Courreges, Hermes, Pierre Cardin and Gucci—surely a heady experience to even the most jaded traveler (Mrs. Roxwell comes to mind). If still not suitably impressed, then the *Jardins du Trocadero*, whose fountain and nearby garden are beautifully illuminated at night, should do the trick.

Earlier, stepping out onto the balcony, with the Eiffel Tower in full view against a backdrop of purple-pink sky I felt so moved as to proffer a prayer of thanks. Not only was I lucky to be offered a top position within a store of merit, but here I was enjoying a breathtaking vista in one of the most beautiful cities on earth. Later, strolling from the hotel along the *Champs Elysees* towards the *Arc de Triomphe*, I could see the Eiffel Tower to my left, but it was getting too dark to take a picture for Kev. Just the idea of him snugly asleep at home (it was well past midnight in North York, Toronto) gave me pause to marvel at the idea of me actually being here, halfway around the world in Paris, France, "The City of Lights." I felt blessed. This experience took place in the early seventies, and not many Canadian women of my generation, none that I knew, had been given the opportunity to see the world through their work. Most were with their families, minding babies, husbands, hearth and home.

Earlier, in the Hotel Plaza Athenèe, after the headache from hell had finally lifted, everything around me took on such color and beauty as to appear dreamlike, surreal. I felt renewed, even reborn, after I came out of my numbed, drugged-out state. It was as though I'd stepped into one of van Gogh's brilliant paintings—the Sunflower series or *Starry Night*, painted in 1889, the same year the Eiffel Tower was built for the World's Fair to commemorate the French Revolution. But surreal or not, what a memorable evening I had!

The April air was palatable with scents of rosemary, thyme and garlic, wafting my way as early dinners where offered at sidewalk cafes. Nearby were petite herb gardens and early spring flowerbeds blooming in such a profusion of color that my migrainous eyes, still sensitive to light, were assaulted by their beauty. Strolling along the Champs Elysees on that balmy spring evening, in April 1971, free to enjoy the sights and sounds of Paris at leisure, I felt happier than I had in years. At that point, comfortably relaxed, I felt hungry. Plunking myself down on a bench alongside the *Arc de Triomphe*, I pulled out the packaged cheese and crackers left over from the plane. Not one to waste, I'd also packed one of the *petite* complimentary bottles of white wine, which I was unable to drink on the plane because I was on medication. Sitting comfortably alone in the middle of Paris, bathed in a pink sunset, I marveled at the beauty of the scene surrounding my humble, delicious repast.

As I sat on my bench, I started people-watching in earnest. The French women were not particularly beautiful—not like the blonde Italian women in their tight Jeans and high-heeled silver sandals on the streets of Firenze, nor like the tall beautiful models that we'd seen at the restaurants and the one disco we visited. No, these women on the *Champs Elysees* were mostly petite and dark-haired, attractive in their own distinctive way. Meticulous in their make-up, fastidious in everything from their neat designer jeans to their pseudo Jean Claude Patou suits and Nina Ricci knock-offs, they each seemed to possess an innate fashion sense of their own. I found my walk that evening informative and timely in light of the zoo that awaited me the next day at the fashion presentations in the Petit Palais, Grand Palais and the other hotels.

Hidden Talent

"Mom, when you're in Paris, maybe you'll get to go to the Eiffel Tower and take a picture please?" Kevin had asked, already fascinated by towers ever since Joanne had shown him the model of the Toronto CN Tower soon to be built. When the tower was completed in 1976, Kevin could see the top of it from his bedroom window—many miles south, next to Lake Ontario. For many years, it was the tallest freestanding building in the world. When we bought Kev some high-powered binoculars, he would stare at it for hours. Then he started drawing it; that's when we, and the school, discovered his art talent.

Years later, in Northern High, his art teacher pronounced Kevin as "one of the best in the school," then promptly failed him. Dismayed, I asked why.

"Well, near the end of the term, Kevin didn't hand in any of his work. With nothing to mark, I simply had no choice," the art teacher explained. When I discovered Kev's final art assignments hidden under his bed, I confronted him. "What's this stuff doing under your bed? Why did you hide it?" I demanded—beside myself with annoyance verging on serious anger.

"Because, Mom, I knew you'd make me go to University or College or something, and I just don't want to go, not right now, anyway," he answered. I was incredulous at his story; his burning honesty spoke to me as an arrow searing through my already vulnerable heart.

"Yikes," I countered, "This is how you see me? You shoot yourself in the foot just to avoid what I consider my primary job as a single parent—looking out for your later independence and your best interests in getting there?"

"I guess so, but please don't be so upset. You know I'll probably go—eventually."

This was back in 1986, when Kevin, almost eighteen, had just finished grade twelve. He'd left private school after grade ten, a year after his father died. Having been in the public school system only two years, I think he felt lost, not ready to face the challenge of college or university. Of course, in my own way, I wouldn't give up. We'd been on our own over three years and I'd been saving like mad for his university. I was disappointed, but I had to stand back, remembering my own independence at that same age. I too had disappointed my parents by refusing to go on with university, attending x-ray studies at the Winnipeg General Hospital instead. Obviously, I'd have to let him find his own way.

Around this same time, I discovered Kev's serious interest in, and talent with, music. With no lessons at all, he sat down at Al's electronic organ and started playing jazz riffs and pops by ear. I was surprised—no, shocked. When I'd studied voice at the Toronto conservatory, I'd struggled through the prerequisite piano classes and barely passed. My instrument was my voice, and that's all I was interested in. I quickly realized that Kevin's innate talent came from his paternal grandmother, Alan's mum, who played the piano beautifully by ear, professionally, in Yorkshire, England, for many years before immigrating to Canada. So now, at least, I had a clue as to where Kevin's "surprise" talent came from. After working at odd jobs and menial labor in the real world for a year, Kev decided to go back to school. This time, I quietly encouraged him from a distance, and on his own, he decided he would like to attend the Humber School of Music in Toronto.

"Great!" I said, trying to hide my glee, "but don't you have to audition to get into such a prestigious school?" He found out that he did, and although he was hoping to attend the jazz program he was told that to be accepted he would have to audition with a classical piece. Here, my heart fell.

"So," I asked tentatively, "what are you going to do?"

"Mozart," he answered, without a pause. "I'll do Mozart."

Unable to read music, with just a month left before school started, Kevin proceeded to memorize Mozart's Sonata in C by ear. Walking home from work that summer when we lived in midtown Toronto, nearing the house and hearing him practice, I'd stop to listen in amazed pleasure, marveling at his talent at being able to play Mozart without one piano lesson. Audition day at Humber College came and went. He was accepted, he said—"no problem."

"But didn't they know you couldn't read music?" I, the practical one, persisted.

"Not really," he explained. I propped up the music in front of me; I'd already memorized where to turn the pages in accordance with the music in my head ... that's how I faked it. And remember, it's the jazz program that I'm interested in. I'll learn as I go along." *Ouch,* I thought, laughing to myself; *this apple has fallen very close to this tree.*

"So, Kev, in my mother's words, you *bamboozled* your way in."

"Whatever," he replied, smiling at my mom's old-fashioned word.

No fuss, no bother. That was Kevin during his childhood and early teens. And all through those years, the CN Tower fascinated him. He kept drawing it, comfortable in its familiarity and permanence in what would soon become for him a disrupted world.

∞ ∞ ∞

"Of course I'll take a picture of the Eiffel Tower for you, Kev, and everything else in Gay Pareé too," I'd promised him back in 1971 when I was headed to Europe on that first buying trip. This was the least I could do for the little guy who grew up never asking for much. In retrospect, what I remember best about Kevin, as a young boy, is how good-natured he was around me and everyone else—not needy, not greedy, not perfect either ... but *easy.*

Chapter 15

Designers of the Seventies

You have made known to me the paths of life;
You will fill me with joy in your presence.
— NIV Bible: Acts 2:28

Visiting the Eiffel Tower, Paris 1971

The Paris Connection

France is renowned for its luxury goods including perfumes, expensive accessories and *haute couture* fashion, to name just a few. Today, the name Nina Ricci is still known for all the above. Founded in 1932 by Madame Ricci and her son Robert Ricci, fashion designer Ricci had become, in four decades, a prestigious name in the French luxury goods industry.

Madame Ricci arrived in Paris from Turin as a young girl but she was forty-nine years old when her only son Robert convinced her to set up her own haute couture house. Apparently success was rapid for this remarkable "dress architect." She started working in a building at *20 Rue des Capucines* with about forty seamstresses, but increased her work force tenfold to include 450 more employees by the outbreak of WWII in 1939—such was her couture success.

Wishing to diversify the couture house's operations, in 1946, son Robert Ricci launched his first perfume. Enclosed in a frosted crystal bottle designed and created by Marc Lalique, the bouquet of sweet-smelling flowers was retailed under the name of *Coeur-Joie*. It was so successful that it set Nina Ricci up in a class of its own in the world of creative perfume. Two years later, following this success, Robert Ricci created *L'air du Temps*, a light, memorable fragrance that would eventually become one of French perfumery's great classics. The rest is perfume history.

I remember one of my older sisters spraying on copious amounts of *L'air du Temps* when she was getting ready to go out with one of her many boyfriends. Always curious, I was interested in what went on in the grownup world of sweethearts. Being small and skinny, I didn't create much of a shadow on the stairwell when my sister and her boyfriend turned the lights low and started smooching. All I can say is that although I was only eight years old, I learned plenty about romance and other grown-up stuff from my watch on the darkened back stairs....

For example, when my mother was around forty-one years old, she started putting on weight around her middle. No one paid much attention, but when she took to wearing a baggy smocked top, loose skirt and started walking funny, slow, that's when we three little kids figured out that there was a baby coming. My older sister, Lessia, a university student and my roommate at the time, didn't notice Mum's extended girth. When my brother, Simeon (Joe) showed up on September 6, 1942, we three kids, Yvonne, Daria and I, were hardly surprised. Not so everyone else: Lessia went into temporary shock; my older brother, Leo, wasn't that interested; my big sister Snow was far too busy with work and boyfriends to pay much attention; and Babka seemed rather grouchy about the whole event. "Too much work for your Mama," she told me. As for us, the three little kids, we were excited; we'd made our plans well in advance:

"If it's a girl," I said, "we're going to dress her up in our old baby clothes that we use for our dolls. We're going to curl her beautiful blonde hair, put on Mama's light rosy lipstick and put pink rouge on her cheeks. Then we'll parade her up and down Main Street to show everyone how pretty she is."

"And if it's a boy?" Daria piped up. Pause....

"Well, then we'll do the same thing," I announced. And when Joey came along, that's exactly what we did.

Oh my, how I adored that baby. I changed his diaper and rocked him when he fussed Once, at my wit's end, I snitched a bottle of my sister's French perfume, something about "Air," it was called, sprayed some on Mom's best hanky and waved it in front of his nose to calm him down—it did. Today, I wonder if my brother Joe, an anthropology professor at Brandon University in Manitoba, remembers the smell of Ricci's world famous perfume, "*L'air du Temps.*" I sure do. Aah, the power of a scent to turn back the clock.

∞ ∞ ∞

In 1970, at the age of eighty-seven, Madame Nina Ricci died. It was soon after, on my first buying trip to Paris, that I had a memorable and telling personal experience with Ricci Couture. In 1971, Ricci was showing their couture and *prêt-a-porter* (ready-to-wear) lines in one of the large hotels where the suppliers would group together to accommodate the buyers. I've always appreciated the irony of the following scene because it encapsulates what soon became clear to me: the European fashion business is, in essence, an epic hypocrisy of mythical proportions!

In order to take the fashion world seriously, one must be naturally narcissistic. Following that, it helps if one is addicted to "affectation" or is, at least, willing to feign it. In order to pull the whole affected act off, one requires the innate desire to be seen as on the cutting edge of fashion—often through a conspicuous manner of behavior and dress. These are the prerequisites of fashion success on the part of the designer and consumer alike. Anything less won't do. Being none of the above, I timorously entered Ricci's very crowded hotel room, interpreter at hand, and scanned the crowd.

Okay, I thought, *it's a zoo*: lots of high-powered buyers dressed in the latest, talking, arguing, some in French, all jockeying for an opportunity to tie up a certain design for their retailers' exclusivity. These buyers were usually from large stores like Marshall Fields, and if they bought a minimum number of outfits, were allowed to copy them, stitch for stitch, into mass "knock-off" lines. This was the name of the game. There were only so many styles in a line and if even *one* was deemed as exclusive to Holt's, then you had bagged something big—bragging rights in your ads: "Exclusive to Holt Renfrew in Canada."

After some introductions and murmurings by our interpreter about "how well the Nina Ricci line is doing in the exclusive stores of Holt Renfrew across Canada" (I detected a distinct lack of interest on the part of the Ricci sales rep), I was ushered into a corner and invited to sit down. *Fine I'd love to,* I wanted to say, but without the French to pull it off, I just smiled and turned around to sit—but where ... on the floor? I looked to the interpreter, but she was already engaged in a flurry of dialogue: "*C'est comme cela,*" said the rep with a shrug of his shoulders.

"*C'est sans important,*" said the interpreter, turning to me to explain: It's like this, Mrs. Small. They had no idea they would be this busy. You know the line has been so successful; they've doubled their haute couture sales through the huge success of their *L'air du Temps* perfume, particularly in Japan and the United States. Today, they've run out of space and chairs—we're lucky to get a rep."

"So, what do we do now?" I queried. "You know, I *can* write standing up."

"Oh no, that won't be necessary. Monsieur Duval has suggested that we all step into the *toilette* and work there. What do you think of that?" The idea was so ludicrous I started to laugh.

"Well, if it's good enough for Madame Nina Ricci, it's good enough for me," I said, knowing full well that Nina Ricci had passed on and was long past caring. Having that thought in mind, with much aplomb I plunked myself down onto the bidet, withdrew my Holt's order forms, pulled out my pen and waited. Not knowing where to go, our translator delicately hinged down the toilet seat next to me, sat down, and side by side we watched Monsieur Duval roll in the rack of Ricci ready-to-wear samples.

Whenever I think of the French haute couture collections being shown and the inference of glamour involved in Paris' *pret-a-porter* buying week, I remember that cramped bathroom: myself on the bidet, the interpreter on the toilet, and the rep on the bathtub's edge—a sobering thought that always brings a smile. Offended? Never! For that you'd have to take yourself and the fashion scene seriously. This inauspicious and whimsical beginning prepared me well for the "The Paris Connection" and the harrowing days that followed.

French Foulard

Christian Dior (1905-1957) was the most influential designer of the late 1940s and 1950s, and as such he dominated the fashion world after World War II. The very first Dior collection, shown in February of 1947 was a spectacular success. American journalists christened it the "New Look". The public loved the hourglass silhouette of this voluptuous new look and demand was instantaneous as the New Look became a post-war symbol of "Youth, Hope and the Future." Known all over the world, Dior's label accounted for half of France's haute couture exports. His client list ran from the sultry movie actresses Ava Gardner and Marlene Dietrich to Princess Margaret and the Duchess of Windsor. But the New Look was not reserved for the elite only.

In the post-war era, women were expected to return to passive roles as housewives and mothers, leaving their jobs free for the returning soldiers. The paradigm of post-war womanhood was a capable, caring housewife who created a happy home for her husband and children. "Waspy" waists and full flowered skirts, re-invented from the beautiful flowered fabrics that Dior's mother had worn in the early 1900s, were well-suited to the post war mentality: Dior was right in assuming that people wanted something new after years of war, brutality and hardship, and so he designed for those whom he called the "flower women." I still remember those fashions through my four older sisters who were all talented at sewing and well able

215

to "knock off" any Dior copy by simply purchasing a Vogue pattern from Eaton's basement. Dior's closest rivals were Pierre Balmain and Cristobal Balenciaga, but as the most prestigious couture house, Dior attracted the most talented assistants.

One of these was Pierre Cardin, an Italian-born tailor who was Dior's star assistant in the late 1940s before leaving to begin his own business. Known for his avant-garde style and space-age designs, Cardin was the first couturier to turn to Japan as a high-fashion market when he travelled there in 1959. Another talented assistant of Dior's was Yves Saint Laurent, a gifted Algerian-born designer, who joined Dior in 1955. Saint Laurent flourished in the feminine atmosphere of the couture house and contributed thirty-five outfits to the 1957 autumn collection. When the fittings were finished, Christian Dior took off for a rest cure at his favorite spa in northern Italy hoping to lose weight; unfortunately, ten days later he died of a heart attack after choking on a fishbone. Over two thousand people attended his funeral, including all of his staff and famous clients, led by the Duchess of Windsor. Just two weeks later, the young Yves Saint Laurent, twenty-one years old, was designated as the head designer for the house of Christian Dior. Saint Laurent's first collection, designed in just nine weeks after Dior's death, was a sensation. His 1958 Trapeze line was a great success, but subsequent collections were less well received, particularly his Rive Gauche (Left Bank) collection in 1960, which was severely panned by the critics.

I personally remember this event. It was a confusing time in fashion because of the onrush of social change—the rejection of conventional styles and attitudes that was being advanced by the hippie movement. In this same year, 1960, Saint Laurent was conscripted into the French army to fight in the Algerian war, which allowed the Dior house an opportunity for change: Saint Laurent was subsequently replaced by Marc Bohan as head designer and art director at Dior's. My first experience with the House of Dior was with Marc Bohan, in 1971.

I must admit that I was in awe—maybe because everyone else was, as well. I remember the hushed atmosphere of the Dior salon, which was lavishly furnished with plush armchairs arranged around an octagonal gilt-edged table. Throughout the showing, I detected a general attitude of respect for our H.R. group. Although Holt Renfrew was not large, still it was prestigious enough to hold the exclusive rights for Christian Dior in Canada. Holt's vice-president, Mr. Dixon, always attended these important suppliers, and for once, I felt a rare sense of congeniality between Madame Roxwell and me. Those present spoke in reverent tones, as though in a holy place, and in the fashion world, I guess it was: today Christian Dior is considered the most important and innovative designer of the twentieth century.

Although Marc Bohan's couture work at the House of Dior was successful, his tenure, from 1960 to 1989, was not without upheavals. In 1989, Bohan moved on, and after a brief stint by the Italian designer Gianfranco Ferre, the bold British designer John Galliano took the reins in 1996.

In 1971, when I made my first trip to Paris and the *prêt-a-porter* fashion showings, Givenchy, Yves Saint Laurent, Pierre Cardin and Marc Bohan of Dior's were the most talked-about couturier designers of the day. But there were many other up-and-coming couture stars launching ready-to-wear lines: among them, Hermes, Jean Patou and Jean-Louis Scherrer. It was Scherrer who provided the most titillating experience of my career as a European buyer fashion buyer—one that best exemplifies the frivolity of the fashion world. Because I had no acquaintance with Parisian, much less Quebecois French, the comments and personal asides, diluted through the interpreter, could easily lose their color and humor. Luckily, in this instance, my interpreter had her own sense of humor. It all started with my daughter Joanne's hat—actually her *tam.*

As described earlier, I was given less than a week's notice by Holt Renfrew to prepare for my first overseas buying trip. In between my job, looking after Alan, the kids, and the house, the passport and my final philosophy paper due at York University, the last thing on my mind was my wardrobe. On a Friday, a few days before leaving, I hiked myself down to Ports International on King Street, where Luke Tanabee, the founder, outfitted me at the wholesale price for the trip. Personally, I thought we did very well. I picked out some sports pants, coordinated blouses, a classic blazer and a couple of dresses, one wrap-around in navy jersey and another in cotton twill—this last, a sample in khaki, was fashioned after the women's uniforms of the Israeli army. Casual, yet trendy, I figured this dress would travel well, but I felt it needed something to complete the look—the right scarf or hat would do—but alas, there was no time.

The night before I was to leave, while in my pajamas packing, I spied Joanne's Brownie tam tossed outside her door (she was *so* untidy); in a hurry, I picked it up, stuck it on my head and kept on packing. Soon after, Al came upstairs, saw me, and started laughing: "So tell me, is this the best outfit you can come up with for your fancy trip to Paris? Do you think Holt Renfrew will approve? At least take your beige PJ's to color coordinate with Jo's tam."

"Too funny," I muttered, "but thanks for a great idea." I searched the closet for my new Israeli army dress, I quickly put it on, adjusted Jo's tam to a stylish tilt, slipped into my new leather walking shoes and after a quick dab of lipstick, stepped out in a model's stance, one arm raised high. *Tar-ah!* I sang out for attention to Al. "So tell me; how do I look?"

"Only great," Al replied. "Of course, anything suits a good-looking girl. They'll love it!"

Leave Your Tam On

In 1962, designer Jean-Louis Scherrer created his Couture House of Fashion after his own name. By 1971, after a successful decade in couture, he launched his new ready-to-wear line; we were advised by our Paris buying office to view it: "Scherrer is great to work with and he is building up an important look. You must see it," stated our senior interpreter—my favorite. She was a lot of fun (how we'd laughed over the Ricci fiasco!) and I was happy she would be coming along.

As soon as we entered the well-appointed suite of Jean-Louis Scherrer, we were greeted by a tall, slim man, probably in his late forties, with dark brown hair flecked with silver. Smiling radiantly, Jean-Louise reached out his hand in a warm greeting, then turned to our interpreter with an impish smile and made some comment about me that I didn't understand—except the part about "*le chapeau est très jolie.*" I smiled and thanked him in broken French, then turned to the interpreter to explain: "You know this is my daughter's Brownie tam." Seeing her quizzical look, I explained: "She's eleven years old, and in Canada, Brownies are the precursor to Girl Guides; I wanted to finish off the look of my army dress, and I thought this worked."

"Apparently it *does* work. Monsieur Scherrer loves the tam, and it seems he would like to examine it," she added, with a smile.

"You're serious? This tam cost three dollars..."

"But he thinks you and the tam are *très chic*."

"Hmm ... Well, who am I to argue with a Paris haute couture designer?" With that I ripped off the tam, and smiling broadly, handed it over. When Monsieur Scherrer turned it inside out to look at the label, I could not contain my laughter.

"Tell him the history of the tam," I said to the interpreter, "he'll probably love it," and he did—but not Madame Roxwell. Apparently she reported the incident to Mr. Dixon, who reported it to the president, Mr. Samson, who called my manger, Mr. Boyd, in Toronto. Three weeks later, by the time I returned home, the story of my daughter's tam had been repeated and embellished to a frivolous point of no return. In Madame Roxwell's words it started out as "a shabby Brownie tam" (it was *new*) which was an embarrassment to the firm; from there it became "so innovative and stylish as to start a new trend," and then the story finished off in a flurry of superlatives to a place where I was practically invited "to design *les chapeaux* for the Scherrer House of Fashion." I must admit that this last over-the-top comment came from my dear friend Wade in the display department. So much for fashion's façade, the obsession with external appearances and the need to buy into it! I was bewildered, baffled and bemused. Here's my "très chic" three-dollar tam creating a fashion stir, and instead of seeing the humor of it all I am reported for "not dressing the part!" So, what do I have to say about fashion's fake façade?

"Only that it is *très malade*," very sick, for sure.

∞ ∞ ∞

I was homesick those last days in Paris, away from home almost two weeks, but I would never have been unprofessional enough to admit it. After the initial hubbub in Italy I was receiving fewer late-night phone calls, but soon I was feeling lonely—out of the family loop and feeling guilty for not being "the perfect wife at home".

Barring my guilt, I was annoyed with the idea of being queried about the calls. At breakfast I was often asked by Mr. Dixon how I slept, and, "Were there any disruptive calls?" I usually ignored the last question, smiling politely in response.

"No, no, I'm quite fine," I'd say, filing my annoyance into my "later" folder—which nestles very close to my migraine folder. As far as management was concerned, it seems that the telephone episodes in Italy had been filed in their hefty "for further discussion" folder, as was the "dressing the part" episode. By now I wasn't as upset with Alan's calls as I was with the involvement of my counterpart, "the undercover agent," Madame R. It seems she just didn't like me and wanted me out.

In contrast, I must admit that Mr. Dixon was trying to be pleasant by way of suggesting to Madame Roxwell to, "take a few hours off tomorrow, our final day in Paris, for a spot of sight-seeing for Mrs. Small's benefit." *The offer was gracious*, I thought. *But how does one see Paris in three hours? One doesn't.*

The Notre-Dame Nod

On an unseasonably warm Saturday in April, after a rushed morning's work, we headed out by cab to see the sights. Needless to say, Madame R. was bored to tears—she'd obviously put in her three-hour tour many years earlier, but I was determined to enjoy myself.

We headed east from our hotel, along the River Seine towards Notre-Dame, one of the three great Paris symbols—the other two, of course, the Eiffel Tower and the *Arc de Triomphe*. I was excited to be driving along the River Seine; I wanted to browse in the myriad stalls and shops that lined the busy *Quai des Tuileries* and when I mentioned this to Mrs. R., I got the usual response. "Oh no, my dear, there's not enough time," she emphatically declared.

The cab was hot, and since there was no air conditioning, one of the few useless phrases I'd retained from high school French came to mind: "Pardon Monsieur," I said from the back seat, while tapping the driver lightly on the shoulder. *"Ouvrez la fenêtre, si'l vous plait."* No response. I repeated my simple phrase—still nothing. At the next light, the cabbie turned to me, apologized in French and followed with, "Just what language *do* you speak?" in well-pronounced English.

So much for my inept French delivered with a Canadian accent, in Paris, France. I should have been embarrassed, but I was not. I was too happy to be bothered. *Yes! At last, I will get to see Notre-Dame*, I thought, as I gulped in the river's cool air from my open *fenêtre*.

"Notre-Dame: The Cathedral of Paris, completed 1345, is one of civilization's greatest edifices; this is more than a building—it's like a book written in stone and wood and glass. It can be read line by line, the Virgin's Portal alone telling four different picture stories." I'd read this in a travel guide while flying over the big pond. And earlier, on this last morning in Paris, I'd read more. It seems that the beautiful picture doors of Notre-Dame did, in fact, take the place of religious texts during the middle ages when very few of the faithful were literate.

"We're almost there," said the driver, interrupting my thoughts. "Where do you want me to park?" But, before I could answer, Madame Roxwell piped up:

"Oh no, we're not parking. Mrs. Small just wants to see it on a drive-by; right?"

"Absolutely wrong," I answered, in something close to a snarl.

"But," Mrs. R. persisted: "you know it's getting late, and by the time we get back to the hotel to get dressed for dinner it will be after five."

Too bad, I thought, as I called out loudly to the cabbie. "Stop the car! I'm going in." Enmeshed within heavy Saturday traffic, the taxi was moving very slowly. By now extremely impatient, I jumped out before it came to a full stop, crossed over to the Cathedral doors and stepped inside. The travel guide was right. Notre-Dame is indeed a "joyous church." As soon as I entered, I felt a peaceful pleasure at the aroma of incense—a comforting legacy of my childhood.

I've since seen many cathedrals larger, but the altitude of the ceiling at Notre-Dame has a transcending loftiness that makes it seem absolutely immense. I stood at the main entrance adjusting my eyes to the candle-lit interior with my neck craned up toward the ceiling, and there my gaze held fast, transfixed by a mass of smiling devils and gargoyles grinning down. This could have been a macabre scene, but instead it jolted me back to reality, as a silly rhyme emerged:

"See Notre-Dame without delay, the gleeful gargoyles seemed to say;

"Be quick about it; if you dally, you're going to score a higher tally."

That's right, chided Sinc. *Your concern with Mrs. R's impatience is ruining your day—with bad poetry, no less. Get moving!* Whoa … Sinc, my critic, is back; and as usual, he's right.

Glancing through the extended centre aisle to the main altar I could see many people crowded around the front, some standing, some sitting. *Something's going on,* I thought, *and my curious self wants to know.* As I started down the right perimeter aisle, I heard a high-volume church bell chime five. *Is this the famous sixteen-ton bell that hangs in the South tower? Oh-oh, if it's already five o'clock, the gargoyles (and Sinc) are right. I'm heading for big trouble with my boss-lady Mrs. R.* But I couldn't pull myself away from the magnificent rose window to my left, on the west facade. *Is this the one that I've been reading about?* I wondered.

I was looking up at the window, searching the right angle to see the famous rose halo meant to be hovering over the head of the Virgin Mary, when I felt something hard bang against my knee. *Ouch, that hurt. There'll be a bruise for sure,* I thought as I felt the pain, followed by a loud metallic thud and the clatter of something rolling—sounding like metal against terrazzo. Looking down, I saw what I had bumped into: to my horror, one of those tall standing ashtrays of weighted metal had fallen over and was rolling fast towards a wedding party in full gear. At the altar, the bride, resplendent in creamy silk with her face demurely veiled, was clinging to her groom who, distracted from his vows by the crash, had stopped and turned in alarm, as did the other members of the wedding. Now, en masse, wedding guests were all staring at me in unified disbelief. Gasping in shame, thoroughly embarrassed, I looked over to assess the damage just in time to see the "holy roller" come to rest against the carpeted stairs leading up to the altar. Breathing a sigh of relief, I turned and fled.

Unfortunately, Madame Roxwell was standing at the front door watching. Concerned about the time, she had come looking for me, she explained. For all I knew, she could have seen the entire catastrophic incident in full play. I didn't know and was not about to ask, but I guessed that my hefty "for further discussion" file just got heftier.

Zurich Zeitgeist

Next on our itinerary was Zurich, Switzerland. I remember very little about my experiences there, except that my hotel room was inordinately small. Beside the narrow bed done up with a pristine white coverlet and eyelet lace pillows, stood a tall walnut dresser that faced a small window looking directly onto a stone courtyard. In the mirror, a tidy oblong of early purple hyacinths bloomed. They appeared to be in the room, but no, they were but a reflection in the mirror facing the courtyard; although they weren't real, still, their cheery image provided a welcome relief to that otherwise colorless room. Aside from the parson's chair, there were no other furnishings—no side table, no desk. Because of the minimalist mentality and dour decor of the tiny room, I had nowhere to write up my orders. In the end, I placed my hard-backed suitcase on the bed, propped it up against the raised footboard, and dragged over the one and only chair to create a pseudo writing desk—one that had to be disassembled each night before going to sleep.

The bathroom, in staid European fashion, boasted an obligatory bidet leaving no room for a bathtub. Consequently a narrow plastic tube of a shower was chiseled into one corner beside a tiny pedestal sink which disallowed any makeup or medical storage. Here I created a shelf by placing my small case on top of the bidet, temporarily denying access to that out-of-date accoutrement rarely found in bathrooms across North America—no great loss.

Aside from the problems created by a miniscule hotel room, I recall the stressful experience of being exposed to three official federal languages: German was spoken by 64 percent of the population, French by 19 percent and Italian by 8 percent, all in the same country and often spoken at the same time. The balance of 9 percent was made up of multi-linguists proficient in all three, or, as in my case, one—English. Swiss German itself has many different dialects, so that any time I dared try my high school German, with a simple *Guten Tag* (Good Day), I could easily be responded to in Swiss German: *Gruezi* (Hello). Or, if I relied on a chirpy Italian *Buongiorno*

(Good Morning), I could be responded to in a basic French *Bonjour*, and so on. After a day or so I got so lost in the minutiae of trying to understand three languages that I called upon our interpreter, who could switch tongues on the pause of a comma and intersperse English in-between. It was truly fascinating to hear her speedy dialect change and see the appropriate body language appear at the same time.

Aside from the language challenges, I was fascinated with the cultural habits and application of Swiss niceties—to ignore them could cause offence. We were advised to always shake hands when being introduced to a Swiss and again when leaving. That was easy for me, because I tend to do that anyway. Formal titles should be used when addressing each other, *Herr* for men and *Frau* for women; and it is customary to greet shopkeepers when entering their domain.

Foreign writers and artists had visited and settled in Zurich, drawn in by the beauty and tranquility of the Swiss landscape, the mountains and lakes, but I do not recall that we were treated to any such memorable vistas. I can only deduce that there was no time *at all* set aside for relaxation, or perhaps I suffer from a lacuna due to some other concerns—the return of the migraine headache and a corresponding fatigue in this, the third week of my European sojourn. I also recall that I had the extra burden of buying dresses, suits *and* coats for Holt's, because I was responsible for all three departments in Ontario and across Western Canada. In retrospect, this was quite a challenge for a rookie European buyer. What I *do* remember are the impressions and details of a particular showing that took place in a large country manor house—a chateau. Although the name of the designer and her firm elude me now, the details of that afternoon remain colorfully clear.

We arrived for the late afternoon showing close to teatime. Everyone was friendly; Madame Roxwell and Mr. Dixon had been long associated with this particular designer, and, as a result, we were given extra attention throughout our time there. Together with thirty other clients, we were seated on claret velvet sofas and chairs placed around a mini catwalk that stretched through a crowded parlor—grand in decor but not particularly spacious. This crowded atmosphere added to the relaxed intimacy. The models, who were very tall, blonde and quite beautiful, mostly of Italian Swiss descent, stepped out from behind a maroon velvet curtain, paused, then turned slowly while the designer explained the fabrication, styling and selling potential of the gowns being modeled. Questions were asked by the buyers and answered in an informal way by the personable designer—a petite woman, mature and attractive in the French style, with brunette well-coiffed hair and meticulous makeup. Wearing a white basket-weave suit trimmed in navy, à la Chanel (her own design), she appeared very relaxed as she conversed and joked with the buyers assembled. This designer, who specialized in gowns and mother-of-the-bride costumes, was world-renowned for her formal wear but what I remember best about her showing in Zurich was the display of Swiss conviviality and hospitality.

After the applause subsided, we were treated to our choice of gourmet tea, followed by an arresting display of pastries that were wheeled out and offered on multi-colored crystal plates. Our energy flagging, the petite designer pastries, based on the fashion colors of the season and copiously swirled with dark and white Swiss chocolate, were definitely the hit of the show.

"Now, Mr. Dixon, these pastries are what I call a *real* fashion statement," I announced. And with this he smiled in agreement as we reached for another—both basking in Zurich's *zeitgeist* and our own agreeable mood.

The above reverie is as fresh today as the day it was born. For over three decades it has been laying low, holding on to its coveted place in my crowded memory, knowing its value—a precious cameo to be retrieved and enjoyed at will. A simple scene on a sunny afternoon in Zurich leaps out of hiding after half a lifetime and triggers the notion that it needs to be written, needs to be heard. Like fine wine, it has a covenant with the past to be enjoyed in the future, a future that is now—as glistening pastries, lined up in perfect rows, colorful as glass beads gleaming in the sun, are wheeled out and offered as a sweet reward in foraging memories.

Chapter 16

London Levity

The life of the soul, as the structure of dreams reveals,
is a continual going over and over of the material of life.
— Thomas Moore, *Care Of the Soul*

The Joust, London, 1971

A Royal Reverie—Rich in Detail

Finally, *English* spoken: in the streets, in the cabs, in the restaurants and in the designer showrooms—what a relief! I'd never appreciated how insecure I felt on my initial trip to Europe until I got to London, England. Just flying into Heathrow, I could feel my blood pressure drop. Impossible, claim the doctors, but I've done my own research. As a victim of high blood pressure for many years, I've learned a little about my own body. Whenever I feel so edgy and nervous that I would gladly exit my skin, my blood pressure heads north while my body temperature dives south. In other words, I feel cold then hot, shaky, wildly hyper and light-headed—and then the headache starts. Ever since that wonderful "awakening" in my Paris hotel room when I was gifted with a spiritual ascension, I'd been feeling better—healthier. Now, on the last leg of my journey, I was looking for something more than relief—what I wanted was *joy*.

Show me the magic, I prayed silently. *When Alan comes to London, let us see, feel and touch our joy again.*

After arriving at Heathrow airport from Zurich, our group was whisked by limousine to Claridge's Hotel—the Mecca for world personages from Saudi Arabia, Singapore, England and America—where celebrities, in their own right, or merely "the filthy rich," have stayed for the past century. Founded in the 1800s, Claridge's is legend with one of the world's classiest guest lists. The friendly liveried staff is never condescending, and all of the rooms are luxurious—even those classed as standard. Today, Claridge's is considered an art-deco masterpiece, but I didn't understand that at the time. Why would I? I'd never stayed in a hotel that charged well over £95 a night, in 1971, the equivalent of $250 CDN—equal to my weekly salary at Holt Renfrew's! Today, almost forty years later, in high season, that same standard room at Claridge's starts at $950 CDN per night. Founded in 1812 and situated in London's grand borough of Mayfair, Claridge's emerged into the city's social scene in 1898. In a recent 45 million dollar renovation, Victorian and art-deco furnishings reminiscent of that period have been invested in and maintained in an effort to preserve the hotel's original charm and comfort. But even back in the1970s there was plenty of comfort and copious charm. I remember my room well.

Although it was probably classed as standard, my room was truly sizable compared to my stringent hotel room in Zurich. It was never explained to me why I had been allotted that sparsely furnished room, nor did I dare ask about it. I was still smarting from my Notre-Dame debacle, which of course had been fully reported by Madame R., so I thought it best to lie low. Claridge's, with its nineteenth century opulence, more than made up for my previous discontent.

Claridge's signature color in 1971 was hot pink. According to legend it was once dubbed "whorehouse pink" by an un-named dignitary. My room, while painted a subtler shade of rose, certainly picked up the hot pink motif in its velvet cushions, satin quilted coverlet, as well as the towels in the spacious en suite marble bathroom. Of special interest to me was the secretary-styled mahogany desk surfaced in leather accompanied by a comfortable-looking Regency chair. What a step up from my makeshift work table in Zurich! Thinking of how I had to hoist my large suitcase onto the bed every night to write up my orders still irritated me. But in Claridge's, sitting at their spacious desk in a beautifully upholstered chair of wine-and gold-striped sateen, writing out orders all night might finally become a tolerable task.

As pleasing as the room was, what I remember most about Claridge's is the combination of well-being and elegance that enveloped me while floating down one of the two grandly curved staircases leading into the main lobby. On my way to meet some friends for dinner, I felt that I looked quite smart in my Ellen Tracy creamy-silk shantung dress and tan snakeskin pumps; and, in keeping with the mood, I clearly recall the Frank Sinatra song, "The World We Knew," that the Muzac was playing during my descent.

Claridge's magnificent lobby is governed by two grandiose staircases that dominate the vast hall from every viewpoint. Descending from either side of four massive copper Art Deco pillars, they form an integral part of the central hall's design. Starting at the foyer, the Great Hall sweeps through a vast waiting room replete with a grand piano then continues to a spacious dining area decorated in rosy hues to finish with an intimate café-bar situated near the hotel's back entrance—a late-night hot spot for the younger socialites prominent in London's society. In the early seventies, this informal café, noted for its petite round tables with hot-pink cloths and matching napkins, was famous for its traditional English tea.

The ritual of "Tea at Claridge's," or anywhere else in Mayfair, is something that every traveler to England should experience at least once. Usually served between three and five PM, this is not just a quick "cuppa"; no, this high-cholesterol repast starts off with a generous variety of delicate crust less sandwiches, featuring wafer thin cucumbers, presented with a huge pot of tea (Fortnum's, I wager) served on the best English china. This delightful array, wheeled out on a floral-bedecked tea table is left for the patron's indulgence, after the first cup of tea is ceremoniously poured by a courteous waiter. After a suitable time has passed, scones, resplendent with golden clotted cream and a side of glistening strawberry jam are presented (wait, there's more!) accompanied by assorted cream cakes and *petit fours*, all to be washed down with innumerable cups of tea. Today, this sumptuous repast will set one back at least £35 ($70 CDN), an ultimate extravagance, but a luxurious experience well worth the price!

London Liberties

Up to this point, my experience in London had been perfect. I was excited and joyful to be in England—no need of an interpreter, free to express myself again. And that's exactly what I did when I floated down those grandiose stairs, danced my way through the Great Hall, the palatial foyer and out the front door of Claridge's on my first night in London.

It was time to go out on the town with my new friend, Vicky Wheeler, whom I'd just met in Florence—a buyer with the Bay in Montreal. We'd found each other while we were peering out of windows facing each other over the piazza of our hotel in Firenze, Italy. At that time Vicky's home was in Montreal where she lived with her husband Michael and her two young children, but she was English born, I could tell from her first greeting. Good-looking, with sparkling grey eyes, she was wearing a pink felt hat, tilted in a jaunty way that invited comment. When I mentioned her "great hat" she'd smiled broadly.

"I know," she said. "I like it too—it makes me feel ... chic, if you know what I mean."

"Yes, I know exactly what you mean," I said, relating the first part of my *chapeau* story about my daughter Joanne's three-dollar Brownie tam and how great it looked with my Israeli army dress. By now we were both laughing, and since we seemed to be having such a good time, we agreed to continue our repartee over a glass of wine—in Italy, a "go" at any time of the day. After that, we saw each other at the Firenze shows and once for dinner in Paris, where we'd planned this liaison. Now in London, we'd been invited out for dinner by mutual friends who were two sales reps from one of the bigger suppliers in Montreal.

"Okay," I said, "but let's not discuss business as usual. Let's go out somewhere special, where we can dance; somewhere I can forget my worries about Madame R., Mr. D. and all of the trouble I'm going to be in when I get home."

Yes, that's what I *said*. But what I *thought*, was, when I get back to Toronto the powers that be will call me up on the carpet for sure, and then I'll have to explain again about the late-night phone calls, and how Alan doesn't take well to my being away. Not that they'll care— why should they? This is business. And that's just *one* of the problems. What went on between Al and Mr. Boyd, or worse, Al and Mr. Samson, the president of Holt Renfrew, is another worry. Apparently they think that Al is interfering with my job. As well, there's the so-called "conflict of interest"—the small shop on Markham Street that Al set up with Ken Vernon, a longtime friend and fashion-rep. Whatever was said, I hope Al behaved and didn't lose his rag ... that's all I need.

And how will I explain to Al that I'm *not* ready to throw in the towel on this career too? Anyway, why *can't* a woman be more like a man and have it all ... a husband, family, baby and a career, even if it does, at times, take her away from home? Why should a woman have to fight so hard for something that men take for granted? When a man has to be away on business, it's readily accepted as being noble because it's "for the family." But just let a woman of the early 1970's leave home, hearth, and husband on a business trip in trying to strengthen her career, and no one is impressed. More than that, they disapprove—they don't *say* it outright but they *think* it:

"Well, what *does* your husband think of you being away for a whole month? On one hand he must be quite proud of your success, but on the other, doesn't he miss you? Who looks after the children, cooks the meals, washes the clothes, prepares Kevin for bed at night and in the morning makes sure Joanne goes to school and doesn't get into trouble. After all, she's almost twelve, isn't she?"

Okay, Sinc pipes up; *enough with the thinking. Start dressing, or you'll be late!*

A Moment Sublime

While enjoying myself in the luxury of my hotel room in Claridge's, trying to pick out just the right outfit for my dinner "date," I couldn't stop worrying and thinking, so I turned on the radio for distraction. Nat King Cole was pouring out his velvety voice with his current hit, "Unforgettable." I stopped to listen and as the familiar words struck home, I started thinking again: *What am I doing here, alone in a hotel room in London, England, so far away from the people I love?*

All my life I've found myself buried in my own situational conflicts. All kinds of lofty thoughts clutter my head as I search for the sublime, the ideal, in a combination of moral, intellectual and spiritual worth, just to find that there is no reprieve for human folly— mine or anyone else's. Human consciousness knows *intellectually* that life on earth must end in death, but how does the psyche, the pragmatic self, face the truth of life's impermanence? It's like some irrevocable fever, this searching—for what? What is it I am looking for? Here Sinc interrupts my thoughts again.

It's all of the above. Have faith and pray—you can certainly do that. Just stop thinking so much. Right now, you can't solve anything by thinking. You are a doer. Soon Al will be in town, and then you can sit down and have a nice heart to heart talk about the "sublime." After that, find out what really happened between him and Holt's in Toronto, but for now, have a little fun. You deserve it! Your friends are downstairs. Go!

I went.

∞ ∞ ∞

"Okay," I said to Vicky and our two supplier friends who were waiting in the lobby. "I want to forget my worries. We're in London! Let's go! Let's have some fun!" And off we headed to the Savoy Hotel, where we drank multiple vodka tonics and danced; then we drank red wine and danced. Following that, we enjoyed a delightful rosemary lamb and goat-cheese salad with more red wine; the men had grilled tuna, crab beignet with saffron sauce and white wine. Following this sumptuous, calorie-laden meal we danced—again and again. And in between the dancing and the drinking, we flirted, self-consciously, as seriously married people are wont to do. It was almost midnight when we arrived back at Claridge's. There was no one in the lobby. The regular quartet had disbanded but the Muzak was playing that same song that Frank Sinatra was singing when I first floated down those regal stairs earlier that evening, "Over and over..."

Through the hazy outlook of too much wine, Claridge's Great Hall transformed into a sixties ballroom. Everything in that vast room, including the walls, moved in a slow dance entwined with Sinatra's voice, and without hesitation my body took up the rhythm. Hips swaying, I turned to my dinner companion with arms outstretched and without a word he stepped in. We danced; bodies locked, thighs touching, hips in perfect rhythm, our feet barely moving. With my eyes closed I entreated time to stand still, to allow me these sublime moments in the sweet ecstasy of wanting—what? A feeling of being young again: guiltless, filled with innocent desire and the object of a longing in return. The music stopped.

With my focus blurred in the moment, I stepped back, orienting myself to the light of my reality and my primal yearning. The others watched as we hugged our goodbyes, lips brushing, both wanting to kiss—but of course we dare not. We didn't see each other for a long time after, and I've always assumed that the sublime midnight moment in Claridge's had passed into oblivion but apparently not, for here it is now, still imbued with its original longing and passion.

So, through a plaintive song, a past memory bursts into consciousness; a moment of human connectedness is recorded in a reverie of emotional truth. Clinging together through body language and music, two human beings are caught up in a momentary desire, a yearning triggered by loneliness and longing—today, as sweet and alive as ever ... reverie's timeless gift.

The Joust

Two days before our buying trip was officially over, Alan arrived in London. It was great feeling his cuddly bear hug again, a place where I'd always felt safe and at home. We'd been together almost seven years and never apart for any length of time and I realized that if the proverbial seven-year itch were to be scratched, it would probably be sooner rather than later.

Stop! Sinc interjected. *Don't think about that now. You came close, but nothing happened. You'd better hope that Alan had the same good sense in your absence. Don't forget how many attractive single women are hanging around the golf club.*

Okay, okay, I thought. *Just don't go on about it. I'm happy that he's here now and we have this time together.*

"So, what do you want to do tonight?" I asked Al on our way to the hotel from Heathrow. When I'd met him at the airport I could tell by his uneven gait that he'd had too many mini-bottles of vodka on the plane, but I wasn't concerned; he doesn't like flying, so I was half expecting him to be off-kilter when he arrived. He was. I carried on.

"This morning the bell captain gave me a pamphlet about a club here in London that features a unique roast beef dinner; it's served in bite sized morsels that you are supposed to eat with your hands while watching a 'joust.' Apparently the male waiters are dressed as knights, as in the 1400s, and the women waitresses, who look especially buxom in the pamphlet, walk about with pitchers of foaming beer, pouring out glasses while they themselves are spilling out of their laced bodices—you know, the kind of stuff you see in the movies."

"Okay, the last part sounds like fun, but where is this "joust" and what the heck is it anyway?"

"Well," I explained, while rifling through my bag to find the pamphlet; "it seems that a joust is a battle between two mounted knights using lances, like a spear—a long wooden shaft with a sharp metal head that is blunted to prevent serious damage. Anyway, jousts are sometimes called 'tilting matches,' which means there is a competition in which one knight tries to knock the other off his horse." I'd finally found the pamphlet, but we were already getting out of the cab and heading up to the room, so I tucked it back into my travel bag, next to my postcard of the *original* David, Michelangelo's masterpiece I'd missed seeing in Florence. (I did, however, manage to catch a fleeting glimpse of the *faux* David, looming left, outside of the Pitti Palace on our way into the fashion show. He is very impressive, over seventeen feet tall on a high marble stand that adds five feet; I promised myself that on my next trip to Florence, if there *is* one, I will see the authentic David at his home in the *Accademia*.)

Now at our hotel room, after fussing with the bell-boy, over-tipping of course, Al looked around the room. Giving a low whistle; I could tell he was impressed.

"Whoa, this place looks too expensive for a 'young lad from Yorkshire,'" he said, while flopping onto the hot-pink satin quilt. "Wait a mo', what's with this color? You know what this looks like?"

"Yes, I do, and so does the hotel; it's their signature color, hot pink. As I said earlier, my travel guide calls it 'whore house pink.' Anyway, it's part of the 1930s art-deco renovation. That same book also states: 'Perhaps Spencer Tracy said it best when he remarked, that when he died he wanted to go, not to heaven, but to Claridge's.' Do you think he was referring to our quilt?"

"Well, let's hope that Claridge's *and* the quilt live up to their name," Al muttered, already half asleep. Meanwhile I kept reading the pamphlet aloud: "Okay, it says here: 'a joust is a type of war game which was popular in the middle-ages.' It also says: 'This is only one way to win. The other way to gain points is by breaking the end of your lance on an opponent's shield.'"

This was too much for Al. He came to, and started cackling.

"My God, I'd certainly like to break the end of my lance on your shield," he spurted out gleefully, reaching for another swig of beer before sinking back into bed. Now *I* started laughing. As rude as his comment was, Al could always make me laugh, and I smiled to myself as I snuggled down beside him, trying to ignore his fitful snoring which had already started up. Burrowing myself spoon style against his body, I realize how much I have missed this familiar, comfortable position, a marital intimacy that takes years to build up and one pulsation of a lonely heart to break down. In some cases just the *idea* of an indiscretion can breed contempt of the familiar—and how close I came.

Shame on you, Sinc chided; *so stupid to endanger the love of your life. Just look at him sleeping in innocence. Why would you compromise your connubial bliss, your state of satisfaction with a stranger—an unknown.*

Because, Sinc, I wanted to retort, you know as well as I that the "connubial bliss" is remiss, derelict, delinquent—lax; but it was too late. I was already drifting towards sleep ... and *the* dream.

A Future Appointment

I've been here before. In this dream, I find myself embedded in fear while standing before a bounded space that fans out into infinity—emptiness. In front of this endless expanse stands a low black wall; I am walking quickly towards it. I find myself thinking that I can climb over this wall, but somewhere, behind the dream, I know I cannot. Yet I keep walking forward in spite of a palpitating fear. Although I see the desolation surrounding the wall, the nothingness in front and behind it, still, something keeps pulling me forward. Forcibly drawn, I walk faster, but the closer I get, the further the wall appears. First jogging, then breaking into full speed I run towards it, but the wall keeps sliding away. Then suddenly it stops. So do I.

I can see something moving behind the wall, a transient shadow that stretches into a tall human shape. Fully robed, hooded and faceless, the shape darts about, transforming itself, so that here it is a black-robed elf, and then a shadowed giant playing a saxophone in front of an orange firewall; slithering low, it becomes a crouching centaur, hissing as it tries to crawl over the wall. I watch, grounded—anchored in fear. Opening my mouth wide, I issue a piercing scream in a laborious attempt to break out of the dream, but no sound comes. Voiceless, I sink back in despair and watch the centaur mutate back into human form.

Huge, black-hooded and faceless, the android turns toward me. With one hand raised high, its forefinger crooked, it beckons, urging me to come forward. Under its spell, unable to resist, I try to walk, but my legs and feet are dead to my will. Powerless, unable to move, I perceive a sliver of light shining through a weakness in this dream's intent. Obedient to its urge, I will myself awake; at the same time, I know this dream sequence isn't over. I know I'll return to this dream's future, but for now we both need a break. I know all of this—even as I wake up.

∞ ∞ ∞

Startled by Big Ben as it loudly strikes eight, I am surprised to see my hotel room bathed in darkness. The next surprise comes when I find Al's robust frame sprawled obliquely beside me, deeply ensconced in sleep. Shaking off my nightmare, I lean over and gently touch his shoulder.

"Hey, we're supposed to be at the joust by eight," I remind him as I slide out of bed and head for the bathroom. Turning the cold water tap high, I douse my face, trying to drown out the remnants of my dream. It helps. When Al appears in the doorway, eyes blinking in the strong bathroom light, hair tousled from sleep, the reality of his presence helps push my depression aside. Sliding past him with a quick hug, I search the closet trying to find something appropriate to wear. *What does one wear to a joust,* I muse; *a costume, maybe? I suppose the brochure talks about it, but, no matter, the best I can come up with is my paisley gypsy skirt, white silk blouse and multi-colored sandals. Kick them high!* I think, smiling to myself as I head back to the bathroom, makeup in tow. On my way through, I see Al slumped in the rose velvet armchair, finishing a beer.

"I'm not sure when we'll eat, but I'll read the brochure in the cab, okay? Boy, you look so tired. Maybe we shouldn't go."

"I'm fine," he mumbles, finishing off his beer as he struggles to his feet. "Okay, what'll I wear?" he asks, looking to me for guidance, as usual.

"I dunno; what did you bring?" Just then, one of my favorite songs, "Seems like Old Times" came on the radio: *Oh my, I love this tune, and the words are so timely,* I thought. Nostalgically, I turn to Al.

"C'mon, big guy, let's dance."

"Okay" Al says, giving me a bear hug after a couple of turns. "We'd better go, or we'll be too late for dinner, never mind the joust. Although I'd love to embark on a personal joust with you right now, I'm too hungry to start up. It'll have to wait 'till we get back. By the way, do we *really* have to eat with our hands?"

"I don't know, but scrub them anyway. And remember, the pamphlet says, 'the tournaments were meant to be a display of honor for a lady,' so please don't behave in an un-chivalrous way tonight. Okay?" I said this as I watched Al pour himself a healthy shot of vodka followed by a spurt of tonic. I knew that he knew exactly what my admonition meant, but I think he was already too far in his cups to care.

Just don't lose your cool, Sinc warns me. *You two have been apart for almost a month, so don't be impatient with him. He seems nervous about something, and that's why he's drinking so much. Okay? Better find out what's bothering him.*

Well, although chivalry was not dead in the show that night, as the formal joust progressed, my knight in tarnished armor drank to the point where he and his chivalry became grievously ill. In spite of Al's laughing and joking, using booze as his handmaiden of humor while buying drinks for everyone at our table, I could tell he was working hard at having a good time. It had been a long day for him and a long night for me. By now I was too tired to enjoy the show or the ribald humor. Ready to leave, I nudged Al,

"C'mon, sweetie, I'll race you to the bed. The last one there loses the joust *and* the lady. Okay? Let's go." In a way I felt badly pushing him to leave, but I had to be up early the next morning for our second-to-last breakfast meeting with Madame R. and Mr. Dixon. Also, I could feel a migraine coming on. By the time our cab pulled out of the restaurant's parking lot, Al was asleep with his head on my shoulder, snoring softly. Later, snuggled under our satin comforter, I breathed a sigh of relief. The first day was over. "Okay," I murmured to myself as well as to Al. "Tomorrow's another day; then we'll play."

"Okay," Al muttered, as he settled in under the whore-pink quilt.

The next morning, groggily late for the breakfast meeting, the small circular tables appeared as giant powder puffs, too pink and perky for this early hour, but at least the silly image forced my smile towards the others who were obviously annoyed at my tardiness. *Why are old people always early and young people always late?* I mused, as I slid under the tiny table's hot-pink skirt.

"Good morning, my dear. And how is Alan. He arrived safely, I hope?" Mr. Dixon graciously asked, as Madame Roxwell produced a wan smile in her best version of friendliness.

"Thank you, he's fine; resting ... jet lag and all."

"Well, that's good. We're almost done here in London. After breakfast, we'll go to our last appointment; it's with Mary Farrin Knits, then you'll be on your own for the next few days. Have a good time with Alan, try to relax and see some sights. We'll look for you in Toronto next week, the second day after you return home, which should be Friday. How does that sound?" It sounded ominous. *Why was Mr. Dixon coming to Toronto*, I wondered, *and why did Madame R. finally decide to be nice? Okay*, I thought. *As soon as I finish working the Farrin line, I'll meet Al for lunch and ask him what really took place between him and Holt Renfrew in Toronto, before he left.*

London in Forty-Eight Hours

You'll have to buy some sensible shoes," Al warned me as we headed out of the pub next to Claridge's after a beer and kidney pie lunch. It was a lovely bright day and I was looking forward to the London sights, especially Westminster Abbey.

"Okay, but where do you want to start? At Trafalgar Square, where everyone else starts?

"No," Al stated, "at Selfridges's shoe department, that's where *you* have to start."

I must give Al credit, he knows my feet well, not only from the toe-nibbling days when we were madly in love, but more recently from my hobbling days when, in three-inch heels, I tried to digest New York city in forty-eight hours—a small feat compared to London's historical feast now spread before us. As my guide states, "London's medieval layout is a mystery of tangled streets in a heady mix of new and old fashioned lifestyle and architecture."

"Yoo-hoo, come back to earth—we're talking shoes," Alan chides....

"Right; it's not that I mind 'sensible shoes.' I mean, they are alright for middle-aged women past forty, but that's not me."

Because I was in view of that watershed birthday, I was entrenched in denial worthy of poetic license. In fact I'd written a poem about these very shoes in one of my writing classes at York. At the time I was in rebellion against my censor/critic, Sinc, who's been with me from my late teens into adult life and, as such, prone to surface at any provocation—like now.

Listen to Al, Sinc ordered. *He knows your feet better than you.*

"Okay, but let's talk about *poetic* feet. They need to be supported, right? And in what way shall they be 'protected, covered and clad?'"

Shoes, I guess; but sensible shoes—they're the safest, warns Sinc.

> Hmm, *safe* presents an enigma—a riddled way of looking at the writer's world.
> If you don't watch out, your life can diffuse through the use of 'sensible shoes.'
> Now take a sandal, fling it high, feather weight—it can almost float.
> But lift a sensible shoe, you'll find, a censor clutching at your throat!
> Shoes can track and shoes can lead, but 'sensible shoes' pay no heed, to writers' lofty dreams.
> So throw away all earthbound shoes, kick high your heels, shout, for glee;
> And ask your muse for sandals light then stretch creative toes—now free!

Very nice, retorted Sinc sarcastically, now in the guise of Al. *But if you want to do London, you'll have to resort to sensible shoes. Okay?*

So, an hour later, there I was, trotting off to Trafalgar Square in a pair of canvas wedgies, the British version of Canada's Tender Tootsies. These were named Fleet Street, which was, in fact, the real enticement for Al, a pseudo-poet, to suggest them:

"They sound prosaic and efficient, what I'd call poetic justice for your poem—which, by the way, wasn't half bad," muttered Al.

"Thanks," I murmured, remembering how long I'd struggled to get it just right.

Standing in Trafalgar Square, Al announced, "Well, here we are in the dead centre of London." When I asked him how he knew that, he patiently explained, "Because this plaque on Strand and Charing Cross Road is the marker from which distances on UK signposts are measured."

Hmm, I thought. *Sometimes Al surprises me. He knows a lot of stuff about a lot of stuff.* This propensity for gathering, storing and retaining details would later be passed on to our son, Kevin.

"Okay, great. I learn something new and useful every day! Now let's go and look at the famous landmark, Nelson's Column. What can you tell me about this one?"

"Well, this has to do with Admiral Lord Nelson's greatest naval victory over the French, in 1805. This famous column—145 feet high and sculpted in granite, is the dominant landmark here in Trafalgar Square where Nelson looks down keeping watch. The statue was done by one E.H. Bailey in 1843, thirty-eight years after Nelson died in the Battle of Trafalgar, in 1805. But you can read all about him yourself ... here, it's written on this plaque."

I knew that, but I've always liked hearing Al read out loud. His rich voice still gives me a thrill, especially late at night when he's on the radio. I found it very pleasant having him along for touristy companionship after the unhappy Paris experience with my disingenuous co-worker, Madame R.

"Well, that may be," I said, "but I like it better when you tell it. It's more interesting."

"Whatever, but right now I'm all talked out. What do you say we stop for a brew, a fag and a little rest?" And that's the way the afternoon went: forty minutes of viewing and twenty minutes of brewing. And in between, we walked through the charming church, St. Martin-in-the-Fields (a current string quartet now named after it), and stepped through Admiralty Arch and the Gateway to the *Mall*—"rhymes with *shall*," Al cautioned me with his broadcaster's penchant for correct pronunciation.

Situated on the southwest corner of Trafalgar Square, Admiralty Arch was designed in 1910 as part of a ceremonial route to Buckingham Palace. Here royalty leaves the frenetic crowds of the square and enters the elegant avenue that leads to the palace. I was interested in this walk because I'd seen it when we first received television in Winnipeg in the fifties; many Canadians became avid Royal watchers, as did I. My fascination with "Lillibet," who became Queen Elizabeth II, began early in grade school, when, as gawkers, our family and many others ten deep along Main Street, waved the

British flag (no Canadian flag yet), hoping to catch a glimpse of the Princesses Royal, Elizabeth, and her sister Margaret. I remember thinking how much my sister Lessia looked like Princess Margaret, and later I remember my Mom's friends commenting on how much *she* looked like Queen Elizabeth II—I thought so too. My early fascination with the Royals continues to this day.

Having entered the Mall, I was anxious to follow its path to Buckingham Palace in order to see pomp and pageantry at work. From behind the front palace gates, we watched the Changing of the Guard with all the ceremony a Canadian monarchist such as me adores—one who apparently has stronger ties to England than an Englishman, judging by Al's indifference. Marching to live music, the guards proceeded up the Mall from St. James's Palace to Buckingham Palace—*the* symbol of the Royal Family.

On the Palace tour, we were given vital statistics: 19 state rooms, 52 royal and guest bedrooms, 188 staff bedrooms, 92 offices and 78 bathrooms! Wait ... this last one stops me in my tracks. Just *when* were these bathrooms put in? Was there indoor plumbing in the palace when Queen Victoria was crowned in 1837?

The Royal Flush

When you consider the contributions that plumbing and sanitation makes to the quality of our lives, then much of the other things that we do just seem so much less significant.
—Jim Olsztynski, *The Legend of Sir Thomas Crapper*,
P&M Magazine

The myth over who invented indoor plumbing and the conveniences therein has been debated for years. To my surprise and interest I have learned that there is a group of Sir Thomas Crapper scholars who have made it their business to prove that *crapper*, today's vernacular for the toilet, stands for more than the slang term brought home by the WWI dough boys. Through research, I am also surprised to learn that the term *dough boy* was derived from the oversized buttons on the uniforms of Americans in their Civil War, 1861-65. Apparently these buttons resembled a "dough-boy": bread dough that is rolled thin and deep fried—the precursor of our doughnut today?

Sir Thomas Crapper, born in September 1836, enjoyed a successful career in England's plumbing industry from 1861 to 1904. Although the myth that Thomas Crapper invented the toilet, as it exists today, abounds, researcher and author Ken Grabowski, who has created a detailed history of Crapper's business life including nine patents for drain improvements, three for water closets—containing a toilet and a washbowl, disagrees. Grabowski claims that the most famous product attributed to Crapper wasn't invented by him at all. Apparently the *Silent Valveless Water Waste Preventer*, a siphonic discharge system that allowed a toilet to flush effectively when the cistern was only half full was issued for this product in 1819 to a Mr. Albert Giblin. Although theories abound, the best one to date suggests that Thomas Crapper bought the patent rights from Giblin (who was at the time an employee of his), and marketed the device himself.

Now, your patience near depletion, you might well ask what all of this has to do with my reverie-driven memoir. Believe me, upon moving to our grand mansion, Tara Hall, a B&B in Wellington, Prince Edward County, Ontario, in 1992, over fifteen years ago, there's been many a time that I've marveled at the invention under discussion.

Tara Hall, c. 1870   *Tara Hall, 2006*

Tara Hall, a sizable mansion over five thousand square feet, was completed in 1839 near the beginning of Queen Victoria's sixty-four-year reign, which began with her accession to the throne in 1837. Every day I spent in our well-preserved home, I thought about the inconveniences suffered by the many souls who occupied the house starting back 167 years. Aside from the seven fireplaces that had to be stoked day and night during the prolonged winters (Tara is directly across from Lake Ontario's icy winds), during the time from 1839 to 1957, there was *no* indoor plumbing at all in Tara Hall! I'm happy to report that today there are six bathrooms; hence, my fascination with early plumbing. How *did* the early owners manage to accommodate their many guests and their own families in those long icy winters?

In its day, Tara Hall was famous between Toronto and Ottawa for its hospitality and entertainment, which included dancing in the second floor ballroom. Yet for 118 years, the sole "facilities" at Tara Hall consisted of one outhouse—fifty feet out front, near Main Street!

Aah, but I digress. Getting back to Buckingham Palace, which today boasts seventy-eight bathrooms; just *when* and *how* were these acquired?

My research indicates that by the 1880s, Crapper & Co.'s reputation was such that they were invited to supply the Prince of Wales (Edward VII) with plumbing at Sandringham, Windsor Castle, Westminster Abbey and Buckingham Palace—which has housed the monarchs since Queen Victoria's ascension in 1837. In answer to my question as to *when* modern bathrooms were installed in Buckingham Palace, it seems that in 1848, after cholera felled 14,000 people in London and 55,000 nationwide, the Public Health Act was passed, primarily in response to the public's concern for improved hygiene. Later, the Victorian reign became known in sanitary circles as "The Golden Age of Toilets."

A lengthy chronology dating from 1775 (here, the use of "swirling water" is described) progresses through details of added inventions to conclude with the launching of the "Unitas." This product, designed by William Twyford and dubbed as a "Perfection of Cleanliness," debuted in Buckingham Palace in 1883, followed by Henry Doulton's "Combination" Closet (similar to the Unitas), which remained in production for another sixty years. By the 1880s, all of the monarchy benefited from Crapper's, Twyford's and Doulton's goods and services. In honor of their product, Doulton's son was granted a "Royal" warrant in 1901, which won him the right to use that word in its name. Aside from his renowned fame for his fine china, I conclude that Henry Doulton should *also* be crowned as "King of the Royal Flush!" Now, turning back to the *real* Royals:

Buckingham Palace gave us a fascinating glimpse into another world—the fabulously gilded interiors indicating pomp and pageantry at work. The Grand Hall, followed by the truly Grand Staircase and Guard Room gave a taste of what was to follow: lines of cool marble pillars, gold-leafed ceilings and bright rooms with massive sparkling chandeliers. While we were all oohing and aahing, Alan lagged behind, looking for a place to grab a quick smoke. Yes, we were all still smoking in the early seventies. My habit wasn't as extreme as Al's, but he'd been smoking longer then me to start with. When he came back, I could tell he was getting tired, still suffering jet lag. Heading for what would be the climax of the tour, the Throne Room, I asked him if he could hang in for another fifteen minutes. "Just—but no more," Al muttered as he found a bench to perch on.

Beautiful in its baroque style, the Throne Room featured the *original* coronation throne of the present Queen, Elizabeth II. The crowning took place in 1953, and I distinctly remember how avidly our family crowded around our tiny black-and-white TV watching this historical event in awe, as much for the wonder of television, as for the event itself.

Brushing up behind me, breaking into my reverie, Al asks, "So, have you had enough of the Queen for today? And how are your sensible shoes holding up?"

"No to the first, good to the second, but how about you? Sounds like you're about ready for another break. Maybe we could stop for a cup of tea, and you might muster up the energy to visit The Queen's Gallery, which is over at the other side of Buckingham Palace. Apparently the Queen herself is not the personal owner, but she has the privilege of holding these works of art for the nation. Sounds like there would be some great stuff to see over there ... what do you think?"

"I think if we're going to do more sightseeing I'll need something stronger than a 'cuppa.' Let's find a place that brews both tea and booze." And that's what we did. But by the time Al had revived enough to move forward, we were too late for the Queen's Gallery. As for my feet, by now they were begging me to throw off my sensible shoes and replace them with *sandals light*, so we headed back to the hotel with Al's promise that "tomorrow we would leave bright and early to do some galleries—followed by Westminster Abbey *for sure.*" But, as I've since found out, nothing in life is "for sure."

Need a Break?

When I'm around Al, there are three little words that I should *never* say. They are far too dangerous, an open invitation to trouble. Every time I ask him, "Need a break?" he always says "Yes," and then it's goodbye to my plans, as they waft away on a cloud of smoke and complacency towards the nearest bar.

While browsing through my guidebook, the first thing I found out about Westminster Abbey is that the origins are "uncertain." The first church on the site *may* have been built by the Saxon King Sebert in the seventh century. After leaving out three centuries, the text explains that there were pre-existing foundations when Edward the Confessor, crowned in 1040, moved his palace to Westminster and began building a church that apparently appears in the "Bayeux Tapestry."

Standing with Al in Parliament Square, I tell him I want to find this famous tapestry.

"So, where do you think it is?" I query.

"Too many questions," Al says. "You're still asking too many questions."

"I know," I shot back. "But I want to learn things. How will I find out if I don't ask? Annoyed, I threw this last comment over my shoulder and headed off, instantly caught up in the middle of teeming tourists pouring out of four British-flagged buses beside Parliament Square. It was stupid of me to move so quickly, but how often have I heard that "too many questions" comment? It started back in grade two for goodness' sake. Calmed down, I turned around expecting to find Al behind me, but he wasn't there. *Where is he?*

Westminster Abbey

Caught up in the middle of the jostling tourist group, I pushed my way out and looked around; I still couldn't see Al. *This is crazy,* I thought, as my concern shifted from annoyance to anger. Matters got worse after another busload of tourists spilled out at the north entrance of the Abbey, where a tour was about to begin. Again, I looked around—he was nowhere to be seen. Bloody Hell, where *is* he? Maybe he stepped away for a cigarette? *This is so bad*, I thought, as my stomach started to churn. Then I remembered something a friend once told me: "When you've lost someone, the best thing to do is stand still—don't move. The place they've lost you, that's where they'll find you." *Well and good*, I thought, but I knew in my heart that this was not a feasible choice for someone as high-strung as me. So, I started searching in earnest.

First I circled the smaller crowds converging around the Abbey's entrance, then, as more tourist buses arrived, my circles got bigger ... until, finally, I couldn't even *see* the entrance. Now, *I* was lost. Panic struck. I could feel bile rising in my throat accompanied by a queasy feeling announcing the start of a migraine. Walking faster, almost running, I searched the perimeter of the square while trying to ignore the burning tears blurring my vision. Soon the sea of Tilly hats, sunglasses and anxious faces merged to become a mass of undulating humanity—too vast for me to contemplate. Moving from concerned panic to full-blown anxiety, more frenzied tears emerged.

Now, just stop that, snapped Sinc, hearkening to my rapid heartbeat that now matched the nervous trot of my sensible shoes. *Just park yourself over by the entrance and wait. Al will show up, and if he doesn't, the worst thing that can happen is you'll take a cab back to Claridge's. Oh, you didn't bring any money? That was smart. Okay, you can put the cab fare on your hotel tab—being Claridge's, they'll cover you. Now, follow your sensible shoes and do as they (and I) suggest. Okay?*

This one-way conversation took less than thirty seconds, and now I found myself standing beside the north door of the Abbey, wishing I'd worn my three-inch spiked sandals so that I'd be tall enough to see over the crowd. It was close to lunch hour, and I expected the mass of tourists would soon thin out. My anxiety, now too heavy to reckon with, had moved from concerned panic to righteous anger, as I processed our combined stupidity: mine, for taking umbrage at Al's comment, and his, for the disappearing act that was now far from funny.

Okay, I thought, *anger I can deal with. I'll give him another twenty minutes, and that's it. If he's not here by then, I'm going in by myself. Luckily, I've got the tickets with me. I always carry the tickets.*

When I finally entered the Abbey's darkened lobby alone, I was still in a blue funk, but this soon gave way in lieu of the lofty architecture that *did* appear as impressive as the guide promised. The entrance was crammed with statues and tombs, full of commemorative tablets, most of which were impossible to read due to the tourists marching ahead and pushing from behind. But that was okay. I'd made up my mind that I wasn't leaving London without doing Westminster Abbey—at least the highlights. At the start of the tour, before I got more involved, I'd lingered around the entrance just in case Al showed up. If he did, he would be *sans* his ticket, and that would upset him, so I waited—which had its side benefits as the tour crowds thinned out for lunch—but still, no Al. As I sidled in at the tail end of a ticketed tour, I could feel my anger finally subside.

Okay, now enjoy! Sinc ordered, resurfacing. *You're finally here in the Abbey; do you remember what the guide book noted?*

"Sort of," I murmured.

Right, so go! Sinc urged.

Hundreds of years ago, kings were the first patrons of the Abbey. That's where they began and ended their rule—first with their coronation then with their burial. And today Westminster is still the centre of government. Queen Elizabeth II was crowned there, and her government still meets beneath the fancy pinnacles of the Palace of Westminster, where MPs engage in fiery debates. All of this information is fine in the reading, but actually stepping onto the hallowed ground of Westminster was an awesome experience.

Upon entering the north transept, I soon found myself part of a formal group of tourists. With little control over individual movements, swept along with the tide, we gravitated en masse to wherever we were led. Luckily I was at the tail end, and was able to wiggle through the thinning crowd at just the right time to catch a stunning view of a huge rose-painted window as the afternoon sun poured through it. I read the plaque and learned that this style of window was "the largest of its kind in existence." Sunning my face in its welcome warmth and relaxing my neck—the usual start-up point of my migraine—I experienced a momentary bliss that energized me enough to strike out on my own, looking for those places in which I was particularly interested.

Proceeding along the north ambulatory, I came to the *Henry VII Chapel*, considered one of the architectural glories of Britain. At the steps I was in a perfect position to see the "hot seat" of power, the *Coronation Chair* ordered by Edward I around 1300—which had apparently hosted (or "hoisted") nearly every regal posterior for centuries since historical time began. After stopping briefly at the tomb of Henry II, I circled and turned into the South Transept and the Poets' Corner. Aah, this is what I'd been looking for. *Just a minute,* Sinc cautioned. *Look at the time. Shouldn't you be looking for Al?*

Nope—I'm not done. Besides, he should be looking for me, was my thought response.

Poets' Corner

> *Time held me green and dying*
> *Though I sang in my chains like the sea.*
> — Epitaph, Dylan Thomas: Westminster Abbey

The first occupant of Poet's Corner was Geoffrey Chaucer, buried there in 1400, not because he was a poet, but because he lived nearby. Apparently his battered tomb on the east wall wasn't built for another hundred-and-fifty-odd years. Another fascinating tidbit was about Edmund Spencer, who was buried in there in1599. (I'd studied him in depth at university and I must admit I *disliked* "The Faerie Queen.") Apparently his fellow poets, Shakespeare may have been among them, threw their own works and quills into the grave with him as a mark of honor. This last detail brought the poets to life for me—through their situation in history and the Abbey's place in time. This happened to me more than once during the Abbey tour, and the best was yet to come.

Others buried in the South Transept under carved angels keeping watch from high, include Ben Johnson (1574-1637), whose friends minimized on space and cost by burying him vertically in the nave in a two-foot-square space; William Wordsworth (1770-1850), Charles Dickens (1812-70) and Thomas Hardy (1840-1928)—who left his *corporeal* heart buried in Dorset. Among those commemorated is a "foppish" figure of William Shakespeare, erected in 1740 which started a trend that continued with a sculpture of William Blake—finally receiving recognition in 1957. Some other honored writers have their memorials here, but not their bones. On my own I found John Milton (1608-1674), Jane Austen (1725-1817), Samuel Taylor Coleridge (1772-1831) and Dylan Thomas (1914-1953). *Aah, now there's a poet.*

Dylan Thomas

Dylan Thomas, the Welsh bard, is considered by many as one of the greatest twentieth-century poets writing in English. As the leading figure in Anglo-Welsh literature, Thomas gave himself over to his passionately felt emotions: his writing is both intensely personal and fiercely romantic. Through extraordinary musical energy and original use of words, with the publication of his first book, *Eighteen Poems,* at age twenty, Thomas was recognized by critics as a brilliant and original poet. Personally, I feel that some readers find his explorations of words and rhythms, applied in unusual ways, too rich for their ear. As for me, when I first heard the lilting rhythm of Thomas' poem *Fern Hill,* I was carried away, actually, carried *home*—filled with nostalgia for the carefree days of my own childhood:

Now as I was young and easy under the apple boughs
About the lilting house and happy as the grass was green,
The night above the dingle starry,
Time let me hail and climb
Golden in the heydays of his eyes...

I well remember being "young and easy" under our own apple tree along the back fence of our spacious lawn in Winnipeg—always green, it seemed, in those timeless summers when I was young and hopelessly in love with life. Our ample house *did* "lilt," never empty, never quiet; and oh, those "starry" nights: the Big Dipper clustered, sparkling against a purple velvet sky. The Aurora Borealis, luminous bands that shone like glittering diamonds as they streamed across the night skies, so that for a moment I could see my father's face illumined with pleasure as he watched along with me. And yes, I did climb "Golden in the heydays of his [time's] eyes," because of course, as a little girl I had no concept of "time" or finitude.

Since time has not yet taken me, I am pleased to reference the importance of Dylan Thomas' work in my life, as now, forty years later, his well-remembered poem runs through my reverie. Sometimes, through a poet's expression, we are given a life-long gift. And so it was for me when I found Dylan Thomas's commemorative plaque in Poet's Corner at Westminster Abbey; after reading his stunning epitaph, I stood dazed ... did not move, did not want to. Now as I write out his fiercely lyrical epitaph, "Time held me green and dying / Though I sang in my chains like the sea," it brings home the pathos of every human being. Life as an oxymoron, an awareness of being alive while dying—so hard to live, *knowing* you're going to die.

Then, as now, I felt a release, a poignant sadness that left everything else behind. Tears start whenever I experience great poetry's uncanny alliance of beauty combined with pain—a classic rendition of the sublime. Through Thomas' poetry and his epitaph, I enter an elite reality that nourishes my spirit and repairs my soul. How is this? Here, I look to Gaston Bachelard for an explanation:

"In waking life itself, when reverie works on our history, the childhood which is within us brings us its benefits."—*Poetics of Reverie*

Today, as "reverie works on our [my] history," I am taken back to that glorious moment in Poets' Corner where, through the lyrical strength of Dylan Thomas' poetry, I was able to discern a key concept of the *finite*—the arbitrary limitation in every life—and as such, the foolishness of squandering the balance of time that one is allotted. For me, this concept guides me through my variegated past where indeed, "I sang in my chains like the sea," and it further allows me to graciously accept and celebrate my life while writing it within reverie's powerful ability "to help put our being to rest."

Hi, and Goodbye, Lovey

After I had experienced the other-worldliness of Poets' Corner, and then stepping out into London's late-day April sun, I found it difficult to retain the annoyance and anger that had plagued me all afternoon. It shouldn't be too difficult to find Al. If there's a bar around, that's where he'll be. Earlier, when I was circling the tourist group looking for him, I noticed The Wesley Café, opposite the Abbey, housed in what was once a Methodist church. Okay, that's the obvious place to look.

Entering the labyrinth-like setting, my myopic eyes took some seconds to focus on the shadowy figures outlined against the low-lying smoke barrier that hung across the room. But I needn't have worried—Al saw me first:

"There she is! C'mon over, *lovey*, and join us, we were just talking about you."

"All bad, I hope," I retorted, while faking a wide smile around the picturesque group. They were all well into their cups. I could tell by Al's reversion back to his Yorkshire expression "lovey," and the raucous laughter that greeted my inane remark. There were three others at the table: two men, tourists, maybe, and one woman—definitely not a tourist, perhaps posing as one. When my eyes became accustomed to the dark, I could see that her plunging knit top was a close color match to our satin quilt—Claridge's famous hot pink. The image of her getting lost in the quilt brought a smile that I shared with Al before he introduced me to his new-found friends.

"So," I whispered, leaning into his ear: "What do you think? Which one of you guys will get lucky? [I was definitely in a sarcastic mood.] Helen's wearing the right color for quilt trouble," I snickered, before sitting down between him and the American guy, Joe, who was tightly squeezed into a black turtleneck and sitting next to Harry, from who knows where—looking quite proper in a striped tie and blazer.

"So-ooh, *watch-you-all* been doing this fine afternoon?" I drawled to all and sundry.

"Waiting for you *lovey*," murmured Al, sidling closer while planting a peck on my cheek.

"Now, ask me," I said, waiting for the same question of interest from Al, or anyone else.

"Al said you've been visiting Westminster Abbey," Harry the suit, offered politely.

"How did you like it?"

"Very much, thank you. There's a lot to like. But it would have been even nicer if I'd been able to share it with *someone*," I said, glaring at Al.

Harry looked at Joe. Joe looked at Al then started to put on his wind breaker. Helen ordered another drink.

Al may have been tipsy but not so intoxicated as not to recognize my anger—now on a slow burn, temporarily held back with effort. He knew, unless harnessed, it would soon explode.

"It's okay, folks, you stay," Al said, while pulling back my chair. "We're heading back to the hotel. It's our last day in London, you know; big night out—right, my flower?"

"Right," I agreed, biting my tongue. I love it when he calls me "flower," and he knows it.

Not a word. No apology, no explanation, no excuse; nothing was said in the cab on the way back to the hotel. That's the way it's always been. "If you don't talk, you can't get into trouble," is Al's motto, not mine. Although I didn't say a word in the cab ride back to Claridge's, I *thought* ... a lot.

PART THREE

The Lost Divine

Chapter 17

Heartache

It is your turn now, you waited, you were patient.
The time has come, for us to polish you.
                    —Jalal ud-Din Rumi, Sufi Mystic Poet

Alan and Joanne Small, 1968

Say Maybe

How much heartache is enough? Is it when your heart-in-love suffers its first or fifth injury?

"Don't worry," the doctor once said about my damaged rib; "it's only a hairline fracture. It hurts like mad, but it will mend like new."

Is that the way of the heart? Is a fractured heart able to "mend like new?" If so, then how many assaults can it sustain? Can we add

255

up a lifetime of emotional injuries? No—too many. Then, how about my marriage to Al? Can I tabulate the items of emotional abuse and add up the damage in the way a store cashier scans items and in so doing, adds up the cost? No—too many.

Okay, I hear you, said Sinc, always listening and hovering nearby. *I'll help you tally up your grievances. I'm good at that, you know....* "I know, I know," I muttered.

Okay, I remember one, said Sinc with relish. *It was the day of your final exam for* "The Modes of Reasoning," *that tough course you took when you first went back to York University. It was the end of August, 1968; you were very pregnant with Kev and it was ninety-eight degrees in the shade. Anyway, Al started up with you about something, you got upset and grabbed a boiled egg, some sliced cheese and a bun, threw them into your briefcase—you know the one that was previously your music case and then your business case for Eaton's—and then lumbered out of the house five hours early for the exam.*

"I'll study at school," *you said, between tears. But what you were thinking was:* "How could he start up with me; I'm so nervous about the exam, I could have the baby right here and now!" *Well,* Sinc went on, *you found a corner in the library and studied right through until seven PM. The exam was very tough, and you still can't forget how nervous you felt as you sat in that huge arena sweating with at least five hundred other students, waiting for the papers to be passed out. I know you were praying that you had studied the right stuff. There was no air conditioning—this was the big campus at Keele and Finch in the late sixties and the building wasn't finished yet. Perspiration was dripping onto your paper; it even smeared the philosophy part about Queen Elizabeth "etcetering" herself ... remember? Anyway, on the way out, you ran into Sam Mallin, your TA at the time, and after you commented on his 'cool' sandals (this was the sixties) you then complained about how hot it was in the arena and how he'd better pass you because you had studied so hard while being very pregnant and all.*

Sam kindly assured you that your class work ensured a passing mark and you felt relieved. As I recall, you came home that night to Al and his brother laughing and joking, again "in their cups"; they asked you to join them and you had a small glass of rye and ginger to celebrate passing the exam. And then you had Kevin, the very next day, on September 1, Labor

Day—two weeks early! Here, Sinc paused then went on: *Frankly, I'm surprised you would drink at that stage of your pregnancy.*

"You know what? I'm surprised too. What were we thinking of? I know for sure that I had stopped smoking temporarily (I quit altogether in 1976), but I guess we weren't fully informed of the risks of drinking alcohol the way expectant mothers of today are. Anyway, Sinc, if you're going to recapitulate every grievance since 1967, we'll be here forever. Let's move on."

Okay, Sinc agreed, then added, *because these hurts are so ingrained in your heart, I'm sure you remember them better than me.*

"Right," I sighed; I could tell Sinc was on a roll. He knows I've been bottling everything up, and this is his way of reminding me how early the hurts had started—even before we were married—so it's at least five years ago. He wants me to stop hiding from the truth. He went on:

And the one about your 'perfect' Dad was a low blow, a lifetime bruise. Anything to do with your family we'd better let go. I know Al loved your Mom very much and he respected your Dad, too. Also he was very good to your younger brother, Joey and his wife, Pat, when they were working on their graduate studies at U of T. After all, there were plenty of good times too, right?

"Right," I whispered to myself, feeling sad. "There sure were."

And there will be again, promised Sinc. *But for now, let's go back to the grievance list. Remember that time in the Pickle Barrel restaurant when Al got sarcastic with you in front of everybody; he'd already drunk too much vodka during the day, at home, when you were at work. That's what he did, you know. The drinking and the golf are all he had. Anyway, forget about the Pickle Barrel. I think we should just put that one to bed.*

"But I can't," I protest, under my breath. "I feel guilty. I should have quit working and stayed at home."

C'mon, that wasn't the first time Al embarrassed you in public, and it won't be the last. What do you expect? He's a drunk.

Whoa! Now there's a low blow, I thought, reacting to Sinc in shock: "It sounds awful the way you say it. Do you have to be so blunt?"

Apparently—what else should I do? Pussyfoot around the problem the way you do?

"But Sinc," I wail, "I love the guy. I can't just give up on him."

Aah, then you'll have to reclaim your heartache list, won't you? Well, lots of luck, my dear ... and with that, Sinc was gone.

Okay, I thought; *as usual, Sinc has a point. I know there have been some mistakes on both sides, Al's and mine. But this is the short list, and it already tallies up to more than I bargained for. My nerves can't afford this anger. I'll have to discard some of my grievances. I'll talk to my "heartache" right now:*

"Sorry, dear heart. I can't pay the price. I don't have the resources. You're willing to wait? Well, thank you, but in the end I'll still have to pay—right? I'm not sure of what grievances to leave out. No, I'm not saying I'll never come back to your heartache list. It's just that, for now, the price is too high. How could I bear implementing the list in all of its intricacies? And, how could I leave Al? What would he do?"

These last rhetorical questions surfaced in my enabler's voice, the one I'd learned to recognize at Al-Anon—the counterpart of Alcoholics Anonymous' twelve steps to sobriety. I remember that I'd had a *lot* of trouble with the first rule: "You have no control over the drinker." I simply could not believe that Al's drinking was not *my* fault.

"Sorry, dear heart, I'll have to leave off for now. No, no, please don't be offended. Your offer to fix our love is wonderful, but I can't afford to reckon with the truth of your complaints right now—another time, perhaps? Alright ... I won't say no, I'll say *maybe.*"

∞ ∞ ∞

The thought process above, the interaction between me and my inner critic Sinc, took place during the cab ride back from the Wesley Café, where Al had hung out all afternoon while I toured Westminster Abbey—alone. The traffic, extremely thick and slow, gave me enough time to calm down. I devised a plan. It was simple and doable, I thought. My big plan was to say nothing to Al about his disappearing act that afternoon ... *nothing.* I know Al prefers drinking to driving so I'll have to take up the helm of our "relation-ship" and steer us home to safe harbor—again.

When we got to our room at Claridge's, the first thing Al did was mix a double-vodka at the mini bar. I watched him while I removed my jacket, threw off my sensible shoes and climbed out of my miniskirt; I was looking forward to a soak in Claridge's "huge luxurious tub in the best bathroom in London," as expressed in one of my guidebooks.

"So, would you like a drink?" Al asked without looking up.

"Sure, why not?" I replied. Actually I was dying for a drink. I needed *something* to prop up my plan. Since when am I able to keep quiet when something (everything) is bothering me? I was getting undressed for my bath, stepping into the fancy turquoise robe that Al bought me last Christmas when I felt *the twinge. Whoa, that's my injury alarm sounding off—probably triggered by my turquoise robe.* And it all came back. *Yup, that was some awful Christmas.*

How to Cancel Christmas

The previous Christmas, right after Al had finished his second Bloody Mary, a pre-breakfast holiday tradition, he proudly brought in my present: a large box expensively wrapped in silver paper bedecked with Holt Renfrew's signature royal blue bow. Inside, there nestled an expensive-looking turquoise negligee and matching nightgown. I *loved* the color and style, so I jumped up and left the room to try it on. I was gone about three minutes, that's all. As I headed downstairs, looking over the balustrade, I sensed that something was wrong. The holiday ambiance had changed; in its place there was an uneasy silence emitting from the living room.

"What's going on?" I called down to my sister, Yvonne, who was leaving the kitchen, heading for the living room. She didn't look up—just shrugged her non-complicity and kept going. I guessed it had something to do with Al. Once downstairs, I followed Yvonne into the living room and quietly questioned her again.

"Well," she hesitated ... then continued; "it's about that brown ultra-suede coat that you liked so much and bought for Al when we were at Ports International the other day. He tried it on and his brother Brian made some joke about the coat looking 'poncey,' so Al left the room in a snit. That's all I can tell you."

Now I hear ice cubes rattling in the kitchen, and I figure Al's heading into his third Bloody Mary of the morning; *hmm, not good.*

"So, how do I look?" I say to Al, snuggling up to him in the kitchen. *He doesn't look good in the coat,* I thought. *It's too darn short and too tight. It will have to go back.*

"Not as good as me," he says, striking a foppish pose. I thought he was kidding, but apparently not. He was upset.

The slightest comment at the wrong moment could set Al off. He took umbrage readily, and the resulting mood was lethal. That morning, before I left our kitchen, Al was pouring his fourth Bloody Mary. I knew then that another Christmas had been ruined.

∞ ∞ ∞

Enigma

Four months after that doomed Christmas, in our tasteful room at Claridge's Hotel in London, while caught up in a vivid memory of that fiasco, I noticed Al looking at me over the rim of his glass. Jolted out of my reverie back into reality, I asked: "What?"

"Are you okay?"

"Sure. I was just thinking about last Christmas, when you bought me that gorgeous turquoise negligee set. You know, I brought it with me. What do you say we order up room service? Being as how it's our last night here in London, maybe we should celebrate."

"Okay. But what'll we celebrate—wh-a-a-at?" he slurred.

"Let's just celebrate being here together, in this fancy hotel for the rich and famous. Did you know that General Dwight Eisenhower stayed one block west of here in Grosvenor Square when he ran the D-Day campaign? Apparently his initial pied-à-terre, here at Claridge's, was a room painted *whorehouse pink*. Maybe he originated the term? For all we know, this could have been his room. After all, he wasn't the American president then. I wonder how *he* felt about the signature color.

Okay, thanks for the drink ... mm, good. Now I'm going to get my bath ready. Can you hear me with the water running? Oh, how I love this deep bathtub," I shout to Al over the running water. "It's so 1930s art deco. The golden clawed feet remind me of that Pablo Neruda poem, you know, the one I love so much titled "Enigmas." It starts with a question asking what the lobster is weaving with his "golden feet." And then, in reply, it answers "the ocean knows this." Isn't that a stunning way to start a poem? Right from the opening line, Neruda plunges us into his poem—to the ocean floor, no less. There, the water symbolism, so deep, so spiritual, sets the scene. We are placed in another world—somewhere in infinity ... you know what I mean? Hey, Al, can you hear me?"

Here, I pause to finish off my vodka tonic propped precipitously on the ledge of the European bidet. As I replace my glass, I wonder: *does anyone ever use this thing? This is the seventies. Get over it! Use the pill!* Okay, now I'm a little tipsy. I don't know whether Al can hear me or not. I'm into my opulent bath, the jasmine scent of the bath salts and Neruda's poem.

"Al, listen," I call out, to repeat. "Here's the best part. In this dark place, the ocean bed, there's this lobster weaving with golden feet.... Yikes! This is so lavish, so, I don't know ... completely irrational—hyperbole at its best! What do you think? Isn't Neruda brilliant?"

No answer.

Relaxing deeper into the water, I dwell on the improbable idea of a lobster with golden claws—I love it! Somehow, through this unusual image, I am taken to another place, a magical place, a romantic place—maybe one of William Wordsworth's *spots of time.* I feel happy.

Okay, the vodka is easing off. Ooh, I'm so relaxed ... if I'm not careful I'll fall asleep. I could drown in this water, it's so deep. Hey, maybe I'll see the lobster! Climbing groggily out of the tub, I'm aroused by the jasmine scent and softness of the huge pink bath towel.

"Hey, Al, what about these towels? Whoop-ee! Your favorite color: 'hmm-hmm pink.' Okay, listen. After my bath, I'm going to put on my frilly night gown and robe, you know, the set you bought me last Christmas, and then we're going to have a fabulous dinner in the room on Holt's tab. Don't worry about the cost, I've been saving my dinner allowance all week—you know how little I eat when I'm working. Okay, when you call room service, see if they have lobster on the menu. Make sure they have one with golden claws! By the way, do you remember how we used to pig out on Tuesday nights, 'All You Can Eat Lobster' at the Silver Rail on Yonge Street? Weren't we crazy then? After all of that aphrodisiacal dining, we could hardly wait to get back to the apartment. Those were great days, weren't they? You know it's almost seven years since we first met. Where did the time go? It's hard to believe, isn't it? Al … Al … are you still awake?"

Silence….

Heading Home

Off we go, into the wild blue yonder, climbing high into the sun.
—Captain Robert Crawford, *Air Force Song*

That last night at Claridge's Hotel Al slept right through—no fancy dinner, no lobster loving, just lots of much-needed sleep for both of us. Now here we are, dodging fat celestial clouds in a jumbo jetliner on our way home to Toronto.

"Al, do you remember that song they're playing?" I shout loudly above the engines' revving noise as I nudge him awake. You know, the one that starts: 'Off we go into the wild *blue*, or is it wild *sky*, yonder'? Anyway, you were a fly-boy in England, in the RAF, weren't you? Isn't that how you got started in radio?" Eyes closed, Al grunts a "yes." He was still suffering an extended hangover from yesterday's drinking debacle at the Westminster Abbey site, and the continuation later at our hotel room. In a way I felt sorry for him, because he missed what I considered the highlight of our London tour—Westminster Abbey.

We'd taken off from Heathrow airport late-afternoon, and now it was time for tea. Although I'd been in London only a week, I was already hooked on the teatime pick-me-up and I was looking forward to it. Of course, after the sumptuous English Cream Tea at Claridge's, everything else would fall short.

"So, how are you feeling?" I ask Al, again nudging him awake. Are you ready for your afternoon *tea?*'

"Absolutely" he answers and I swallow a sigh of relief.

See, everything will be okay, whispers Sinc.

This Thing Called Love

Some stones are so heavy only silence helps you carry them.
—Anne Michaels, *Fugitive Pieces*

After we got home, I never talked to Al about how upset I was with him and his drinking indulgence in London. It would only start trouble. He would get offended and start insulting me, then I would get angry and off we'd go.... Trying to reach him in that place that only liquor could appease was a battle I'd lost long ago. There were other problems to concern ourselves with. Although Al had been away from home just a week, Carminda reported that Joanne was acting up: "skipping school and lying about it too," she stated emphatically.

"I guess the two go hand in hand," I whispered to Al. "You can't do one without the other, can you?" Also, Kevin was not eating, not even "shiken"—which is what Portuguese-born Carminda had taken to calling everything from hamburger to steak, because chicken (*shiken*) was all Kev thought he liked. Of course, I'd prepared myself for these domestic problems; a month away is a long time for anyone, but a lifetime for a two-and-a-half year-old.

When we got out of the cab at our driveway, I noticed how Kevin shied away when he first saw me. Well, maybe it was because of the shocked look on *my* face when I first saw him. Gone were the blond silky bangs and long curly hair I'd tearfully kissed goodbye a month ago. Instead there was this inverted blonde-colored sugar bowl sitting on his head, styled so plain, so meager and boyish, that today I still remember my anguish: it was couched in a combination of betrayal at not being told, guilt at not being there and anger at the idea that they would cut his hair "while my back was turned." (I'd been fighting "them" about cutting his hair for weeks before I left.)

"But what did you people do to his beautiful hair?" I shouted. They all looked at me as though I was crazy, and in some ways I guess I was. Away for a month, I had missed them all, especially Kev. I'd been left out of an important rite of passage—the cutting of his baby hair marked the end of his baby years, and I just wasn't ready for that. As guilt kicked in, I could feel a migraine thumping close behind. Locked arm in arm, guilt and migraine always march in tandem to a rhythm that I've come to know only too well. I'd have to calm down, or I'd be facing that unwelcome beat for a long time.

"C'mon kids, give Mom a big hug and a kiss—I really need one."

The Best Is Yet To Come.

After I returned from that first trip abroad, a lot of things changed. Yes, I was called up on the carpet, but it wasn't as bad as I had imagined. I must say Mr. Boyd was, as always, a perfect gentleman. First of all, we talked about the "retail situation" with Al: the small store on Markham Street behind Honest Ed's would have to be dissolved. Then we talked about the late-night phone calls and I explained that we'd never been apart for any length of time and the calls *did* stop soon after Madame Roxwell's concern for my welfare was expressed. I tried to minimize my righteous indignation at Madame R.'s interference in my personal affairs; I understood that we would not be travelling together again, so there was no point in aggravating Mr. Boyd. The next part about my wardrobe, including the infamous Brownie tam, actually turned out to be fun. Personally, I think Mr. Boyd was as bemused over the three-dollar tam incident with Jean Louise Scherrer in Paris as I was. In some ways, I felt that he was proud of the way I'd handled myself in Europe—my independent nature and all. After all, it was he who had hired me for the job, and, as his European apprentice, I think he was quite happy with my performance. We seemed to be getting along famously; I thought it was time to leave, but, as it turned out, the best was yet to come.

"Well, Mr. Boyd, before I leave, I want to thank you for your support and understanding through these last weeks. I know that you had to fight "city hall" on my behalf more than once, and I want you to know that I fully appreciate it."

"Well, thank you very much, Mrs. Small, for the way you handled yourself around Madame Roxwell and for that matter Mr. Dixon too. I think he rather appreciates your spunk, although he would be the last to admit it with the president, Mr. Samson, looking over his shoulder. What I want to talk to you about is the latest development in the wardrobe 'saga.'"

Here I could tell Mr. Boyd was starting to relax, and even enjoying himself. It must be that he has good news to impart. Maybe, in spite of the Montreal group's grievances, I was actually going to get a raise. *Well, I've been with the company over a year now and surely, with an advancement quickly followed by a promotion, a raise is in order?* While

I was thinking about this, I was smiling at Mr. Boyd, waiting for him to go on.

"Saga, Mr. Boyd? There's a 'wardrobe saga?'" Now I was getting interested.

"Well, Elaine, it's about the Israeli army dress and the other outfits from Ports International that Madame Roxwell didn't think were quite up to Holt's standards—particularly for our overseas buyer. I'm sure you looked very nice, you always do, but still—"

"Oh," I interrupted, "now I see; it sounds as though you want me to wear designer, high-fashion clothing on the European trips and here in the store too. Well then, I guess you've been thinking about giving me a raise. I've been with Holt's over a year now, a year this last March." After a slight hesitation, Mr. Boyd continued,

"I did bring that up with Mr. Samson when we were discussing your wardrobe, but he wants to review your orders and your work in general before going ahead. No, what he's offering is a one-time clothing allowance; something that would allow you to buy a designer suit, maybe two, also a pair of designer shoes. How does that sound?"

"It sounds as though I'll need a designer bag to go with the designer shoes. Remind Mr. Samson that that's the trend. You know I did buy a pair of Ferragamo shoes right from the company in Firenze, but unfortunately, they're a little tight. So ... how much do you have in mind?"

"Well, let's see what the wholesale price for a suit from the House of Dior would be. We have the Canadian exclusive with them, as you well know. Did you see anything you liked?"

Mr. Boyd was being most pleasant. As for me, I was vacillating between appreciation and annoyance. The former because I think he really was trying to solve the clothing dilemma caused by Montreal's snob factor and his own perception that I always dressed nicely for the job. (He once commented that the French import blouse I was wearing most likely cost more than his suit! On the street it would have cost double, but that particular blouse was the actual sample off the model's back, and the manufacturers practically give those away.) At this point, I felt that Mr. Boyd had mixed feelings regarding my parvenu wardrobe—obviously not up to Holt's self image. Of the latter feeling (my annoyance), this was due to the way the prestige of Holt's is held up to the highest standard while their employees' stipend is held down to the lowest among the major retail boutiques and department stores in Toronto.

In keeping with my mood, still lagging from the exhausting flight and pressured month I'd just put in, I decided to go for broke: "Yes, Mr. Boyd, Dior was showing a classic pant suit, a quality wool knit in a dark chocolate collared style with a long structured jacket and a well-cut cuffed pant. This suit will retail just under six hundred dollars." (Here Mr. B.'s left eyebrow raised slightly, the merest expression of surprise in his otherwise impassive face.) I went on:

"However, the landed *wholesale* price, all taxes included, will run around $250.00, which is, coincidentally, the sum of my weekly salary. Well, the way I see it, the suit, the shoes and the bag could be supplemented with a classic designer scarf from Saint Laurent and perhaps that stunning off-white Stetson that's on display downstairs in our hat department. That will complete my Holt's fashion statement. I'll do your store proud, and that should only set you back a dollar amount equal to my two-week salary. How does that sound?" Again, the eyebrow was raised, but this time accompanied by the slightest quirk of a smile.

"It sounds fine, my dear; I'll send the request in to Montreal today. Is there anything else for us to discuss?"

"Well, please mention the raise again to Mr. Samson and tell him that 'soon I won't be able to afford the luxury of working for his store.' Does he have a sense of humor?"

"I'm afraid not."

"Good. Tell him anyway," I said, half-smiling over my shoulder as I headed for the door.

The outfit was a big success at the European *pret-a-porter* that fall. Not only were the scarf and brimmed hat a hit in Europe (even Madame R. approved), but in the end that fashion statement was instrumental in obtaining my *next* fashion job with The Bay, at Bloor and Yonge in Toronto. But before that happened, I had some serious soul-searching to do. The situation at home was worsening.

Angel Eyes, Devil Shoes

From the first time I met Joanne, I considered her my surrogate child, a gift from God. I loved her from the start, through agape love I'm unable to explain in human terms. But even before our wedding, her Dad's and mine, there was trouble looming. As a blonde blue-eyed five-year-old, Jo had the look of an angel and the edgy temperament of a devil; from her first day at school to her last, she had hassles; consequently, we had hassles with her. She just didn't like school—and the prescribed tranquillizers didn't help. Fortunately (or not), the school was just down the road at the end of our street. Every day I'd walk her there, and every day, a minute or two after the bell, she'd be back home banging on the front door, sobbing and begging to stay home. Soon we were all on "tranqs" (these were the late sixties, and everyone was on something), but they didn't help us or her. Nothing worked, nothing changed. Much later, just after Joanne's first teen birthday, a watershed year in any girl's life, our fragile household came close to collapsing under the strain of her shenanigans ... too many to relate, but one in particular comes to mind.

Jo had just turned thirteen. I guess the teen-time hormones (Greek--*hormon*: *to urge on*) had kicked in, because they were certainly doing their job—running rampant through her slim body, now too curvy for her own good; she was beautiful, ripe enough to find trouble if that's what she was looking for; for a start there were frequent "absent without leave" hooky offences of which we were rarely informed, or, if so, usually after the fact.

"We tried to call you, Mrs. Small; we were really worried about Joanne. She seemed so upset over her grandmother's death that we sent her home after lunch yesterday. And how did the funeral go? Do you think she'll be coming to school tomorrow? If not, we'll understand, and thanks for your note. I wish more mothers would show such compassion for their teenage daughters' problems."

"Note ... death? What grandmother? There's only one, my Mom, and she's alive and well and living in Winnipeg."

"Oh, my goodness, there must be some mistake," murmured the grief counselor. "Perhaps we should talk about this. Would you like me to set up an appointment?"

"For me or for her," I sarcastically exclaimed, just before we were cut off. (I found out later Joanne was listening in.)

Although I was not always patient with Jo, her father was even less so: "Playing hooky again? Writing notes? That's it!" Al shouted. "You're not going out tonight. You're only thirteen years old. And what about that boy up the street? He looks younger than you—and what's with his hair? Tell him if he wants to come around here, he'll have to get a haircut. I'll be happy to pay for it. I've had it. Where are your shoes? Give them to me," and with that, Al grabbed Jo's red Adidas and stomped out of her room.

"This should keep her in," he muttered, going into our bedroom and tossing the shoes on my side of the bed before throwing himself down on his side.

"You mean I have to sleep with her shoes under *my* pillow?" I laughed provokingly. If nothing else, Alan always had a good sense of humor—but not today.

"It's not funny. That girl has turned into a devil. What's the matter with her?"

"At least she's got an excuse: *hormones*. But what's the matter with *us*?"

"Not hormones," he murmured; but, just as he turned to me, I heard the back door slam—hard. Jumping up, I plunged down the curved staircase, cursing my slippers as they held me back.

"Too late," I hollered, from the bottom of the stairs. "Jo's gone!"

First we searched the house. Kev was in his bedroom sketching the CN Tower in downtown Toronto, which he'd been drawing ever since it got high enough to be seen from our house in North York. Now almost six, Kev paid no attention to the bedlam over Joanne—he'd grown up with it. For the last few years, he'd minded his own business and although he loved his "Anno" (a dyslexic version of Joanne) and she was crazy about him, still, he was already too smart to get involved in her domestic hubbub.

Walking over to the Bayview Mall, half a block from our house, I could sense Alan's fatigue. He was withdrawing into one of his depressions, I could tell. Ever since I'd left Holt's and gone to work at the Bay, he'd been getting worse, but there was no sense in bringing that up now. Whenever I'd mention his "distancing," he'd brush it

Priests in the Attic

aside. "There's nothing to talk about," he'd say ... but I knew there was.

Come Out, Come Out...

I loved my job with the Bay but travelling to Europe twice a year on a regular basis was taking its toll on our family. As before in my life, I was torn between two loves. Earlier I'd been led to give up my music for the love of Craig. Then I gave up my job at Eaton's in order to "do the right thing." In the sixties that meant being a stay-at-home wife. Now I was facing similar choices again.

Al was semi-retired. He'd left the radio station and now spent half his time at the golf club and the other half doing free lance commercials. Even though we could afford live-in help, I was still made to feel guilty for being away from the house too much, a house that I regularly contributed to in the way of the monthly mortgage, some of the kids' clothes, my own clothes and some food too. Anyway, how could I stay at home? I just wasn't ready to give up this job too. We walked on in silence.

First we swung through the Pickle Barrel restaurant; it was uncommonly empty, but then again, it was past nine, near to closing. Jo didn't appear to be there, but Al insisted I check the washrooms, saying, "Remember that time five years ago when Jo was in grade three, and the school called you to say they couldn't find her after recess? You had to come hurtling up north from downtown, and you were smart enough to search the bathrooms, every one of them. You finally found her by standing on one of the toilets in your high heels and looking over the cubicles. She was there in the last one, crouched down on top of the seat, so that her feet wouldn't show—what was she hiding from?"

"Who knows," I answered ruefully. "Where should we look next? Remember, she's not wearing shoes. She can't be far."

After searching the mall, going through the drugstore, peering into the doors of Loblaw's as they were closing, we realized we had a problem. "It's past ten," Al said, anxiously, "Where the hell is she?"

"Wait a minute," I said, "maybe she's with that boy who has been coming around the house. You know the one with the pageboy hair-do." Now desperate, we searched the crowd of high school boys

269

hanging around the pool hall. James (today, my dear son-in-law!) wasn't there, so we pushed our way into the dimly lit hall. Dense clouds of yellowed smoke, filtered through amber lighting, hovered over the emerald tables, closing down on the players so that they all appeared headless, like figures out of a Stephen King movie—only plausible because of their context in the wake of our own horror story. Fully concentrating on their game, the partially disembodied paid no attention to us—two suburban interlopers frantically searching for their kid. Finally, after a couple of Al's impatient coughs, one of them looked up:

"Who are you looking for? Oh, a young girl, you say. What would an underage girl be doing in here?" he asked, as he turned back to his game.

By now I was really upset: "The same thing those two girls, who look around thirteen, are doing over there huddled in the corner, smoking and flirting. C'mon guys, give us some help … *please,*" I emphasized, now close to tears. Watching the headless honcho finish his play, staring at each ball with impatient fascination as it travelled smoothly, obediently, into the selected pocket, I thought, *He's got too much control. Look how cool he is, he must know something.* By now I was so irritated I wanted to strangle him. Instead, I said: "Okay, if you're not going to help us, I guess we'll have to call the police. Come on Al."

"Don't bother. She's here," was the headless response. And, in a déjà-vu moment of when I first met her, Joanne came creeping out from under the table. Shoeless, with her tear-stained face and disheveled hair, she looked around ten years old instead of thirteen.

"Okay, Jo, let's go home," Al said, calmly. "We'll talk about it there." But we never did.

∞ ∞ ∞

I've always maintained that Joanne's early behavioral problems started with the loss of her birth mother, Patricia Small, *nee* Walley, who died of cancer at age thirty-three. After two years of suffering, primarily at home, near the end, Pat's pain was buffered by strong doses of morphine. Although I wasn't around at that time, I was told by my brother-in-law Brian, Alan's younger brother who, at age twenty-one, had emigrated from England to join his widowed mother and Al in Toronto, that upon his arrival he'd immediately felt a palpable stress in the household. Brian also told me that he was not surprised by all of the drinking ("to calm my nerves," Al said) that took place in the last stages of their loss. Patricia Small's tragic illness and early demise had taken its toll on many, especially Alan, his mother, Pat's mother, who had come from England to be with her terminally ill daughter, Brian and of course, little Joanne—at that time two-and-a-half-years old. When I first met Alan a year and a half later, I could readily sense the pain that had been experienced by the family as a whole.

For Al, Pat's early death manifested in a tilt towards alcohol that soon developed into a full thrust quickly followed by a serious spill-over into heavy drinking. Having been warned by the doctor at age thirty-five that alcohol was exacerbating an existing pancreatic condition, Al was unable, or unwilling, to stop drinking—undermining his promising future with alcoholic riffs of bad humor that in the long term compromised his job, his health and finally our marriage.

Always a loving father, but burdened with "bad nerves," Alan was weak in the realm of punitive discipline with Joanne, who had been cared for by her two doting grandmothers during her mother's illness. Astute in a child's way of discerning truth, Joanne quickly caught on to her Dad's weaknesses and played on them, wreaking a trail of havoc in a household already threatened by life's vicissitudes. In retrospect Joanne's teen-age pranks were generally harmless except for her inclination to skip school.

A reluctant student from the start, Joanne grew up to be a professional truant—a distinct artist at the game, so that years later, only half in jest, I used to tell anyone who asked: "Oh yes, my daughter Joanne has already graduated *cum laude* from the Sheppard Mall. It's conveniently located next to her high school, you know."

By that time, in fairness to Joanne, the delicate balance of our marriage had collapsed, compromised by Alan's excessive drinking habits and my obsessive work habits. Our individual addictions had surfaced early in our marriage and were already implanted by the second year, soon after Kevin was born. And what had my censor

Sinc whispered to me before that time of "suburban bliss?" *Beware of what you dream for* (or was it *pray* for?).

In any event, can an unheeded warning reverberate after so many years? Can reverie's voice echo a warning *ad infinitum*? Apparently so, for I'm still hearing it now....

Chapter 18

Love, Labor and Loss

Honoring Symptoms as a Voice of the Soul: 'Soul' is not a thing,
but a quality or dimension of experiencing life and ourselves.
—Thomas Moore, *Care of the Soul*

Kevin, Joanne and me, in the late '70s

Symptoms

Too soon, our marital feast had been devoured and picked clean; the marrow sucked dry, succulence diminished. A decade into my marriage with Alan, the passion between us had settled into a predictable pattern, vacillating between work and parties and revived in times of need. Otherwise it was sustained by a cold politeness on my part and tempered by sarcastic humor on Al's. Still, the bones of a family remained—dried out and bleached, fragile but intact.

For long periods of time, the problems between Al and me were safely buried, simmering within their own contexts; then suddenly, on the slightest provocation, they would surface, ignited by superficial arguments that quickly escalated into angry discussions driven by an alcoholic's rancor on Al's part and disappointed resentment on mine. Our marital issues, too difficult to take on singularly or together, were a mystery to us then, and remained so to the end. There was no doubt that we loved each other but, for me, our future together appeared clouded. The idea of an eternal relationship—till death do us part—was murky, out of focus, beyond my vision. In those days I perceived myself as a consummate problem solver, and considering our mutual love for the children and each other, my inability to reconcile the emotional insolvency of our marriage within a comprehensive context—say a loss of faith or love for each other— frustrated and baffled me. As the demise of our family progressed, all hope of meaningful confrontation appeared doomed, to be replaced, instead, by heavy doses of denial on both sides.

While I worked, fretted and argued, Alan drank. While I attended Al-Anon (a support group set up by AA for the partners of alcoholics), Al drank. And in between my frenetic activity designed to mask my sadness, Al drank. Oh no, he was not an obvious out-of-control alcoholic; he was, as the doctor explained, a "sipper," and this is what made it so difficult. Al managed to hang on to a golf club, his Ford commercials and *Untamed World*—a successful documentary series on wild animals and their habitats at which he was very good—"one-take Al" they called him. But, regarding his personal relationships, he had no handle on them at all. As for me, I am not pleading innocence. The softer Al got, the harder I grew and the more difficult the conditions at home became. It was a no-win situation all the way around.

Concrete Lady Crumbling

The breakdown of our family was slow but steady, in all probability aided and abetted by my own frequent absences from home. By now I was the head fashion buyer for the new Mirror Room at the Bay, in midtown Toronto, at Yonge and Bloor. There were seasonal buying trips to Montreal, New York and, again, Europe, when I was away four weeks at a time. The days of stalling a decision about Al's and my future were impatiently filled: fashion work, house work, child work, church work and writing university papers were the order of the day, including Saturdays and Sundays. In retrospect there were some good days. At times our relationship was tolerable. At other times it seemed beyond repair, filled with work as a way of stalling discussions about our respective addictions—me as a workaholic and Al as an alcoholic. Vacillating constantly, I swung indecisively between deference and disregard. After a particularly busy day, coming home around seven, almost dark, I'd found Al, Joanne, Kev and Carminda watching TV in the family room. They hardly glanced up when I came in; the dinner dishes were washed and put away and I felt like a stranger in my own home. It wasn't their fault; they were living their lives and I was living mine. The breakdown in Al's and my relationship affected the dynamics in our household and it was showing up in the kids. What to do?

Do better, try harder, Sinc my vigilant self-critic urged. So I took on *more* responsibility: I spent hours sorting through Al's shoebox of tax receipts. He worked under his own company, and back in the '70s, unlike today, almost everything was deductible—including the meal and alcohol receipts received for entertaining many "clients." Assuring Al, who always freaked out at tax time, that I would take care of it, I would hike myself and my briefcase (my brown music case doubling again) downtown to our accountant's office, where Marty would counsel me as we haggled through lunch trying to reach a dollar amount financially doable for Al and acceptable to the tax department.

In many areas, Al was generous to a fault. Unconscionable numbers of dollars were spent on gifts for our family, especially after a quarrel, followed by a wholesome amount on liquor for himself and anyone else who crossed our threshold. He was popular and liked to party. The more frivolous Al became with his earnings the more sober I became with mine—I always paid the mortgage. There was never enough communication about money or anything else between us and after a particularly bad bout of Al's drinking and my retaliation, I phoned my Mom in tears:

"I can't help it Mom. The 'concrete lady' is crumbling, and I don't know how to build her up again."

"Don't even try," was my mother's sage advice. "You don't have to be all things, to all people all of the time. Remember the therapist

Rose and her advice? I liked it. She told you: 'Once in a while, do your worst, because in your case it will probably be good enough.'"

"Oh Mom, I protested as I murmured goodbye, "I'm not sure that anything I do will *ever* be good enough again."

Those were the days of "MacArthur Park," (the LA song where the cake was crumbling in the rain), and that's probably where my metaphor, *Concrete Lady Crumbling* sprang from. Okay, it's silly, but that's how I saw myself: I was an accomplished career woman, a good mother, a darn good scholar and often a loving wife—so why wasn't I happy? Why was I crumbling, melting in my own rain of sadness? Today I see things differently. Then, I was busily involved in what I perceived as a great recipe for self-fulfillment, but I've found out since that it was a bad recipe—a guarantee for failure—the exact opposite of an accessible, open, caring human being with time for loving self and others.

∞ ∞ ∞

The trouble built slowly but steadily, and in retrospect I see that I was as guilty as Al for our failing marriage: I was wrapped up in my fashion job, including the month-long biannual trips to Europe. Although I perceived myself as a thoughtful and reflective person I don't remember having *any* time to think during those hectic forty-something years. What I do recall is heaving a sigh of relief every morning, once I was finally in the car headed downtown to work.

The mornings were always hectic: organizing Joanne and Kev for school then trying to look "just right" for my fashion career (false eyelashes, stiletto heels and hairpieces were the fashion of the day). I'd often leave for work fighting a headache born of '70s guilt, running out of the house to the beat of my own drum—which was now centered in my head. Ten hours later I'd arrive home late for dinner, often too worn out to be social. Relieved at getting through another hectic work day, I would hide in our bedroom and "relax" with my hobby—studying, as a philosophy major, for the night classes at York U. In a mysterious way, my real self, my spiritual self, received important nourishment from studying the ancient philosophers, Socrates and Plato. Their question and answer method towards self-knowledge provided digression and relief from the indiscriminate world of seventies pop culture in which I was immersed. By now, my earnings were a necessary contribution to a household whose emotional axis rested on the holy dollar and the speed with which it could be dispensed. For Al, now semi-retired, the mantra "only the best is good enough" took on new meaning as it hummed along in a voracious mode, feeding an ever-increasing golf and alcohol habit that knew no bounds. For a long time, this was Al's lifestyle and I adapted to it by blindly pushing myself away from his addiction only to delve deeper into my own addiction—work.

Led by a worldly spirit, the frenetic activity of my present was taking a serious toll on my future both spiritually and physically although I was far too busy to notice, until, in my mid-forties, I received an unexpected diagnosis.

"Young lady, you are perfect material for a serious stroke," the doctor stated as he wrote out a prescription to lower my precipitously high blood pressure. Fearful that my work-driven nature would lead me into a hazardous illness, I realized that I'd have to make a change.

The next day, during a particularly long and tedious drive home, I was struck by a simple but profound realization. For the first time I was thrown into an area of soul-shock—a finite place of compromise and health concerns—a place I'd never been before. It seems that while I was busily fighting my life-long fear of "wasting time and growing too old to achieve my goals," I had erratically tumbled into middle age without a parachute, thereby hastening the early demise I so dreaded. Rather than enjoying my life I was losing it through feverish activity born of frustration and fear. Meditating on the paradox of time's tyranny—losing your life while living it—I took on the seriousness of the doctor's pronouncement. *Okay*, I thought, *I'm in trouble. What can I do? What should I do? I need help.*

"Too much guilt," pronounced Rose, a great gestalt therapist, the wife of a doctor who Al met at the hospital after an "unsteady" fall against a radiator.

"And please forget the word *should*," Rose further admonished. "Drop that one out of your vocabulary as soon as possible. Replace it with *could*—that's the past tense of *can*, used to indicate ability, possibility or permission—*self-permission* too—a concept that I can see you're not clear on. We're going to have to work on that."

We did.

Addictions Anonymous

I used to maintain that I was unaware of Al's chronic drinking problem, but was I? I don't know. All I'm sure of is that the addiction slid in unnoticed, creeping through the cracks in Al's ego, edging stealthily, covertly, under his armor of will, so that none of us were aware of its progress until it was too late. As the strain of Al's addiction played havoc with his physical health—by now a serious inflammation of his pancreas had been diagnosed—my own physical and emotional health suffered in tandem, exacerbating my high blood pressure and chronic migraines to an intensity that continued well past my forties. After some therapy sessions with Rose, I learned that one solution lay in the realm of self-acceptance—work-warts and all; I admitted to Rose and to myself that my work was my escape: I found pleasure in it and relief from the tensions at home. But to keep some control over the kids, Joanne, fifteen and Kevin, eight, I would have to quit work or bring my work closer to the house. *Maybe I could do something crazy like open up my own store in North Toronto* I thought. And so it happened that on my way to work on January 2nd, 1976, this last idea was born in prayer.

I'd been toying with a plan to quit smoking for the past couple of years, but like all powerfully-driven addictions my resolve always weakened under duress. So there I was, puffing away at eight AM, physically and emotionally exhausted, trying to face that day's tedious task of taking inventory of the Mirror Room at The Bay, the high-fashion ladies' department in the new store at Yonge and Bloor where I'd been employed as a buyer-manager for the past two years. Although I liked my job and was treated well, I knew in my heart that a change was due—both my home life and marriage were faltering. Contemplating the entrance of a new year, feeling guilty over being away too much from the situation at home and frustrated at my own ineptitude, I suddenly burst into tears. *What's the matter with you?* Sinc whispered.

I don't know. I just feel so frustrated, so annoyed, so helpless, so....
Anger rising, I called out, chastising God,

"Where are you? Why don't you hear me? I need help! And, how about this stupid habit," I shouted, shaking my fisted cigarette out of the half open window. Blinded by tears and feeling guilty at my outburst, I hardly noticed the cigarette being torn out of my tight hold; but then I knew something was going on when my other hand followed suit by pitching a just-opened pack out of the same window.

By the time I finally arrived at work I was excessively calm—not myself. I passed through the day in a dream-state, nodding and smiling benignly each time my dear friend and assistant, Mrs. Sarah Shilton, asked, "When can we stop for a cigarette?"

"You go ahead, I don't feel like one," I heard myself repeatedly reply in some otherworldly voice. And so it went for the rest of that day and the days that followed; I seemed to be operating above the natural sphere. Covered by an unusual calmness I floated about in a smokeless realm until the third day, at which point I landed back into reality with a gentle thud. Yes, I wanted a cigarette, but I realized that something more important was going on. For the first time, in twenty years I had not smoked for three days in a row! This was, for me, a miracle.

Aah, I marveled, *I am not doing this by myself. This is the answer to my angry fist-shaking prayer—a dramatic, amazing answer! Yes, I realized I could finally quit my disgusting smoking habit through prayer … I was not alone.*

With the realization that my angry fist-shaking prayer was heard, I knew that anything, everything, was possible. I felt free, out of bondage for the first time in years, and it was through this newly born energy that my old idea of bringing my work closer to home took on new life.

Through a series of prayers and good luck I was led to a store on Cumberland Street, off Bloor, that was closing down. I purchased all of the fixtures: racks, hangers, counters and chairs—everything that was needed to open up shop, by using all of my savings. I then leased a commercial space on north Yonge Street, just south of Finch, and after handing in my required notice to The Bay, I opened my first fashion store by mid-July.

Alan was very helpful throughout; he not only installed the fixtures and new carpet, but he came up with a name too: "Alaynes Fashions" it would be—a combination of our two first names. So, after wrenching months of indecision, looking for solutions to our unstable home environment, I'd found my answer through prayer. I was much closer to the house—less than two kilometers away, close enough to jog or cycle to and from the store. This gave me over three extra hours of family life every day. Out of an overcrowded twenty-four, this seemed like an excellent start.

Appointment with Death

The ensuing years were somewhat easier. The extra hours at home each morning and evening lifted some of the daily pressures of running an active business and household. My first fashion store at 5645 Yonge St. took off nicely that summer, and a few years later I purchased a building and opened a second store further south, Alaynes II, at 3435 Yonge St. in Lawrence Park. I recall that life was less stressful except for a persistent shadow of unease that loomed over me: I was dogged by a dream, an ongoing premonition of disaster involving Al, and although I never talked to him about it, I lived its reality every day.

The dream is always bound up with premonitions of death; a desolate feeling cast against fear, first presented as anger then shame which in turn dissolves into wrenching sadness: tears for vows committed in the throes of passion, then lived out in denial—a sly force hidden from view but not from feeling. This denial resides in my dream as a black wall of fate which morphs into a dire omen, a death wish, not my own, but one buried within an ailing psyche relying on alcohol for sustenance. In this dream, as in all of my dreams, I am physically and emotionally unable to intervene—dead-locked, without power. And in my own life, within my own reality, I found myself in the same place. I would suffer this dream many times over the years.

Later, in the same dream sequence, I am being transported on a moving sidewalk along a dark shaded path that leads to a blackened archway. Paucity pervades as the dream's other occupants appear resigned to their purgatorial fate. In spite of the presentiment of evil, the dearth of hope permeating my path, I know that I'm not included in this phenomenon of early death—a death that is essentially self-inflicted and premature. Five years later in the final dream of this sequence, I would wake up sobbing, stricken with an inexplicable sadness and a knowing that this dream was prophetic: all that was shown would come to pass.

Meanwhile, in our personal life, past deceits lay dormant in a landscape of jealousy and blame where suspicions spread until even those that were *not* false could no longer bear witness to truth. Growing to mythic proportions, the resentments of our past and the anger of our present engulfed a future too bitter to embrace. For a little while longer, we played at being happy, but those times gradually faded in a prolonged haze of liquor and lies. Locked in an emotional disaster, with seemingly no power to fix or even change, I was stuck between a rock of love and the hard place of Al's addiction. Believing the vividness and truth of my recurrent dream as a presentiment of the future, I took the only choice I believed I had. I woke up from my dream of love-ever-after, accepted the foreboding truth of love-lies-bleeding and walked out the front door of our Willowdale manor in the naive belief that my leaving would trigger a healing. *After all, Alan loved me so much he would be able to stop drinking.* I was wrong.

Six months later, after a brief reconciliation attempt, the drinking worsened and finally, after another month of Alan's infuriated insinuations (by now they held some merit), and my angry rebuttals, I left for good. Then, even then, trying to save our love, he'd scratched and pounded at the car as I backed it out of the driveway—its phantom driver unresponsive to his pleas. And so the divine was lost—to me in a cloak of hostile silence and to Al in a haze of liquored despair.

A year after our separation the fatal illness emerged and the year after that, all came to pass as predicted in my dream. The last time I saw Al he was in the Toronto General Hospital, waiting for the end. During those days we visited him many times. After a few weeks, on August 3, 1983, Alan Joseph Small, father of Joanne Muir and Kevin Small, succumbed to pancreatic cancer and passed away at fifty-two years of age.

Chapter 19

As Time Goes By

And his voice descended over me like a silken sheet descending over a sleeper's dream.

—E. A. Small

Our wedding; July, 1967

One Day, When We Were Young

Two decades after Al died, while I was driving along Don Mills Road in early June, I passed by George Henry Boulevard and caught sight of their house. Having lived away from the east end of Toronto—how long was it? Almost twenty years—I could never have anticipated the powerful surge of memory that emerged and soon blurred into stinging tears. Compelled by this primal pain, I backed up and parked alongside the curb. After Al and I had been separated

282

for some time, he had ended up living with his lady friend in the place where I was now parked.

What's the matter with you? My critic, Sinc, barked. *Get over it! Isn't it time?*

"Apparently not," I muttered, annoyed at his interference. *Okay, I thought, maybe it's time to open the past; write about what I've been avoiding, finally close in on the pain.*

The memoir I'd been writing was thus far "selective" in an effort to be fair and judicious to all. But deep down, I knew that selectivity discriminates. It is the wrong way to reach the right of anyone's life, especially my own. So, settling down in my seat I pulled out my note pad, planning to write the *there*, of then, through the *here*, of now—hoping this time to "write it right." Uncertain of how to start, I opened the window, closed my eyes and as the sweet smell of early June peonies invaded my memory, I slipped into a reverie of another spring—one day when we were young. It was early June....

I was with Kevin, my youngest son, who had just graduated from junior high. Home from private school in Brockville, Ontario, Kev had suggested that we go together to visit his sick Dad at his house in North York, where he was currently living with his lady friend. Still anxious and protective of the raw pain induced by our painful separation, I had reluctantly agreed to go.

As we parked alongside the driveway, I could see the peonies that lined the side garden.

"You know Kev, I love peonies; they remind me of our big house in Winnipeg. When I was little I would sit beside them for hours and watch the ants crawl around. My dad once caught me eating the pink petals; I remember how he smiled as he pulled them gently out of my mouth, chiding me for eating "pink dirt." And peonies also bring back the days when you were a baby and we were all living together in the big house on Patina Drive in Willowdale, not far from here. Your father had planted peonies in the side garden that fall, just before you were born. He knew I loved them. Now look, here they are again, at this house—that same gorgeous deep pink color, and so many of them! I wonder if I dare ask her for some."

"I don't think so. And remember Mom, you promised to be nice to her," he admonished, in the tremulous tones of a worried thirteen-year old. "Anyway, she's probably not here." Sensing his anxiety I tried to reassure him, but before I could do that we'd reached the front walk.

I could see Al sitting on the side veranda squinting at us through a shaft of noon sun that was falling across his face. As he raised his beer bottle in a gesture of greeting, a point of light caught the amber liquid transforming it to a brilliant gold, and for a moment it appeared as a trophy held high in a proud victory salute—another award for broadcasting excellence. That's how it had once been. In Toronto there had always been praise for Alan Small of CFRB, well known by his listeners and peers as a broadcaster of merit, skilled in his craft. *Ah, those were the glory days*, I thought. *We were young and so much in love the world should have been ours.*

Radiating through Al's essence was that special voice: strong, resonant, and oh so sensuous. We could be apart for a hundred years, Alan and me, but I'd fallen blindly in love with his voice on his first phone call and throughout our marriage, and even after, the mere sound of his voice carried it all. I remember the very first time he called. Although expecting it, I'd waited through five rings to pick up.

"Hi," he said, in that deep lovely voice. "I got your number from your cousin Eleanore."

"I know, she asked me first."

"I've heard a lot about you," he murmured, "first from Eleanore, then from reading the article and seeing that picture of you on the cover of the *Toronto Star Weekly*. What was it called? *Stop the Merry-Go-Round, I Want to Get Off*, something like that, I think; but, isn't that the name of a new Broadway show?"

"Sort of; I borrowed it. But that stuff is all in the past now ... a lifetime ago," I muttered.

"It is? What happened?"

"Nothing, everything.... That's why I quit singing."

"Well, maybe one day you'll tell me about it. Sounds like the article left something out."

Hmm, I thought, *this guy, Al, is smooth*. Separated from Craig's dad, being down on men, I hadn't been dating. But something about this guy was different. And what a gorgeous voice! *Maybe, just maybe....*

Did You Think I'd Forget

"Mom, say Mom, are you okay?" With Kevin's voice I was startled out of my reverie.

"Sorry sweetie, the sight and scent of the peonies at this house carried me back to when I first met your father. I'm okay now; let's go. Your dad's looking at us. He's trying to stand up."

With an unlit cigarette drooping in one hand, Alan clutched at the arm of a plastic chair with the other. Hunching forward, trying to get up, his unbuttoned shirt fell open to reveal his chest, once bulky, now thin—each rib to be counted as it pushed out against taut skin, white except for an angry purple mark on his midriff. *Oh no, it's in the place of his pancreas,* I thought, recognizing from my years as an x-ray technician, the tell-tale color of gentian violet used for healing. Seeing the x-ray burn, I felt a shudder of shock. *Oh my God, it's cancer,* I thought. *He's left his shirt open on purpose. He can't bring himself to tell me, so he's showing me instead.* Saying nothing, I turned away, but not before catching his rueful glance.

"Hi," Al said, looking at Kevin.

"Hi Dad," answered Kevin, as he walked over and leaned down to give him a hug. "Maybe we should go around to the back. It's cooler there. What do you think?"

"Not much," his dad answered in his usual sardonic way ... and that gave me hope. *I guess he still has some fight left in him,* I thought, as I tried to calm down. As Kev led us around to the back I fell behind, and walking next to Al asked him in a low voice: "But how is it you didn't tell us? Don't you remember when I worked in x-ray, treating cancer? Maybe I could have helped." But he looked away, maybe into the past—maybe to that place I'd just been.

Stepping ahead to join Kevin, I noticed Al's uneven gait as he shuffled over to the other side, once there, hanging firmly onto Kev's arm. Although he was only fifty-two years old he looked tired, beaten—a disheveled boxer leaving the ring. Stepping aside, I glanced at them together, marveling at Kevin's gentleness and sweetness with

285

his dad. At thirteen, approaching his manhood, innocent but not naive, Kev walked in love but with obvious trepidation amidst our marital chaos. Tall, slender, his piercing blue eyes appeared dark and guarded as he took on his self-prescribed role as a peacemaker. *He's a symbol,* I thought, *a beautiful symbol, but, of what—our dependent love, our terrible need? And oh, how disorderly we'd been while recklessly throwing those young years away.*

As the three of us circled slowly to the back of the house, I could hear a woman's voice, sad and plaintive, singing from the pool-side radio—melancholy as it floated over the sun-jeweled turquoise water: "O how I'd love to be a diamond in your eyes," was the haunting plea that brought back the sadness of my own summer dreams. *It's unimaginable,* I thought, *that the miracle of our love could so seriously dissipate as to lose all sincerity—its fire burnt out by coldness and neglect. Dying to self, love removed its presence and receded. Why?* Hearing the mournful music, remembering how *I* used to be the diamond in Al's eyes, I wanted to weep.

As Kevin helped his dad sit down in a tattered velvet chair, I realized that it was the light blue one I'd bought him that second anniversary when we were still crazy in love. Out of the past, I still hear myself flirtatiously declaring, "Why, it's a near perfect match for your eyes," as he tested it with obvious pleasure. Now worn and faded, it had been dragged out onto the back deck for his comfort during the wracking illness of the x-ray treatments. Seeing the chair, I felt my face flush with the memory of how passionately we'd celebrated its arrival. Before today, I had to leap over half my life to remember those fervid times, but now, seeing Al's frail body barely filling the chair, sadness over our lost love came spiraling up. I tried to speak: "How are you feeling?" I stammered.

"How do I look?" he answered, in sharp reply.

But from behind those faded blue eyes, I saw something different: he was looking at me knowingly, in the old way. In the past, when we had looked at each other like that, we had felt such a drowning need for love that our minds were lost to understanding. Our bodies would dissolve into each other and briefly our world would feel secure— unconcerned with the duplicity of the past or the guile of the future. But then the clock would chime or the dog would bark and our spent passion would drift away on a cloud of reality, recalling our individual needs, reposing in our separate anxieties—our future disrupted by our past; our present a shambles.

"I called you the other night," Al said in a hoarse whisper as we followed Kev around to the front of the house. "I was feeling so miserable—unusually depressed and lonely. It was two o'clock in the morning. You answered 'hello' but you didn't speak. Didn't you know it was me?"

"You called? That was you? But why didn't *you* speak?"

Silence....

As Kev and I were walking toward the car after our visit I'd turned back to look at the house. I noticed how the newly shingled black roof shimmered against the clear June sky; I remember gazing longingly at the peonies, wanting to pick some. Turning to Kev, I'd given him a questioning glance but when I saw him with his head low, stumbling towards the car, I changed my mind. I could see how upset he was about Dad.

Twenty Years Gone By

And though I have all faith, so that I could remove mountains,
and have not love, I am nothing.
—Bible N I V, First Corinthians 13:2

Twenty years later, sitting in the car curbside, looking at the house where Al lived that summer before he died, I notice how shabby the roof looks: its shingles are a dirty grey, some loosened, others gone, their newness surrendered to time. Its left upper window boarded over, the house stares at me with a vacant wink. Benignly accepting its age and the vagaries of time, it urges me to do likewise, and I might have done so except for the peonies still lining the side garden—lush, in full bloom. *Aah, just see how they've persisted through time,* I marveled. *Someone has loved those peonies as much as I have.* Enduringly tall and proud, the pink blooms smilingly raise their heads toward the sun, while a soft breeze wafts their scent my way, bringing with it a wave of nostalgia followed by unexpected tears.

Amazing, I thought, *after so many years of fighting love's loss, feeling it recede and finally burying it, only to have its passion so readily awakened, bringing with it a visceral memory of love, as alive at this moment as then.* Through reverie, my emotional truth, so long dormant, will apparently have its way. As tears burn, words prod my memory—words I'd written some twenty years ago while still lost in our anguished separation. I reach for my pen:

> *Did you think I'd forget your golden hair,*
> *the glazed despair of your pale blue eyes?*
> *Did you think I'd forget to remember your face,*
> *while I searched for someone to take your place?*

But something's wrong, I thought. *I am not the poet; oh no, Alan was the poet.* And oh, how I loved him loving me; I remember every scene. All of those times he waited so patiently, sitting in the darkened fantasy of the Silver Rail Café, sipping his drinks while writing soppy love poems on pink napkins and humorous limericks on purple mats—every lunch hour the same. Breathlessly late, I would slide into the booth, always excited to see him, hungry for his first kiss of the day, faint with last night's vodka and this morning's beer but delicious all the same—a prelude and promise toward that night.... My poem presses on:

> *Twenty years gone by since you said goodbye,*
> *dragging our love through the door.*
> *Flying through space, tearing through sound*
> *and myself flat-footed screwed to the ground,*
> *While you high and mighty ascended with ease,*
> *taking your leave in the sky....*

Reading those words, I am, at first, confused: Who left whom? Does it matter? No. Here I console myself with a new truth, an emotional truth—an understanding of love that withdraws to survive, but refuses to die. Here, endowed with reverie, I relive the past. I accept love's passion and console myself with the sure knowledge that true love persists and survives all—suspended in memory, outside of time....

Did you think I wanted to leave you
in a place that was never home?
Did you think that you were the only one
who could never make it alone?

Twenty Years Gone By

Chapter 20

Rock of Ages – the Blessing

That day, I did not have so much a vision as a mythic memory…
Something ancient renewed.

—E. A. Small

Dad and me; Winnipeg, June, 1983

The Visitation

On October 28th, 1984, a year to the day after my father died, I saw his face again. I was in my bedroom, snuggled comfortably in my old velvet chair, trying to relax into the meditation session that I had been promising myself all day—but I couldn't let go. Catching sight of a small cigarette burn on the arm of the chair, my thoughts went back to the early days, when our family lived in the big manse at 7 St. John's Avenue in Winnipeg. Dad used to sit in a similar chair, smoking and hiding behind his newspaper, trying to get some privacy. At that time we numbered eight children and I guess he was attempting to escape from the commotion that always ensued when everyone was hungry and noisily waiting for dinner. Our large family had burgeoned to include my grandparents on a permanent basis and my dear Aunt Mary, living there part-time. We totaled thirteen, an unlucky number for some but not for me—as a child, I always felt lucky, at home in a crowd. Sinking further into my chair, my breathing slowed down and I could feel myself drifting:

∞ ∞ ∞

I was young again, sitting next to my darling Dido, and surrounded by my family at our huge dining-room table in Winnipeg. There was lots of noise and excited laughter. It must have been Christmas Eve because Babka was bringing to the table our good faux-crystal dishes filled with *kutya*—chewy wheat cooked with poppy seeds and honey—the first of our twelve-course feast, celebrated every year on Christmas Eve, January sixth, in accordance with the Byzantine Eastern Orthodox calendar. This delicious appetizer would soon be followed by steaming ruby-red *borscht* (beet soup) accompanied by platters heaped high with *holubtsi* (cabbage rolls with rice), and plump *pyrohy* (dumplings filled with sauerkraut or potato and cheese—my favorite) drizzled with golden onions and spread over with thick sour cream. Then, *pidpenky* (mushrooms in a rich creamy sauce) were served together with jellied fish stuffed with salmon and pickled herring and broad beans on the side. For dessert we'd be offered a variety of stewed fruits and *pampushky* (akin to donuts), *kolach* (sweet egg bread) and honey cake along with tea or coffee.

This distinctive feast was always followed by traditional Christmas carols sung in Ukrainian with the three little kids, all clustered around Daddy at the head of the table, trying our best to sing in a language that I, for one, barely understood. No matter; the intrinsic comfort of that early tradition instilled in me a deep love of all sacred music, which today still moves me to tears, in any language.

After singing, while the dishes were being cleared, Dad would excuse himself and vanish "to buy cigarettes" at Oscar's (our corner deli). He'd not to be seen again until well after the appearance of an over-padded Santa who would sing loud "Ho Ho's" in tandem with steady stabs at the doorbell, then clatter noisily down the dining room steps lugging a huge sack of gifts to be dispensed with gusto to the older kids first—leaving us, the three little kids, in a state of near hysteria as we waited our turn. By today's standards the gifts were meager: hand-knit woolen mittens in distinct colors for each of us, carefully selected inexpensive books and small boxes of chocolates— nothing fancy, but much appreciated as we showed them off to Dad, who always re-appeared after Santa had left.

Deep in the midst of my meditation about our Christmas Eve feast, and before I could lift the first savory mouthful of *kutya* to my mouth, I woke up—salivating and shivering at the same time. Seeing the window open, I moved to close it while taking in huge gulps of autumn air before sinking back in my chair. With a deep sigh, I closed my eyes. As my breath slowed down, so did my racing thoughts. The flotsam of my mind spilled out and I could feel the nagging details of the day dribble away. Finally relaxed, only vaguely aware of traffic noise and TV sounds, I felt myself sink into another space—free-floating, dream-like while still awake. In this half-conscious state, my thoughts returned to my father's house and my childhood. I yearned for those days and sensed that if I could retrieve them I might reclaim my childhood innocence and my natural intuition for the holy—my *lost divine.*

Mythic Memory

Years ago, in my father's house, I kept the two worlds I lived in separate and distinct: the Ukrainian traditions inside our house were not discussed outside, because I thought they would make me "different"—less Canadian. And the happenings outside, in the "real world," I rarely discussed at home, because there was not much interest and very little time. As a result, my two selves were in chronic conflict and rarely came together to match my circumstances—a dual connection that operated independently, at times with falsity, often with compromise and always with guilt. After leaving my father's house, as a young adult, I thought that if I could capture those distanced selves, my split psyche could be transformed into a single entity—a Canadian who could reclaim the richness of my Ukrainian Orthodox tradition and, through my father's faith, revive the divine message of God's love that I had first sensed as a small child. With this hope, I tried again to unwind. Chanting a simple prayer, "Show me the way," I finally relaxed into meditation.

Free-falling in space and time, I descended through a tunnel into a warm cave. Here, surrounded by translucent colors, lulled by waves of peace, I fell into a reverie, a twilight sleep. Tranquil, finally at rest, I was suddenly nudged into awareness—a movement, some air displaced—as though someone had entered the room.

Did someone come in? Why didn't I hear the door open? My eyelids were heavy, too massive to lift, but like a nerve prodded, I sensed the quiver of a shadow pass by. *Something is happening; someone's in this room,* I thought, and then I heard it—strange and eerie, the creak of a rust-worn hinge. With terrible effort I opened my eyes.

Turning toward the noise, I stared in amazement as a huge door, heavily carved, slowly opened to emit a beam of light that gradually widened to a thick shaft of gold. Luminous, shot through with silver beams, the shaft became a mercuric form: darting, slithering, it spilled through space—a kaleidoscope of neon brilliance that kept refilling the room as a new sequence of colors dived, danced and dissolved into a twirling wraith. Gradually, the wraith slowed down to reveal a huge god-like creature that took on the shape of a man. The figure was of mythical proportions, bathed in incandescent light and surrounded by a blue aura that separated him from the reality of the room. Although the vision was blurred, I was enveloped within a comforting love—distant yet somehow familiar—and as the figure moved closer, the blue light dissolved so that I could see more clearly. With one arm raised high, in the way of a priest's blessing, the huge creature emerged into view, resplendent in gold and silver vestments, wearing a miter of high rank—perhaps that of a bishop. All was quiet and peaceful, as in a holy place.

Gazing upward, I gasped in a shock of recognition. Here was a face, as familiar as my own—the face of my beloved father one year dead. I stared in awe as, surrounded by an incandescent glow, he smiled at me in that same wide open smile he always gave when, as little girl, my poems would please him. With overwhelming love, I reached out to touch him; but he faded back, his arm still raised high in an invocation of divine blessing, a consecration of God's infinite love.

"Daddy, is that really you?" I whispered as he vanished into the shadows of the doorway. "Wait!" I called out—but it was too late, he was gone.

With tears flowing, I opened my eyes to joy, sadness, love and hope all mingled together within a revelation, a manifestation of divine truth—finally, an acceptance of my own mortality, and the sure knowledge that my earthly father's love is immortal and everlasting. On that day, the faith of my youth had been awakened, my *lost divine* retrieved through a mythic meditation and the honor of my father's blessing. And, on that same day, my Heavenly Father's love shone forth: openly abundant, inviting and infinitely available—full access confirmed.

AFTERWORD

In the evening of life, we will be judged on love alone.
—St John of the Cross

In my middle years, the title, "The Minister's Daughter," reappeared to strongly influence my evolving search towards a renewal of faith. In looking back I can see the evidence of a life fully informed by the phrase itself. After all these years of being a minister's daughter, I now believe that life's meaning lies not within the combined evidence of a seeker's life, but rather, in the actual *process* of life itself. In repossessing my narrative, an understanding has emerged of who I once was, who I imagined myself to be and who I would become.

In the words of Thomas Moore, *Care of the Soul*, "The point of art is not to simply express ourselves, but to create an external, concrete form in which the soul of our lives can be evoked and contained." As such, as a consequence of writing this book, my life has, in many ways, ended up righting itself—towards forgiveness of self and others. In spreading out my history, reviewing its process and reaching deep into my soul by way of reverie, meditation and dreams, a new understanding has surfaced to illuminate a shadowed self—an alternative voice with an emotional truth that benefits this writer, and perhaps, in some small way, the reader alike. This, at least, is my hope.

The twenty years following the stories chronicled above have proved to be the happiest of my life. In retrospect I see that my life story, so far, has been full of expectations—many fulfilled, spread with success, some dismal failures, soaked with tears—and in between, familial love, faith and most importantly, joy! I have fulfilled many of my desires, not only in my active worldly life, but here in reverie, writing this book. I have looked for spiritual help throughout my life and have found it. As a young girl in my father's house, when I first saw the crude black and white film depicting Christ's passionate journey with his stilted cross, I sensed the sacredness of the scene, and although I could not have named it as such I was, at that moment, mystically graced with a desire towards the Holy.

Today, I honour the faith and spiritual vitality of my father, Reverend Dr. S.W. Sawchuk, and his early influences toward what I now regard as my religious sensibility—secure in the knowledge that there is more to life than that which is available in today's crass, secular world. In writing these reveries, my imagination and memory have enabled me to move deeply into my soul, and when we honour our soul, we honour God—the source of love and hope—the source of life itself.

SOURCES

Every effort has been made to contact the copyright holders; in the advent of an inadvertent omission or error, please notify the publisher.

REFERENCES:

Gaston Bachelard's *The Poetics of Reverie*, translated by Daniel Russell; published by Beacon Press in 1971, used by copyright permission from the Penguin Group (USA) Inc.

Article "Why I Quit the Merry-go-Round," by Peter Sypnowich, Canadian Weekly magazine (May8-14, 1965 issue), used by permission of Torstar Syndication Services.

Fern Hill by Dylan Thomas, from THE POEMS OF DYLAN THOMAS, copyright ©1945 by The Trustees for the Copyrights of Dylan Thomas; reprinted by permission of New Directions Publishing Corp.

Thomas Moore's *Care of the Soul*, copyright 1992 by Thomas Moore, first printed by Harper Perennial, 1994, used by permission of HarperCollins Publishers.

"Bird on the Wire," *Songs from a Room*, by Leonard Cohen, copyright © 1969, Sony Music Entertainment (Canada) Inc., RK Management, LLC, used by permission.

Fugitive Pieces by Anne Michaels, published by Random House, Inc; used by permission.

An Introduction to the Ukrainian Orthodox Church: *The Legacy of Fr. Semen Sawchuk*, by Oleh W. Gerus published by St. Andrew's College, Winnipeg, Manitoba, 2008.

The Coming Together of Four Ukrainian Pioneer Families in Canada, by Joseph R. Romanow, printed by DocuLink International, Ottawa, Canada; copyright 2003, Joseph Romanow; used by permission of J Romanow.

The Legend of Sir Thomas Crapper and Jim Olsztynski quotation, published July, 1994, used by permission of P&M Magazine

INTRODUCTION:

"By certain of its traits..." *The Poetics of Reverie*, "Introduction," Gaston Bachelard, Beacon press, 1971, used by permission.

"Reverie extends history precisely..." *The Poetics of Reverie*, "Reveries toward

Childhood," Gaston Bachelard, Beacon press, 1971, used by permission.

EPIGRAPHS:

All *quotations* used as epigraphs, are listed in Chapter order:

Chapter 1: "In my Father's house..." The King James Bible: John14:2.

Chapter 2: "I learn by going..." Theodore Roethke, "The Waking," published by Doubleday, 1953: New York.

Chapter 3: "As the hart panteth..." The King James Bible: Psalms 42:1.

Chapter4: "One needs, and sometime it is very good..." *The Poetics of Reverie*, "Introduction," Gaston Bachelard, Beacon press, 1971, by permission.

Chapter 5: "Time held me green and dying..." Fern Hill: By Dylan Thomas from The Poems of Dylan Thomas, copyright ©1945, reprinted by permission. (Epitaph, Poet's Corner, in Westminster Abby.)

Chapter 6: "Out beyond ideas..." Jalal ud Din Rumi: Sufi Mystic Poet, 1207-1273.

Chapter 7: "I will extol You, O Lord..." Bible, New King James Version: Psalm 30:1-2.

John: 14: 27 "Peace I leave with you; my peace I give you...," New International Version Bible.

Chapter 8: "I have swept away your offences..." NIV Bible: Isaiah: 44:22.

Chapter 9: "Sell your cleverness..." Jalal ud Din Rumi: Sufi Mystic Poet, 1207-1273.

Chapter 10: "Within us, still within us, always within us..." *The Poetics of Reverie*, "Reveries Towards Childhood," Gaston Bachelard, Beacon Press in 1971, by permission.

Chapter 11: "I waited patiently for the Lord; ..." NIV Bible: Psalm 40:1.

Chapter 12: "Whether you turn to the right or to the left..." NIV Bible: Isaiah 30:21.

Chapter 13: "Brief were my days among you..." *The Prophet*, Kahlil Gibran, Knopf Doubleday Publishing Group, Sept. 1923.

Chapter 14: "I will lead the blind by ways..." NIV Bible: Isaiah 42:16.

Chapter 15: "You have made known to me the paths..." NIV Bible: Acts 2:28.

Chapter 16: "The life of the soul, as the structure of..." *Care of the Soul*: Thomas Moore, copyright ©1992 by Thomas Moore, used by permission of HarperCollins Publishers.

"When you consider the contributions that plumbing..." *The Legend of Sir Thomas*

Crapper, Jim Olsztynski, P&M Magazine, July, 1994, used by permission.

Chapter 17: "It is your turn now, the time has come..." Jalal ud Din Rumi: Sufi Mystic Poet, 1207-1273.

"Some stones are so heavy only silence helps you carry them..." *Fugitive Pieces*: Anne Michaels, copyright ©1998. Random House Inc; reprinted by permission.

Chapter 18: "'Soul' is not a thing, but a quality or dimension..." *Care of the Soul*: Thomas Moore, copyright ©1992 by Thomas Moore, reprinted by permission of HarperCollins Publishers.

Chapter 19: "And his voice descended over me..." *Priests in the Attic*: Elaine A. Small, 2010.

Chapter 20: "That day, I did not have so much ..." *Priests in the Attic*: Elaine A. Small, 2010.

AFTERWORD:

"The point of art is not to simply express..." *Care of the Soul*: Thomas Moore, used by permission.

SONGS REFERRED:

"Bird on the Wire," *Songs from a Room*, by Leonard Cohen, copyright © 1969, Sony Music Entertainment (Canada) Inc., RK Management, LLC, used by permission.

"Don't Rain on My Parade," from the Broadway musical, *Funny Girl*; lyrics by Bob Merrill, 1964.

"There is a fountain full of blood..." William Cowper, c.1771.

"Canto Karabali," (known as "Jungle Drums,") written by Ernesto Lecuona Casado, Carmen Lombardo and Charles O'Flynn.

"Something's Coming" from the Broadway musical, *West Side Story*, music by Leonard Bernstein, lyrics by Stephen Sondheim, 1957.

"You're So Vain" written and recorded by Carly Simon; first released in December, 1972.

"The Sweetest Sounds," from *No Strings*; Music and lyrics by Richard Rogers: March 31, 1957, CBS.

"O Mio Babbino Caro," *Giannini Schicci*, by Giacomo Puccini, Publisher: Schirmer Ricordi, 1918.

"Voi Che Sapeta," (*"Say, ye who borrow"*), is from the opera, *The Marriage of Figaro*, by Amadeus Mozart, 1786.

"Seems like Old Times" by Carmen Lombardo and John Jacob Loeb, recorded November 15, 1945, New York, NY.

"Why Don't You Do Right," by Kansas Joe McCoy, 1936, recorded by Peggy Lee, 1942, in New York, NY.

"Hey Look Me Over," from *Wildcat*, music by Cy Coleman and lyrics by Carolyn Leigh, 1960.

"Just in Time," from *Bells are Ringing*, music by Jule Styne and lyrics by Betty Comden and Adolph Green, 1956.

"Goodbye..." from *I Wish You Love*, music by Charles I. Trenent and English lyrics by Albert A. Beach; recorded by Keely Smith, 1957.

LaVergne, TN USA
07 October 2010
199838LV00002B/2/P